CENSORIUM

CENSORIUM

CINEMA AND THE
OPEN EDGE
OF MASS PUBLICITY

WILLIAM MAZZARELLA

Duke University Press   *Durham & London*   2013

© 2013 Duke University Press

All rights reserved

Printed in the United States of America

on acid-free paper ⊖

Designed by Amy Ruth Buchanan

Typeset in Minion Pro and Monotype

Gill Sans by Keystone Typesetting, Inc.

Library of Congress Cataloging-in-

Publication Data appear on the last

printed page of this book.

CONTENTS

ACKNOWLEDGMENTS

A great many debts have accumulated over the near decade that it has taken me to research and write this book. I have had plenty of opportunities to reflect on the preposterous timescale of academic production and to marvel at the willingness, nevertheless, of so many people to engage so generously with such an apparently open-ended and uncertain endeavor.

The lifeblood of any ethnographic project is, of course, the kindness of all those interlocutors who submit to the anthropologist's ill-formed questions and impertinent conjectures with grace, patience, and wit. In India, I was fortunate enough to speak with Javed Akhtar, the late Vijay Anand, Shabana Azmi, Nupur Basu, Dev Benegal, Shyam Benegal, Rahul Bose, Anupama Chopra, Bishakha Datta, Shobhaa De, Anil Dharker, Shanta Gokhale, the late M. F. Husain, K. P. Jayasankar, Ammu Joseph, Vikram Kapadia, the late B. K. Karanjia, Girish Karnad, Anurag Kashyap, Anupam Kher, Ram Madhvani, Anjali Monteiro, Pritish Nandy, Kiran Nagarkar, the late Pramod Navalkar, Pramila Nesargi, Anand Patwardhan, Adi Pocha, P. Sebastian, Kalpana Sharma, Rakesh Sharma, Saurabh Shukla, Rohan Sippy, Sunhil Sippy, the late Vijay Tendulkar, and Paromita Vohra. Anand Awasthi, Udita Jhunjhunwala, and Jerry Pinto made some invaluable introductions for me. The Sathe family has for years offered me the warmth and comfort of a home away from home in Mumbai.

For nimble archival assistance I would like to thank the staff at the Maharashtra State Archives in Mumbai, the National Archives of India in New Delhi, and the India Office Library at the British Library in London, as well as Jim Nye at the Regenstein Library at the University of Chicago. Debashree Mukherjee dug up valuable material in Delhi early on. I owe John D'Souza and the others at the Centre for Education and Documentation in Mumbai and Bangalore a double expression of gratitude. I spent countless days absorbed in their clippings files for my first book, *Shoveling Smoke* (2003), and again for this one. The fundamental importance of material from their collection to my projects over the years makes it all the more mortifying that they were somehow omitted from my acknowledgments last time.

A scholar's work, particularly in the writing phase, is often solitary if not solipsistic. At the same time, it does offer opportunities to interlace the rigors of labor with the deep pleasures of friendship. For critical readings of the manuscript as it emerged, as well as for support, conversation, and illumination over the past few years, I want to thank Hussein Agrama, Brian Axel, Amita Baviskar, Lauren Berlant, Amahl Bishara, Rob Blunt, Dominic Boyer, Nusrat Chowdhury (Cosmo says thanks, too), Jean Comaroff, Lauren Coyle, Vikram Doctor, William Elison, Kie Ellens, Judy Farquhar, Leela Gandhi, Sangita Gopal, Thomas Blom Hansen, Keith Hart, Jim Hevia, Laura-Zoë Humphreys, Raminder Kaur, John Kelly, Shekhar Krishnan, Brian Larkin, Rochona Majumdar, Joe Masco, Meredith McGuire, Meg McLagan, Madan Mohan, Raj Mohoni, Christian Novetzke, Anand Pandian, Chris Pinney, Sean Pue, Arvind Rajagopal, Andy Rotman, Danilyn Rutherford, Adam Smith, Martin Stokes, Eli Thorkelson, Ananya Vajpeyi, Rihan Yeh, Karin Zitzewitz, and especially Dipesh Chakrabarty, John Comaroff, Shannon Dawdy (who got the last word), Dianna Frid, Don Reneau, and Jeremy Walton. I also want to acknowledge two sets of extraordinarily useful comments by anonymous reviewers. More generally, it has been an incomparable privilege to be part of the Department of Anthropology at the University of Chicago, which despite all the bromides about the "life of the mind," really does nurture intellectual vitality in the finest sense.

I shudder to think what Ken Wissoker, editor-in-chief at Duke University Press, must have thought over the years as my talk about what this project might eventually turn out to be meandered inconclusively and the bar tab mounted. His intelligent forbearance and (flexible) sense of timing have been exemplary. Most of all, I want to thank Ken for giving me the space to write a *book*—that is, not a collection of more or less free-standing essays yoked together around a common theme, but an integral sequence of interdependent chapters. I also want to thank several other people at Duke for their diligence, taste, and understanding: Leigh Barnwell, Amy Buchanan, Katie Courtland, Jessica Ryan, and Susanne Unger.

My field and archival research was funded, at various stages, by a Law and Social Science research fellowship from the National Science Foundation and, at the University of Chicago, grants from the Adolph R. and Marion J. Lichtstern Fund, the Social Science Division, and the Committee on Southern Asian Studies. I originally wrote up much of the historical material as a fellow at the Franke Institute for the Humanities at the University of Chicago and eventually finished the book with the help of a fellowship from the National Endowment for the Humanities. Earlier versions of some of the arguments and materials in these chapters have appeared in "Between Sedition and Seduction: Thinking Cultural Regulation in South Asia" (co-authored with Raminder Kaur), "Making Sense of the Cinema in Late Colonial India" (both in Raminder Kaur and William Mazzarella, eds., *Censorship in South Asia: Cultural Regulation from Sedition to Seduction* [2009]), and "The Obscenity of Censorship: Re-Thinking a Middle Class Technology" (in Amita Baviskar and Raka Ray, eds, *Elite and Everyman: The Cultural Politics of the Indian Middle Classes* [2011]).

On a personal level, I would like to think that the demands of this project have encouraged me to try to emulate some of the qualities I most admire in my parents: my father's loving attention to and respect for the material indices of the past and my mother's mercurially incisive gift for critical interpretation. It would only be a slight (yet certainly sobering) exaggeration to say that my children, Amelia and Jacob, grew from toddlers to teenagers during the gestation of this book; I am so very proud of you. Finally, Dianna, my work on this book started not long before I found you. You helped it unfold as part of a dialectic whose other scene is your studio. In love and in work, then: the playful and startling seriousness of beauty.

INTRODUCTION

THE CENSOR'S FIST

> There are always reasons to spare for every censoring
> act, and the inner heart cannot be placed in evidence.
> —John Collier of the U.S. National Board of
> Censorship, 1915 (quoted in Jowett 1999:30)

Acknowledging a platitude does not make it any less platitudinous. On April 13, 1937, the Indian film writer and actor Dewan Sharar addressed the East India Association at Caxton Hall in central London on the topic, "The Cinema in India: Its Scope and Possibilities." Like so many before him and like so many who would follow, he noted that "the immense power of the cinema, either for good or for evil, is so well known that reference to it is a platitude."[1]

Dewan Sharar did not, at least on that occasion, feel moved to inquire into the basis of this "immense power." Such an inquiry has, however, been one of my guiding obsessions while researching this book. Again and again, from the cinema's first appearance in the 1890s through to the time of my fieldwork more than a century later, the unique and inherent power of the cinema, for good or for ill, has been asserted. It is the basic premise on which the cinema has been mobilized as a means of education, entertainment, nation building, and propaganda. And it is equally the first (and often the last) excuse for censoring it. Being that the claim has so often been made without further elaboration, I decided to pursue the possibility that this bald and repetitive assertion of the cinema's immense power might be something more than a lazy justification for the censors' own authority. Perhaps, I wagered, it is a kind of constitutive symptom at the heart of the discourse of film censorship, a sign of something important about the condition of mass publicity—the broader space in which the cinema breathes—something that the censors must constantly acknowledge and yet for some reason cannot fully explain.

My pursuit of this "something" takes the form of an imminent critique of film censorship. By "immanent" I mean that I explore censorship discourse from within. I take the internal tensions and impasses of what the censors and their critics say and do as my point of entry rather than establishing a stable point outside censorship from which to critique it. Unlike many writers on censorship, I do not, for instance, measure it against a standard of free expression. While my own inquiry has certainly benefited from the rich literature on Indian film audience practices,[2] I likewise do not believe that the social influence of what censors say about audiences can simply be countered or refuted by what actual audiences say about themselves. I start from the by now commonplace assumption that censorship is just as much about making meanings as it is about suppressing them. And yet I do not presume that we can somehow defeat censorship by exposing the internal inconsistencies of its assumptions and claims. Indeed, the ideological tenacity of censorship discourse in the face of—or better, *because* of—its many inner contradictions is one of my central preoccupations in this book. I try to show that the apparent incoherence of the censors' discourse is, in a way, more truthful than the censors themselves have any reason to acknowledge.

My approach is also dialectical. I suggest that the discourse of censorship works by repeatedly staging impasses—that in a way it succeeds by failing. I do not read these impasses only as evidence of the fraudulence or political cynicism of censorship (even as I acknowledge that film censorship is, in practice, often politically cynical). My way into censorship is at the same time my way out to a much broader set of questions. In brief, I argue that thinking through film censorship discloses basic problems in the grounding of political and cultural authority in mass-mediated societies. I develop a theory of *performative dispensations* in order to show how any claim to sovereign power is also a claim on a particular relation between sensuous incitement and symbolic order. One of my central arguments is that the kind of mass public culture within which we all now live, imagine, and work makes such claims more difficult to sustain and that there is something about the cinema as a medium—and consequently attempts to censor the cinema—that makes this difficulty uniquely palpable.

The project started as an attempt to explain why censorship had become such a burning topic of public controversy in India during the decade that stretched from the mid-1990s to the mid-2000s. But I soon realized that in order to make sense of that moment, I would have to go back to the colonial origins of Indian film censorship and, beyond that, to the cinema's arrival in India and, beyond that, to the emergence of mass publics in India. This genealogical excavation eventually allowed me to return to the recent past with fresh eyes and to understand that Indian film censorship is not, as is often claimed, just an inert survival of archaic colonial practices. Indeed, one of my aims in this book has been to rethink the relations of continuity and transformation between the colonial and the postcolonial periods.

This is not a history of Indian film censorship.[3] I have, by and large, arranged my material thematically rather than chronologically, except where developing the argument coherently has demanded otherwise. Nor have I taken upon myself the responsibility of granting evenhanded coverage to different periods. Instead, I am most consistently concerned with the relationship between two periods of transition: one colonial (the 1920s–30s), the other postcolonial (the 1990s–2000s). I also beg the indulgence of those readers for whom the analysis of film form is a prerequisite for any serious discussion of the cinema. Although my thinking has benefited enormously from the work of Indian cinema scholars like Ashish Rajadhyaksha, Ravi Vasudevan, and Madhava Prasad, this book is not in that sense a work of film studies. I do, of course, discuss film content at various points in the book, but I have been more concerned to follow an intuition that was present at the birth of this project: that while, at one level, film censorship is certainly about which image-objects can or cannot be allowed to circulate, at another level it keeps returning to the problem of the cinema as a medium that, whether in a register of promise or of panic, makes palpable potentials that exceed any enumeration of contents.[4]

Ultimately, as a contribution to the political anthropology of mass publicity, this book proposes some new ways to think about old problems. What is the place of affective intensities in modern mass-mediated democracies? What is the importance of the fact that we are called upon to belong at once to concrete crowds and to abstract publics? And what happens to political authority when it can no longer reside in the physical body of a singular sovereign and has to find its feet in the intimately anonymous space of mass publicity?[5]

THE PORNOGRAPHER, THE MAGICIAN, AND THE DEMON-KING

The censor's fist came crashing down onto his desk, startling me and rattling the dainty tea service that had only just been placed between us. It was November 2003. The censor and I were sitting in a small, dark office in the Mumbai seafront suburb of Juhu, a neighborhood that had long been home to many of the big players in Bollywood, the Hindi commercial film business. The man across from me was Vijay "Goldie" Anand, brother of the 1960s matinee idol Dev Anand and himself the director of a series of hits of the period, among them *Guide* (1965), *Teesri Manzil* (1966), *Jewel Thief* (1967), and *Johnny Mera Naam* (1970). Actually, by the time of our conversation, Vijay Anand had not been involved with film censorship for more than a year. In the summer of 2002, after less than a year in the job and amid a flurry of scandalous publicity claiming that, as part of a comprehensive reform of Indian film censorship, he was planning to introduce pornographic movie theaters in Indian cities, Anand had resigned his post as chairperson of the Central Board of Film Certification (CBFC), better known as the Indian Film Censor Board. But he was still furious.

Perhaps I, for my part, should have been better prepared for surprises. After all, only five days earlier I had interviewed the then–Censor Board chief, character actor Anupam Kher. Kher had, during our interview, rather disconcertingly been dressed in a full magician's costume, complete with flowing cape, pigtail wig, and twirly moustache. (In fairness, I should mention that he was at the time in the middle of a shoot for a film called *Abrakadabra*, billed as a kind of Hindi *Harry Potter*.) Our conversation took place in Kher's dressing room at Swati Studios in Goregaon, a Mumbai suburb known for its film lots. Outside, what seemed like hundreds of child extras lined up for lunch at a refectory in their regulation wizarding school robes.

It was hard not to reflect on the aptness of such conjurous trappings for my encounter with the head of an organization that is widely lambasted by Indian filmmakers for spiriting away entire sections of offending movies. In contrast to Vijay Anand's bitter emphasis, Kher spoke lightly, even dismissively, about the anxieties and difficulties of censorship. His was the voice of a man who had been in the job for less than a month, a man convinced that the *hangama* (uproar) around censorship amounted to little more than the champagne-fueled frothing of a hypocritical elite.[6]

In the wake of Vijay Anand's resignation in July 2002, the English-language Indian media turned him into the kind of tragic hero it has always loved best: an enlightened, worldly liberal sacrificed on the altar of political cowardice and cultural reaction. *India Today*'s cover story had the Ministry of Information and Broadcasting, which oversees the workings of the Censor Board, "recoiling in Victorian horror" at Anand's proposals (Bamzai and Unnithan 2002:57). The claim was clear: in a globalizing age, the government's cultural politics were regressive and outmoded. Its censorship practices were holding India back from the kind of world-class cosmopolitan future it deserved.

As if to confirm the liberals' diagnosis, the government played its part by appointing, as Anand's interim successor, a former member of Parliament and actor by the name of Arvind Trivedi. Here was a man the secular liberals could comfortably love to hate. For starters, he was most famous for playing the mythological demon-king Ravana in the smash-hit late 1980s televisation of the *Ramayana*. Trivedi thus seemed to embody the kind of mass-mediated, affect-intensive mobilization of Hindu mythology that had assisted the cultural right wing's rise to national power in the 1990s (Rajagopal 2001). And as if that were not enough, there were the quotes. Trivedi lost little time in presenting himself as the traditionalist corrective to Anand's irresponsible, immoral cosmopolitanism. Regarding the mooted X-rated theaters, he told the press:

> I am completely against such a suggestion. It goes against our Bharatiya [Indian] tradition. What do we want to prove by having such theatres? That we are modern? What kind of culture are we trying to promote? Following Western countries shouldn't be our aim. What about people who will have to live in the vicinity of such theatres? Is this the kind of landmark we're looking for? *Samaj mein kalank lag jayega.* [It will be a blot on our society.] (Martyris 2002)

Trivedi proceeded to invoke an unstoppable prurient escalation, a spreading stain of infamy: "There will be no end to it. First kissing, then pressing, then whole bedroom. What effect will it have on the kids?" As a concluding rhetorical flourish, he equated films with the very apex of spiritual and physical purity, the source of the river Ganga itself: "Films are the Gangotri of our society. They are something holy. We shouldn't soil them" (Martyris 2002).[7]

research paper quote => commercializing photography? Lo Benjamin.

CULTURAL EMERGENCY?

On the face of it, then, it seemed that the furor over censorship was a struggle over the acceptable terms of cultural globalization in which some form of (more or less profane) liberalism faced off against some variety of (more or less sacred) conservatism.[8] From the mid-1990s through the mid-2000s, it seemed that one could not turn around without coming across yet another story about a magazine editor being harassed or beaten by right-wing cultural activists, about cinemas being trashed for showing the films of Deepa Mehta or Mira Nair, about Bollywood starlets or saucy models being summoned to court for obscenity or indecency, about offending books, paintings, and articles being slashed and burned amid saffron flags and TV cameras (Kaur and Mazzarella, eds., 2009). Hindi film director Mahesh Bhatt, ever handy with a sound bite, called it a "cultural emergency" (Bhatt 1998).[9]

On the one hand, the Government of India was being accused of brandishing censorship as a weapon of ideological intimidation and cultural reaction. On the other hand, as I discuss in chapter 3, the very idea of censorship as a state prerogative was being called into question as all manner of activists and enthusiasts, with more or less tenuous connections to formal political parties, competed to capitalize on the spectacular possibilities of the twenty-four-hour news cycle that cable television had brought to India in the early 1990s (Kumar 2006; N. Mehta 2008). To name only some of the most visible controversies during these years: purported lesbianism and Hindu widow sexuality in, respectively, Deepa Mehta's films *Fire* (1996) and *Water* (2005, which was stopped before shooting had properly started and subsequently filmed in Sri Lanka)[10]; ambiguously "traditional" obscenity in the film song *Choli ke peeche kya hai?* (What's behind the blouse?), from Subhash Ghai's action romp *Khalnayak* (1993); purportedly immodest public displays of femininity at the 1996 Miss World pageant in Bangalore; sexual explicitness in the 1995 Tuff shoe ad featuring two well-known models naked but for sneakers and a snake; obscenity, defamation, and violence in Shekhar Kapur's feature *Bandit Queen* (1994) and an unseemly reference to the royal "quinny" as well as a beheading in his *Elizabeth* (1998); sympathy for Mahatma Gandhi's assassin in Pradeep Dalvi's Marathi play *Mee Nathuram Godse Boltoi* (1998; originally written in 1984); cultural imperialism in the form of Valentine's Day; injury to Hindu religious sentiments by James Laine's scholarly study *Shivaji* (2003) and upset among Christians following Ron Howard's movie version of *The Da Vinci Code* (2006); alleged incitement to sedition and communal conflict in critical political documentaries like Anand Patwardhan's *War and Peace* (2003) and Rakesh Sharma's *Final Solution* (2004); and so on, and so on.

Many explained the censorship struggles of this period as symptoms of a clash between two formations: on one side, the processes of globalization and economic liberalization that had opened up Indian consumer markets and brought a deluge of eroticized mass communication, and on the other side, the rise to mainstream power of an aggressively conservative form of Hindu nationalism—shorthanded as Hindutva—in the form of the Bharatiya Janata Party (BJP), the political wing of the larger Sangh Parivar (Family of Associations). The historical conjuncture of these formations seemed too precise to be coincidental. To be sure, economic liberalization had already gently gotten underway in the 1980s, but the decisive reforms in 1991 happened right between BJP leader L. K. Advani's incendiary *rath yatra* of 1990 and the storming and destruction of the Babri mosque in Ayodhya in 1992.[11]

Apparently, the clash had produced a new confrontation between a (threatened) liberal politics of tolerance and secularism and a (surging) chauvinist politics of intolerance, of which the intensification of censorship was one outcome. Superficially, a case could perhaps be made linking Hindu nationalist rule to this new politics of intolerant divisiveness (although only by downplaying earlier Congress-led governments' experiments with mobilizing religious sentiments for political ends in the 1980s and, indeed, later Congress-led governments' continued clampdown on political criticism after the BJP was voted out of national power in 2004). Mumbai was, for example, the site of many controversies during the period 1995–99, when the BJP, in coalition with the aggressively chauvinist Shiv Sena, ruled the state of Maharashtra. And some would claim that this coalition, although it lost power at the state level, served as a kind of laboratory for cultural policing techniques that were then "scaled up" when the BJP led the national government in New Delhi from 1998–2004.

Long-standing left-secularists like Anand Patwardhan, the doyen of Indian political documentary film, charged the Hindu right with having "taken our country to the abyss. . . . Let it openly declare that it does not believe in democracy or in the values propagated by Mahatma Gandhi" (Borpujari 2002). His colleague, Rakesh Sharma, warned that the number of attacks on artworks and critical voices would only continue to escalate as long as the Sangh Parivar held the reins of power: "they are hydra-headed, but they all conform to this politics of intolerance."[12] For others, the intolerance manifested itself first and foremost in the right wing's resistance to the new freedoms of style and bodily comportment that liberalization had brought and that deserved to be protected as indices of cosmopolitanism and progress. Ram Madhvani, a director of feature films and commercials, reflected that

> because of Fashion TV and STAR TV[13] and all that has happened over the last ten years, I think that we have a new middle class. We can see it in the hairstyles that people have. We can see it in the cars that people have on the road. . . . What I *do* know is that you can see it on the road. There is a change in the way women are dressing. . . . There is a lot more risqué kind of brazenness to that whole sense of dress.[14]

Others cautioned that the gleaming, ostensibly liberated erotic envelope of satellite television programming and the new Bollywood coexisted quite happily with the stock soap operatic image of the stoically long-suffering devoted wife, the *sati savitri*, complete with *sindoor*—even as ever fewer urban Indian women actually marked their married status by placing a streak of vermilion in their center partings.

At the same time, some members of the liberal media intelligentsia blamed their own class for having allowed the onrush of advertising-fueled liberalization to distract them from their responsibilities as guardians of a critical public sphere. Advertisers had no interest in media stories about poverty, development, or political reform. And the Hindu nationalist right had, in the words of Nupur Basu of NDTV,[15] capitalized on the opportunity: "It was a vacuum, an open canvas. Anyone could step in. Of course, who better to step in than an aggressive Hindutva force, which has filled that gap with all sorts of slogans and orange colours."[16]

Even when Hindutva was not the main bogey, many felt that the mainstream censorship debate's fixation on the regulation of sexually suggestive materials worked as a kind of smokescreen for the continued, and much less questioned, suppression of properly "political" content. So, for example, I often encountered the argument that the central government was only too happy to have the press wax indignant about Vijay Anand's X-rated theaters proposal because it deflected public attention onto the supposedly trivial area of sex. The Ministry of Information and Broadcasting could thus play a comfortable game of cat and mouse with the media—tightening its grip here, relaxing it there—instead of having to address truly awkward points in Anand's plan, like his demand that the government's power to appoint members of the Censor Board and its regional advisory panels be curtailed (Bhowmik 2003, 2009; D. Bose 2005).[17] Political distraction through smut was, after all, a well-established authoritarian tradition. During the height of Indira Gandhi's Emergency in the mid-1970s, her press censors are supposed to have followed the motto "porn *theek hai*, politics *nahin*" (porn is fine, but not politics) (K. Singh 2002:259).[18]

Now of course Anand Patwardhan had every right to ask why, when Vijay Anand was being celebrated as the sacrificial hero of the liberal intelligentsia, hardly anyone tried to hold him accountable for his refusal to support politically sensitive documentaries like *War and Peace* (I return to the Patwardhan/Anand encounter in chapter 3). And it was certainly true that even in those censorship cases that generated some sustained and serious discussion of sexual politics among cultural critics and public intellectuals, for example the controversy over Deepa Mehta's *Fire*, directors themselves often beat an apolitical retreat into neoliberal platitudes about "lifestyle" and "choice" (Bandyopadhyay 2007; Ghosh 2010; Gopinath 2005; John and Niranjana 1999; Kapur 2002; Kishwar 2008 [1998]; Upadhya 1998). Daily newspapers and current affairs weeklies were, to be sure, increasingly choosing to splash sexy celebrity-driven stories across their covers rather than engaging their readers in sustained discussions of government complicity in communal violence or the displacement of indigenous peoples by hydroelectric dam projects (Joseph 2002).[19]

At the same time, the sex-as-smokescreen argument is problematic on at least two counts. First, it implies that there is a "truth" to politics—its "really real" sublime dimension—that always lurks behind the shadow play of ideology (Hansen 2001; Mazzarella 2006). Second, the implicit ontological claim—that "sex" and "politics" refer to entirely distinct kinds of objects—is, of course, problematic. My point is not only that sex is always already political, but also, as I will be arguing in various ways throughout this book, that the distinction is in fact a conceptual obstacle to understanding the development of film censorship. The regulatory roots run deep here. As an emergent colonial legal category in the mid-nineteenth century, "obscenity" brought together concerns about immorality and sedition. Nowadays, it is often said that colonial film censorship in India between the 1920s and the 1940s was primarily concerned with stopping politically seditious films and that the concern with Indian on-screen sexual propriety was a largely postcolonial invention. (Kobita Sarkar puts the matter tartly: "Along with foreign rule, we banished the kiss from our films as if there were some deep-seated mystical connection between the two" [1982:55].) But as we shall see, the colonial censors' objections to "political" films often had a great deal to do with the sensory erotics of their spectacular appeal. By the same token, the spicy social dramas of the 1920s that the British called "sex films"[20] were not only controversial because of their daring thematic content but, perhaps more profoundly, because of the subtle and unpredictable ways in which they seemed to unsettle the spectatorial and sensorial habits on which the everyday legitimacy of colonial authority rested.

WHY PICK ON THE CINEMA?

The question inevitably arises: why focus so tightly on the cinema, when censors—official and self-appointed—frequently take aim at other media too: magazines, artworks, television, books, etc.? Already in 1937, Ram Gogtay, editor of the trade paper *Lighthouse*, protested on behalf of the film industry: "If through the written word in magazines and through the spoken word on the stage immoral impressions can be flung at the public, why should the motion picture be singled out for annihilation?"[21] Am I not artificially isolating the cinema from a broader ecology in which it operates alongside media that are both older and younger?

 My answer is yes, I am—but with good reason. To begin with, the cinema is the one medium that in India is thought to reach everybody. The force of this claim rests less on whether people in every part of India really do go to the cinema than on the fact that cinema spectatorship is a way of belonging to a mass public without having to be literate. Ashish Rajadhyaksha points to the Indian cinema's long-standing "role in rendering *publicly intelligible*, narratable, the administrative and technical operations of modernity—namely, the modern state, the modern political process (including modern systems of cultural resistance) and the modern market," and "the further role of spectatorship as a process of initiating the filmgoing citizen into the larger protocols of organizing public action in new national spaces" (2009:69, 87; emphasis in original). By the time I started this project, satellite television had already been in India for more than a decade, and the state television network Doordarshan reached many more homes again (Farmer 2003; Mankekar 1999; Rajagopal 2001; Shah 1997). The Internet was beginning to make inroads (Mazzarella 2010d); radio, long a government monopoly, was being opened up to private players; and the Indian-language press had never been so lively (Jeffrey 2000; Ståhlberg 2002).

But nothing could compete with the all-embracing cinema that, as film writer Anupama Chopra remarked, "thanks to the touring cinema and the guys that set up tents in the villages, is everywhere."[22] Here, the sense of general access was crucial, even as urban multiplexes were increasingly sequestering more affluent audiences from the rabble. Journalist Kalpana Sharma argued, "In a way it's a democratic form. It gives access to everybody—a) you don't have to be particularly rich, b) you don't have to be literate, and c) actually the form is such that even if you don't know the language particularly well, you can still relate to it."[23] Perhaps even more important was the sense of the Hindi cinema—despite the regional standing of the South Indian film industries—as the closest thing to a genuinely inclusive and powerfully affective South Asian popular culture. Chopra observed that

> Pakistanis watch Hindi movies, Sri Lankans watch Hindi movies. . . . For non-resident Indians, that's what keeps them linked to the motherland, so to speak.[24] . . . It has an across-the-board appeal. I think songs have a huge part to play in it because it's the only kind of pop music we know. So at weddings, at parties, that's what expresses your emotions for you: a Hindi film song. You know? So it's amazing how completely consumed our lives are, how *drenched* they are in Hindi movies! . . . It's just all-pervasive.

These perceived characteristics of the cinema in India—its reach, its cultural influence, and its affective resonance—help to explain why it has been hedged around with such an elaborate censorship apparatus and why its regulation continues to generate such impassioned debate. On one level, the introduction of systematic Indian film censorship in 1918–20 crystallized a series of anxieties about the management of the affective potentials of public performance that went back to the second half of the nineteenth century (chapter 1). On a different level, and despite the proliferation of other media during the past couple of decades, cinema censorship remains, in a fundamental sense, the model for Indian public cultural regulation today, the template for how the emergent potential of the encounter between mass publics and mass media is imagined. I choose the cinema as my object for thinking through censorship, then, partly because successive colonial and postcolonial governments' confrontations with the cinema have so profoundly influenced how censorship works and is understood.

By the same token, my aim is actually not really to plead a special case. The more I studied film censorship, the more I realized that the regulation of the cinema had become a way for censors and their opponents to talk about public affect management *in general*. In a sense, the censors' attribution of unique characteristics to the cinema is misleading—not because the cinema is not distinctive as a medium, but rather because the exceptionalist claims made around the cinema and the need to regulate it often have the side effect of making noncinematic publics appear less affect-intensive, less performative, and more symbolically stable than they actually are. What I pursue in this book, then, is a double task: on the one hand, to explore the specific characteristics of regulatory encounters with the cinema during periods of heightened anxiety in colonial and postcolonial India and, on the other hand, through this exploration, to attempt a more general theorization of the problem of public affect management vis-à-vis modern mass media.

THE PISSING MAN

The other side of the cinema's universal resonance is the attribution to Indian publics of an excessive permeability to affective appeals and its presumed corollary, an underdeveloped political rationality. Centuries of foreign domination, the argument goes, have beaten ordinary Indians into a state that oscillates between abject servility and overcompensatory assertion. In the words of Pritish Nandy, film producer, journalist, poet, and member of the Rajya Sabha (the upper house of the Indian Parliament):

Being a colonized nation for something like five hundred, six hundred years—three hundred under the Mughals and a couple of hundred under the British—we lost our self-confidence and therefore all this that you see happening today is an attempt to rediscover a sense of identity and a sense of self-worth. . . . Being a colonized nation actually makes you see the state as a paternalistic figure who you think should decide for you—what is good, what is bad, what is right, what is wrong.[25]

If the British, in particular, had plundered India's resources and retarded her cultural development, then successive post-Independence governments had done all too little to bring enlightenment to the citizenry. Of course, Indians now had the vote. But were they mature enough to use it? Vijay Anand, for one, thought that the larger failure of independent India to educate its people was nothing short of scandalous:

It is true. That's why some of our very silly mythologies are superhits. But then that is bad! How dare we keep our people illiterate after fifty-one, fifty-two years of freedom? . . . I have an educated vote, but somehow our politicians have kept this country illiterate, saying "this [i.e. the franchise] is not good for the illiterate." How long are we going to do that? . . . Politics has got so much significance here, more than in any other country in the world. And yet we are not a politically mature country. . . . I don't think the voter is intelligent enough to vote.[26]

Naturally, authoritarian censorship was going to thrive amid a servile citizenry. With finely tuned irony, Javed Akhtar—the legendary Hindi film scriptwriter and lyricist—argued that the Indian system was essentially a kind of soft dictatorship that only formally resembled a democracy:

In India, we have developed a very fine system, you know? In the [Persian] Gulf countries, they have dictatorships. We have *all* the paraphernalia of democracy, and we give freedom of expression as long as it does not challenge the status quo. The moment that the status quo is really threatened, you are [barks] *curbed* mercilessly! These [other countries] are not that discreet. They have constant dictatorships. We don't have that. We don't need it. We are a very discreet people. We know how long we should give this rope of freedom of expression, and when we should pull it in. We are smarter![27]

Such censorial "discretion" was, in turn, necessary because of the assumed immaturity of the vast majority of Indian citizens. Anupam Kher, whose breezy populism in most respects contrasted with Vijay Anand's troubled liberalism, was nevertheless of one mind with Anand when it came to the helpless vulnerability of the Indian masses, although his illustration was peculiarly graphic: "An illiterate mind is much more prone to getting affected by [provocative images] than a literate mind. If you are an illiterate man, and I tell you that this is where you have to piss, [then] because you are not literate you will go and piss there. . . . But a literate man will say 'no, no—I know where the toilet is.' That's the kind of illiteracy that India has, unfortunately."[28] For Kher—and here he was, as we shall see, drawing on a long tradition of censorship discourse—illiteracy equated not only with ignorance but, more fundamentally, with a lack of autonomous judgment.[29] Vijay Anand complained that such ignorant heteronomy had gotten India stuck in a narrowly identitarian public life: "The considerations for voting," he told me, "are not political judgment, but some other. 'He belongs to my caste, he belongs to my religion.'" In Kher's terms, the ignorant man would piss where he was told because his lack of letters left him with no way to achieve a critical, autonomous distance to the immediately given situation and the immediately given command. And the command "this is where you have to piss" is, in the censor's discourse, a stand-in for the cinematic image that, for the ignorant spectator, is not so much a sensuous provocation as a literal, irresistible commandment. *what.*

It is, of course, notable that the figures that my censor informants tended to invoke were almost exclusively male. Does not the pissing man have female accomplices? Does not the censor's discourse, preoccupied as it is with questions of sexuality and decency, thematize the dangers of women's looking? This, it seems to me, is one of the places where the discourse of Indian film censorship remains unreflexively patriarchal. While there is certainly a great deal of discussion of how women may or may not be represented on screen, the regulation of their behavior as spectators is imagined as the primary responsibility of male relatives. According to this line of thinking, male viewers are inherently public and, *qua* pissing men, crowd-edly so. But for the Indian film censors—and this despite several recent female CFBC chairs—women are under the care of men and thus, as it were, private even in public. A "public man" is an actively engaged citizen; a "public woman" is a prostitute. Indian female friends would often mention their discomfort at the kind of salacious attention they would attract if they ventured alone into any Indian movie theater that was not upmarket and urban. Exhibitors occasionally respond by arranging special "ladies' screenings" of films that women might be embarrassed to view even in the company of male family members—such was the case, for instance, with Mira Nair's *Kamasutra* in 1997. Either way—and, interestingly enough, unlike some other markedly public situations like, for instance, political demonstrations—the censor's discourse does not imagine the public space of the movie theater as a place where women and men can enact spectator-citizenship on equally autonomous terms. I use the term *pissing man* throughout this book, then, not to mask this imbalance but to register its inscription in the censor's imagination.

THE IDEOLOGICAL LOOP OF CENSORSHIP

A circular logic thus begins to emerge: First, one acknowledges that censorious, repressive governments and a lack of education have kept the masses immature. Then, one proceeds to insist that, for this very reason, further censorship is necessary in order to protect these illiterate unfortunates from their own worst instincts.

A classic example of this ideological loop appears in the *Report of the Working Group on National Film Policy* (1980). The report defines Indians as vulnerable and thus in need of censorship: "Particularly in the context of a hyperconservative society like India, which has rigid social and religious norms of behaviour, where the political consciousness has still not matured and where harsh economic conditions inhibit individual growth, there are bound to be serious limitations on the freedom of expression" (quoted in B. Bose 2006:3). From there it is only a short step to insisting that Indian cultural policy must, therefore, not get ahead of itself: "Censorship can become liberal only to the extent [that] society itself becomes genuinely liberal" (quoted in B. Bose 2006:3).

Certainly, a handful of my informants unequivocally and absolutely rejected censorship. The late great playwright Vijay Tendulkar was one:

> My experience with censorship tells me that censorship *per se* is absurd. I have yet to come across a single example where censorship has been responsibly and wisely used. The things that probably deserve to be stopped are let loose. The things which probably are different, which have a serious purpose, which are trying to tell something, are stopped. And even by banning something you don't finish the thing. You create a wrong interest in the whole thing. That does a lot of damage.[30]

When it came to the cinema, however, no one believed that commercial filmmakers could put aside their petty rivalries so as to regulate themselves. Many advocated an American-style ratings system on the principle that it would allow both filmmakers and viewers to make their own decisions rather than be bossed around by a paternalistic state agency.[31] But many more expressed some version of the ideological loop: in principle, they were opposed to censorship because it stunted the development of mature democracy, but in practice India was simply not ready for a more liberal regime.

For Anupam Kher, censorship was one of the necessary restraints that kept India's multitudes from each others' throats: "India is the only democratic country in the world where every five hundred miles the food habits, the cultural habits of the people change. And yet we have been managing to live for the last fifty-seven years together." This sense of a volatile diversity, perpetually on the brink of combustion as a result of stray cinematic sparks, goes back to the colonial period. An editorial in the periodical *Chitra* satirized it in 1935:

> A clean-shaven Hindu hero may unknowingly offend the Sanatanis [neo-orthodox Hindus], a kiss on the screen may incense superannuated spinsters, and fighting may rouse the righteous wrath of pacifists. History is in danger too; [sixteenth-century Maratha warrior-king] Shivaji's beard may not be liked by Muslims who might object to that Kaffir disguised as a Mussalman and rabid Sanatanists may be sore at [sixteenth-century Mughal emperor] Akbar and his Hindu wives.[32]

Kher, notably, emphasized that this was not a peculiarly Indian problem: "Religion is the basic problem all over the world today. . . . It's important not to let the violence erupt, riots erupt, problems erupt. . . . You can make fools of people anywhere in the world in the name of religion." But most of the people with whom I spoke felt that India exhibited an unusual—and unusually explosive—blend of democracy, religious/cultural diversity, and underdevelopment. Actor Rahul Bose, a vocal critic of film censorship in principle, nevertheless also argued that this blend had produced a kind of overheated public sphere in which film-makers needed to tread with tremendous caution. Having been left without the education that was their due, the Indian masses remained ignorant, oppressed, and frustrated and, as such, "in a morally and physically weakened state. At that point you can use any stick to drum up frenzy."[33]

From this standpoint, then, India was a country of pissing men, incapable of the kind of critical reflexivity that was the sine qua non of coolly deliberative public reason. Qua citizen, the pissing man was at once passive and hyperactive: easily duped by any passing demagogue and constantly on the brink of violence. Again, for this reason, even some of the most tireless critics of the CBFC nevertheless stopped short of demanding an abolition of censorship. For example, Anand Patwardhan—a man who had turned the act of taking censorious state agencies to court into a kind of public art practice—felt that someone still needed to regulate the "hate speech" disseminated in Hindu nationalist propaganda.

Prefiguring my argument in chapter 2, I want to suggest that the legitimation of censorship—whether in the regretful liberal mode or the less apologetic conservative mode—depends on a diagnosis of being in a historically liminal state of transition. In the past, the argument goes, face-to-face communities regulated themselves organically by means of tradition. In the future, mass-mediated societies will once again regulate themselves, either by means of mature democratic civility or through the strength of moral community scaled up to the nation. In the liminal present, though, Indians are adrift in a rudderless mass society, buffeted by provocative image-objects and solicited by all manner of shrill mass moralizers. Under such conditions, many justify censorship as a pragmatic, albeit lamentable, way of preventing things from spiraling into complete chaos.

But as veteran filmmaker Shyam Benegal noted with characteristic perspicacity, such a justification would never lend censorship a sense of popular legitimacy. He offered me a story of the end of tradition and the modern predicament of incomplete reflexivity:

This is why censorship is so hypocritical, see? Because there *is* a censorship. That censorship has to do with society itself. Each society, depending on what its own cultural values were, would practice an ideal. Create their own rules. And most people function within those rules. And if they start to function outside those rules, that community will automatically keep them out. They'll throw them out. Once [this organic system of rules] is displaced, it becomes an object of questioning. Otherwise [i.e., earlier] it's not. Because it's contained. It can be contained within that system. There are many diversities within India. All of them have many unspoken rules. The way it is managed is that when somebody else has a rule, you don't step into that and proclaim your rule. It's flexible; there's a certain ease to the process. There is not fundamentalist fanaticism in this process. But the moment you get somebody who becomes fundamentalist, then you know you're not going to be able to manage anything. Because you're going to get people's backs up. And suddenly you go out of that area of self-restraint into something else. Then unspoken rules have to become spoken rules. And when they become spoken rules they become a) exterior to you, and therefore punitive in the manner in which they function, and b) something that you will rebel against. You will fight against that because it is not part of you. It's from outside now, it's on top of you. It's not part of you. It's no longer a participatory process.[34]

Between the vanished organics of "unspoken rules" and a distant future civility, in the face of "fundamentalist fanaticism," modern state censorship attempts, without much credibility or success, to enact a kind of preemptive mass judgment. Benegal's reflection points to a central concern of this book: the grounds of the censors' judgment and legitimacy. But in his version, the question of media and their role in making publics is absent; the change happens because of the sudden appearance of an intolerant type of moralism that demands that previously tacit norms be spelled out and externally codified as rules. Starting in chapter 1, I attempt to explain this shift as a function of the rise of mass-mediated publics. One of my arguments will be that the condition that my informants so often imagined as a state of transition between vanished tradition and future civility is a permanent symptom of the structure of modern mass publicity.

THE ENUNCIATOR'S EXCEPTION

How is it that the censors, or even just the persons dispassionately discussing the problem of censorship, are able to exempt themselves from the condition of the pissing man whose consumption needs to be regulated? For the ideological loop of censorship does not only say "censorship should be abolished—but not yet." Its enunciator also—almost invariably—says "censorship is, for now, necessary—but not for me."[35] This is the gesture through which the censor differentiates between public and crowd at the movies. As S. V. Srinivas (2000) remarks: "The cinema hall was perceived as a space within which the respectable member of a 'public' came face-to-face with a collective, a mass, which was an object of curiosity/contempt. The distinction that emerged between the audience at large and a section of 'enlightened' viewers who constituted themselves as a public is critical for discussions of the nature of cinema's audience." This kind of split, whereby a temperate public sets itself off from a rampant mass, had already taken place in India during the second half of the nineteenth century around literature and the theater. But for reasons that I will explore in chapter 1, the coming of the cinema brought regulatory anxieties that had been emerging vis-à-vis print and the stage into a most explosive juxtaposition.

It is not as if the enunciator's exception went unnoticed by the enuncia-tors themselves. Pioneering film journalist B. K. Karanjia, who started writing about the industry in the 1940s and who had on many occasions held up the censorship regime to ridicule, reflected: "If you ask me 'do you believe that there should be no censorship?' then for myself I would say 'yes.' But I would not be able to say so much for the illiterate man who has never seen a woman naked because society is so conservative."[36] (Paren-thetically, it is important to note here that Karanjia, like many of my infor-mants, also suggested that subaltern Indians, whether those city dwellers whose families lived in cramped single rooms or those whose rural ways did not impose bourgeois conventions of female sartorial modesty, were far more likely as youths to have seen naked women in the course of everyday life than most of the "educated" people who were otherwise thought to be more immune to the provocations of the cinema. The naked woman at issue here, then, is a publicly visible nonsubaltern woman.)

The standard "critical" reading of the enunciator's exception is to mark it as symptomatic of the double standards of a middle-class intelligentsia that insists on granting itself different rights of citizenship than it will allow to the majority of its compatriots. First a nationalist avant-garde during the closing decades of the colonial era, then a developmentalist elite during the first few decades of the post-Independence period, this intelligentsia emerged embattled into the post-liberalization period. From the 1960s on, a panoply of subaltern movements challenged its claim to public cultural hegemony. By the 1980s and 1990s, it also had to find its feet within a consumerist public culture in which the affect-intensive, sensuous lan-guages of advertising and performative spectacle were increasingly com-peting with properly "civic" deliberative discourse for recognition as a plausible idiom of citizenship (Mazzarella 2003, 2005a).

On the one hand, liberalization returned upper-middle-class desires to a place of public prominence that they had not enjoyed since the earliest post-Independence years. On the other, the voluptuous idiom of consumerism, as conveyed in advertising, television programming, and films, was a sensuous language of the body. Therefore, it was, potentially, a language in which even the illiterate—even those pissing men—could be recognized as fluent speakers. Vir Sanghvi, editor of the *Hindustan Times*, pithily summed up the sense of contradiction that this shift in the meanings of citizenship had produced in the post-liberalization period: "How does it make sense to argue that an illiterate person can decide who will be the next Prime Minister of India but has no right to gaze deeply at [beauty queen] Sushmita Sen's navel?" (Sanghvi 1999). And yet when it came to censorship, Sanghvi did not claim immunity from the enunciator's exception: "I've spent many years arguing about censorship with anyone who will bother to listen but eventually I've reluctantly come to accept some basic facts: we all have double standards. We may want total freedom for ourselves but we will draw a *Lakshman rekha* [idiomatically, a line to be crossed at one's peril][37] where the middle class ends" (Sanghvi 2003).

On the face of it, then, it would seem that the ideological loop of censorship and the enunciator's exception are the hallmarks of a hypocritical and self-serving ideology that helps to justify the public cultural authority of a small intelligentsia over the vast majority. And before that, under colonial rule, it was a hypocritical and self-serving ideology that helped to justify not only the public cultural authority but also the political sovereignty of one race over another. In either case, it would seem to rely on a picture of the present as a moment of dangerous liminality, between a ruptured traditional past and a posited future of harmonious, modern civility—a picture that justifies the installation of a privileged minority as the authoritative pathfinders on the path of progress.

The problem with this explanation, superficially plausible though it might be, is that it reduces the justification of censorship to an entirely cynical discourse, a discourse of domination pure and simple. No doubt the discourse of censorship does in fact help to perpetuate an aspirant middle-class hegemony, but if we press no further than that, I suspect that we will miss what is most interesting about it. As Theodor Adorno points out in *Minima Moralia*, "Where reasonable people are in agreement over the unreasonable behavior of others, we can always be sure to find something unresolved that has been deferred, painful scars" (Adorno 2005 [1951]:51).

I often had the peculiar sense, while listening to justifications of censorship, that they were being offered with utter sincerity and yet, at the same time, with a tacit acknowledgment of their own inconsistency. What I propose to do, then, is not to assume the insincerity of the censors' discourse but rather to do it the favor it least expects: to take it seriously. To be sure, it hardly makes that easy. The very language of Indian film censorship so often seems willfully archaic, referencing, as it does, the legal terminology of another epoch: baroque stuff about moral turpitude, depravity, and corrupted social fabrics; a language that in its very utterance seems excessive, theatrical. But what René Girard once wrote about the deceptive obviousness of sacrifice as a social institution is just as applicable to censorship: "First appearances count for little, are quickly brushed aside—and should therefore receive special attention" (1977:1).

In that spirit, I pushed my informants time and again on the censors' central articles of faith, and especially on the repressive hypothesis—the idea that by blocking provocative but "frank" representations, censorship helped to give rise to repressed and infantile forms of cultural production. Some of my informants would at this point grow irritable with what they took to be my over-intellectualization of something that was really just a "simple" matter of pleasurable entertainment.[38] Anupam Kher, notably, snapped: "To me, these are all very intellectual terms. I don't agree with all this. To me, it's *bookish*. It's a conversation of high society. To me it is [adopts mockingly pedantic tone] 'repression of the art of depression of society.' Pardon my language—but I want to say 'fuck off.' *Real people* do not talk like that."

As a hardened veteran of that particular accusation, I persisted. And with informants more inclined to take an analytical tack, I often ended up in a puzzling, compelling place. A place where both of us knew and all but acknowledged that the discourse of censorship was, as such, logically and empirically indefensible. And yet also a place where we both felt that the discourse of censorship nevertheless registered a trace of something emergent that happens when an audience engages a screen image, something perhaps inexpressible within the terms of censorship discourse yet clearly palpable in its restless articulation. As B. K. Karanjia put it to me: "There is something to [the fear that films will have a bad effect]. I am bitterly opposed to censorship, but I feel there is something to it."

Anil Dharker, longtime journalist and commentator, was in 1975 invited by the then minister of information and broadcasting I. K. Gujral to serve on a high-powered panel of "super-censors" appointed to help make Indian film censorship more aesthetically discerning (see the more extended discussion in chapter 2). He only served for a few months before the Emergency brought in a more reactionary dispensation at the ministry, but the experience was enough to make him reconsider his previously untroubled liberalism. Rehearsing the familiar liberal point about censors being middle-class people who hypocritically "condescended" to administer the aesthetics of "the pit class," Dharker initially surprised me by continuing:

> And there's something to that. Because if you see a movie in a cinema, and there's a scene of rape or romance or physical closeness, the front-benchers[39] look at it in a completely different light than you would want them to. They are whistling and stomping their feet. Cat calls. So they're enjoying the spectacle of a woman being raped. There's no doubt about it. I don't know what the answer is. When I went into the Censor Board, I went in with an extremely liberal attitude, to the extent of thinking that there should be no censorship. I changed my mind.[40]

Again, it would be easy enough to dwell on Dharker's sense of middle-class moral shock: how can people who enjoy watching rape scenes be trusted with provocative fare (let alone with being responsible citizens)? And there is also an element of disappointed moral-aesthetic paternalism (the frontbenchers who "look at it in a completely different light than you would want them to"). But what also marks Dharker's reflection as characteristic of the censor's discourse is its foregrounding of the flamboyantly rowdy behavior that the cinema seems to trigger in subaltern audiences: "They are whistling and stomping their feet. Cat calls." Dharker links this cinematic *jouissance* to the immorality of the audience's enjoyment of a specific kind of content, again a characteristic regulatory move. But this vivid affective intensification deserves to be considered in its own right because it remains, as we shall see, a consistent feature of descriptions of the cinema's power from the earliest days of Indian cinema censorship in the 1910s to the present. Part of my argument in the chapters that follow will be that just as the propositional content of censorship ideology never quite "covers" the sense of affective urgency with which it is delivered, so in the same way the practice of censorship also continuously produces the recognition that the powerful sensuous potentiality of the relation between cinema screen and spectator remains irreducible to the particular "content" of any film narrative or theme.

Liberal critics often argue that censorship has no place in democratic society because it is incompatible with free speech.[41] In the words of Sheila Whitaker, former head of the UK National Film Archive and director of the London Film Festival: "Democracy, at its best, will inevitably promote a healthy balance in society. Censorship, whether it be against the act of creation or the act of viewing, is unacceptable" (1997:3).

In India, freedom of speech and expression is ensured by Article 19(1)(a) of the Constitution but is also limited by Article 19(2), which allows the government to place "reasonable restrictions" on this right "in the interests of the sovereignty and integrity of India, the security of the State, friendly relations with foreign States, public order, decency or morality, or in relation to contempt of court, defamation or incitement to an offence." As Someswar Bhowmik points out, the capaciousness of these limitations on the freedom of speech and expression effectively allows the state to retain extensive control over what can be said and shown in public, subject only to the—not inconsiderable—discretion of the courts. The guiding question for Bhowmik then becomes: "how far is film censorship in India compatible with the constitutional provisions regarding freedom of expression and the forms of democratic principles by which the Indian society and polity is guided[?]" (2009:x).

In a broad sense, this is of course a pertinent question. But it is also ultimately an unsatisfying one, since censorship is at least as much a practice of producing authorized forms of truth as it is of silencing speech and expression. Here, of course, it is in one sense misleading to speak of "censorship," or even "film censorship," in the singular. Struggles over free speech and the dynamics of governmentality have their distinct regional and national histories (Bernstein, ed., 1999; Couvares, ed., 1996; Leff and Simmons 2001; Oshima 1992; Petrie, ed., 1997; Trevelyan 1973; Vasey 1997; Wittern-Keller 2008). And yet, as Priya Jaikumar (2006) and Brian Larkin (2010) point out (see also M. Sinha 2006), the history of the cinema—and thus also of its regulation—is from the beginning a global history, not just because the cinema swallowed the world at a shocking speed, but also because the terms by which it was managed were inextricable from the broader cultural politics of empire. I am, then, indebted to those scholars who, following Michel Foucault, have explored film censorship as a disciplinary technology that proliferates normalized understandings of subjectivity, sexuality, and citizenship (e.g., Kuhn 1988; Liang, Suresh, and Malhotra 2007). At the same time, however, I want to resist the implication—so unforgettably staged in the opening diptych of Foucault's *Discipline & Punish* (1977)—that bureaucratic discipline at once contains and overcomes the unstable corporeality of sovereign spectacle.

One of my guiding precepts in this book is that we should not mistake the ideological discourse of modern disciplinary power for its actual modes of operation. In the space of mass publicity—a space that the cinema captures most acutely for the historical period that concerns me here—disciplinary power both confronts its own continued reliance on spectacular, affect-intensive performativity and seeks to disavow it by displacing it from the state's self-description onto the bodies of various subaltern others. Studies of modern governmentality—colonial and otherwise, in the realm of censorship and elsewhere—typically portray the consolidation of power as a matter of disciplining the unruly and emergent affective energies that appear to emanate from empirically identifiable subaltern groups. Likewise, critiques of Jürgen Habermas's (1989 [1962]) account of the emergence of the bourgeois public sphere have typically taken aim at how Habermas seems to presume a form of public discourse that relies on a disembodied ideal of universal reason, thus tacitly reproducing an unmarked hegemony of white male rationality (Calhoun, ed., 1992; Robbins 1993). One of the earliest critiques of Habermas's apparently incorporeal public sphere was Oskar Negt and Alexander Kluge's (1993 [1972]) "proletarian public sphere," a formulation with which I am in substantial sympathy insofar as it recognizes how mass media continue to mobilize and activate currents of public affect that are not typically recognized as public "speech" or "expression" (cf. Vasudevan 2010:412; M. Hansen 1991, 2011). S. V. Srinivas (2000) argues that the cinema hall provided an early arena for both the consolidation of a bourgeois public discourse on citizens' rights and appropriate comportment and the political mobilization of new subaltern claims to public space.

A problem arises, however, whenever the relation between unruly affect and public reason are mapped straightforwardly onto a division between subaltern lifeworlds and bourgeois publics, as if public communication actually depended upon policing a boundary between a bourgeois public sphere from which affect is evacuated and subaltern forms of expression, inadmissible to the spaces of polite public discourse. One of my arguments in this book will be that while this is an important *ideology* of the public sphere (maintained by defenders and critics alike), it is in fact not how public communication works, in India or anywhere else. Rather, just as David Hume once insisted that what we call rational thought is actually grounded in passions that it largely disavows, so the deliberative reason of the bourgeois public sphere, notwithstanding its own ideology, rests on both routinized and emergent currents of public affect. Part of the historical shock of the cinema was that it made this fact palpable at a time when affectively evacuated bourgeois conceptions of public reason had become hegemonic yardsticks for judging what counted as acceptable and unacceptable public speech.

This is the terrain in which film censorship has always operated, in India as elsewhere. It is a terrain that is, as we shall see, easily and frequently classed, raced, and gendered, so that subaltern groups are made to bear the burden of responsibility for the unruly emergent energies of public affect. For this reason, too, critics of censorship, seeing the censors' phobic relation to public affect as nothing but a prejudicial rhetoric of class domination, have often avoided any serious consideration of the affective dimensions of public culture. In so doing, they have in effect entertained the terms of the censors' discourse—that is, uneducated people are uniquely vulnerable to affective provocation at the cinema—only in order to dismiss them.

My assumption in this book is that these unruly energies are everywhere. They are not "in" subjects or objects, and consequently they are not "in" one group of people rather than in another, or "in" one or another category of image-objects.[42] Rather, they are triggered as emergent potentials in performative settings, all the way from the most banal ritualized interactions of everyday life through the most elaborately staged performances, whether on screen, on stage, or in the streets. I am writing here both with and against a neovitalist mode of theorizing affect, an intellectual lineage that stretches from Baruch Spinoza through Henri Bergson to Gilles Deleuze's writings on cinema (Deleuze 1986, 1987; cf. Pandian 2011; Rai 2009; Rodowick 1997; Shaviro 1993) and from there on to more recent elaborations by Brian Massumi, Michael Hardt and Antonio Negri, and Nigel Thrift (Massumi 2002; Hardt and Negri 2000, 2004, 2009; Thrift 2008; cf. Clough and Halley, eds., 2007; Gregg and Seigworth, eds., 2010). I draw on this line of thinking insofar as it foregrounds the importance of emergent corporeal and sensory potentials in our engagements with media. But I reject its defensive antidialectical insistence on valorizing emergence and potential as integral sites of freedom against representation and mediation (for more detail, see Mazzarella 2009, 2010c).

I am perhaps most indebted to the tradition of thinking about the public potentials of cinema that emerged from Siegfried Kracauer and Walter Benjamin's conversations with Theodor Adorno, was carried forward by Negt and Kluge, and more recently was elaborated by Miriam Hansen and Susan Buck-Morss (Adorno 1997, 2001; Benjamin 2008a; Buck-Morss 1977, 1989, 2000; M. Hansen 1987, 2011; Kluge 1982; Kracauer 2005; Mazzarella 2012b; Negt and Kluge 1993). In particular I draw on the intimation, in these writings, of a dialectical (as opposed to an antithetical or hierarchical) relationship between the social meaning and the sensuous potential of cinematic image-objects—of film as, in Miriam Hansen's terms, a "sensory-reflexive matrix" (2011:71). Kajri Jain describes a locus of inquiry that resonates closely with my own: "the switching point between the 'textual' or representational register of the visual idioms of commerce and the performative efficacy of these images in their animated and animating capacities as objects" (2007:117).

At a metatheoretical level *Censorium* emerges from my long-standing hope that a productive conversation might yet take place across the lamentable divide between Francophone-vitalist discussions of affect and Germanic-dialectical explorations of aesthetics (particularly in the ancient Greek sense of *aisthesis*, i.e., of pertaining to sensory experience; cf. Eagleton [1990]). I would not be altogether embarrassed, then, if someone accused me of being that rather peculiar monster: a "dialectical vitalist."[43]

All this matters to a book about film censorship because it helps us understand exactly what it is that the "film sensors" are responding to and why they are never quite able to articulate it. And it matters much more broadly to how we think about public authority. If there is a theory of power or ideology at work in this book, then its central proposition would run something like this: it is true that ideological claims are often made as if they are watertight and unassailable. But it does not follow that we can liberate ourselves from these ideological claims by pointing to the places in which they are incoherent. Rather, we are already invested in much more inarticulate fields of corporeal disposition, affective inclination, and emergent potential. These fields take on an appearance of ideological coherence only at the level of explicit articulation—and, as we shall see, sometimes not even then. These inarticulate fields of disposition, inclination, and potential are therefore not places from which one might reliably "resist" power. Rather, they are *both* the unspoken—but strongly felt—fundaments of ideology *and* the places in which ideological discourse grapples with qualities that far exceed its grasp.

EMERGENCE AND EMERGENCY

In January 1925, at the height of a moral panic around Hollywood films in Indian theaters, one Rattan Barorji Cooper, a worthy member of colonial civil society, fired off a strongly worded letter to the editor of the *Bombay Chronicle*:

> Sir, with all fairness and frankness I strongly protest against our modern cinema shows. I do not for a moment claim the abolition of this innocent and favourite public resort [although Mr. Cooper would nevertheless go on to call for more stringent censorship]. But it is only when this innocent pleasure house is turned into a veritable infernal dungeon where vilest trickeries and rogueries are taught to its frequenters that any one has every reason to protest, and protest vehemently and emphatically. For so many years I have been visiting cinema shows, but with the lapse of every day my abhorrence for them gets greater and greater. I go everytime [*sic*] with a hope to see something new or original but I am eternally disappointed, and by this time I am practically disgusted. All that I see, and so many others see, is women, wine, gambling, staking, racing, plotting, scheming, murder, roguery, rascality, robbery, trickery, prudery, sycophancy, pomp, magnificence and a host of other vices.[44]

Mr. Cooper's "vehement and emphatic" tone strives for a pitch that might convey something of the sensory intensity of cinemagoing itself. At the same time, he tries to enumerate the determinate forms of the cinema's crimes, as if an adequately capacious taxonomy might contain, and thus somehow control, its provocation. Nothing could be more characteristic of the movement of the censor's fist: the force with which it pounds the table, the frustration with which it tries to grasp and thus to contain the image-object. Censorship tends to generate lists of Bad Things That Must Be Banned: unacceptable words, images, gestures, situations, implications, and procedures. And much discussion of censorship stays on this overt level of content-lists, pointing out their inconsistency and their hypocrisy. In this book, conversely, I take these lists as one side of a dialectic, as necessarily frustrated attempts to "get a fix" on something provocatively mobile in the cinema as a medium of public culture. Sometimes, as I show in chapter 2, these attempted fixes enumerate forms of subjectivity that render certain kinds of people vulnerable to images (audiences) and others resilient to their provocation (censors). Sometimes they categorize certain kinds of images as harmful objects that must be restricted. But in either case, I will argue, the censor's discourse intuits, against itself, that the provocation resides neither "in" the subject nor "in" the object but rather in an emergent relation between the two—a relation from which the ideological appearance of preexisting subjects and objects is subsequently derived. As such, the provocation can be understood as a *tendency* activated by the peculiar public mediation of the cinema. (This is the core of my argument in chapter 5.)

As I argued just now, the ideological loop of censorship typically proposes that we are in a liminal period of instability, a moment between the vanished stability of tradition and a future state of sociomoral order that always lies just beyond the horizon. Censorship is thus, in its very bones, a discourse of permanent exception. One might say that it deals with the emergent provocation of images, their affective potentiality, by perpetually proclaiming an emergency. And yet it is clear that while the justification of censorship structurally relies on the claim that we live in exceptional times, some times clearly seem more exceptional than others—for instance, the moral panics of the 1920s–1930s and the cultural emergency of the 1990s–2000s. These were periods during which the ever-present gap between the emergent affective potential of mass-mediated representations and the public dispensations through which that potential could—always provisionally—be harnessed became particularly obvious. During these periods, various discourses of danger heightened the sense of living in exceptional times and thus also the stridency of the censors' call. But, in fact, the only exceptional feature of these times was the intensity with which a permanent feature of public cultural communication was being registered. I say "intensity," not "clarity," because while I believe that censorship in a certain sense "speaks the truth," it does so more by registering an impact than by seeing clearly. It is the trace of this impact on the censors' discourse that the constant platitudinous invocation of the cinema's "immense power" indexes. And it is this red thread, winding its way through a moralizing discourse, which I pursue in the pages that follow.

CHAPTER 1

PERFORMATIVE DISPENSATIONS

THE ELEMENTARY FORMS OF MASS PUBLICITY

This chapter presents a history of the censors' present. I explain the emergence of film censorship as a response less to particular image-objects and more to a structural challenge that is inherent to mass-mediated societies: *the open edge of mass publicity*. Part historical fiction, part genealogy, this chapter ends where the introduction began, with the so-called cultural emergency at the end of the twentieth century. I argue that we can understand neither the cultural emergency nor its earlier iterations without understanding the peculiar way in which the cinema intensified and consolidated regulatory anxieties that took shape vis-à-vis print and theater during the second half of the nineteenth century. From the beginning, these anxieties touched on the volatile relationship between performative force and representational meaning, a relationship that, I suggest, preoccupies censors because it lies at the heart of any claim to authoritative cultural order or, in the terminology of my own argument, any claim to a *performative dispensation*. My argument thus implies that while at one level these anxieties were specific to the context of colonial India, at another they are both continuous with the Indian present and relevant to the problem of legitimating sovereign authority in mass-mediated societies everywhere.

At the beginning of this history lies a myth.

OUTLINE FOR A SHORT FILM IN FOUR SCENES

SCENE I
The First Play, Ancient India, Mythical Time

We join the action as the sage Bharata and his sons, enchantingly assisted by a group of celestial dancers created for the occasion by the god Brahma, are putting on the first play.[1] Or to be precise, they are staging the first play that aspires to the status of "dramatic art," with all the aesthetic—and in this case also moral—ambition that this implies. There have been earlier, rustic performances in a vulgar mode of lowbrow comedy; indeed, the general vulgarity and dissipation of the age is what has prompted the god Indra to ask Brahma to create a theatrical diversion that might reach beyond the educated classes (who have access to the laws of the Vedas, even if they could do more to follow them) and bring the increasingly insolent subaltern classes to heel by instructing them even as it entertains them.

And thrillingly crowd-pleasing the new theater certainly is: full of fights, explosions, roaring voices, singing, dancing—in short, all the spectacular action that ordinary folk enjoy. But Bharata's theater also takes its ideological duties seriously. Having given Bharata his dramaturgical instructions in the form of a new treatise on stagecraft, a "fifth Veda" called the Natyashastra, Brahma points out that a most convenient occasion for the first play would be Indra's Banner Day—the day commemorating the time that Indra, together with a host of other deities, defeated the forces of the demons, thus safeguarding the social and cosmic order. Having rehearsed his one hundred sons and his dancing girls, Bharata duly resolves that his first play will be a dramatization of this noble triumph of good over evil.

The show comes off exceedingly well, and the gods who have been watching are delighted. They shower Bharata and his players with gifts: Indra gives them his banner staff, Brahma gives them a crooked stick, Varuna a gourd, Shiva blessings, Vayu a fan, Vishnu a throne, and so on. But other onlookers are not so happy. The demons whose defeat has been so conclusively depicted are furious at their humiliating (mis)representation and round up some goons with whom they rush the stage, screaming that they will not tolerate this kind of thing and casting a spell on the performers that paralyzes their ability to talk, move, and even remember. Indra, who had been taking great pleasure in Bharata's dramatic celebration of his military prowess, is livid at the intrusion of this rowdy mob; he seizes his banner staff and bashes most of them to smithereens with it. Still, the surviving rowdies refuse to be cowed and proceed, in their uncouth way, to heckle and harass the blushing heavenly dancing girls.

Bharata is exasperated and asks Brahma to figure out a way that he can put on his plays in peace, without constant interruptions from the demons and their ruffians. Bharata gets his friend Vishvakarman, the celestial architect, to design and build a proper theater for Bharata's company, a separate space under the protection of the gods, each of whom takes responsibility for overseeing some part of it. Indra installs himself as divine patron, officer of order, and exemplary spectator and seats himself on one side of the stage, right next to the action and quite visible to the rest of the audience. His banner staff, still warm from pulping the demons and their hired heavies, stands as a constant warning to those who might presume to breach the integrity of his divine patron-police powers.

Having ensured proper protection for the playhouse, Brahma then decides to give the assembled spectators—gods, demons, and ordinary folk all together—a little tutorial in appropriate spectatorship. He addresses everyone, but he is mainly speaking to the remaining and rather sulky demons, who have clearly not yet learned to back off, to not get so worked up, and to start treating hegemonic ideology as art. Smilingly, Brahma tells the spectators not to take what they see on the stage so literally, but rather to understand that it is fiction. He asks them to remember that the theater belongs to them all, that it serves all of their interests, and that it offers a reflective and refined engagement of all the senses with all the attitudes and arts in creation. Finally, he reminds Bharata and his actors that the Natyashastra requires that the sanctity of each performance be preceded by a sacrificial ritual of devotion to the stage, lest the talents and wisdom of the players be wasted and all involved be reincarnated as beasts.

A Parsi Theater Performance of the Indar Sabha, 1860s

The scene begins with a shot of a crowd milling around outside the entrance of a Parsi theatrical production in a North Indian town.[2] The walls of the theater are plastered with lurid handbills loudly broadcasting the spectacular attractions of the show. This is clearly a new kind of crowd. The spectators at Bharata's play in scene 1, whatever their actual behavior, were expected to adopt a devotional relation to the stage. But the crowds gathering around the entrance to tonight's production are members of a modern public. They have bought their tickets on the open market and come expecting value for money.

The camera follows the crowd as it winds its way inside. We see an interior arrangement in all essentials corresponding to our modern notion of a commercial theater. The spectators find their way to seats arranged in rows facing a curtain that will rise to reveal a breathtakingly lavish stage set, clearly separated from the audience by the invisible fourth wall of the proscenium arch, creating the impression of a self-contained dramatic world that presents itself to be seen by spectators who themselves remain anonymous members of a crowd rather than a devotional community.

And yet the play that they have come to see, a production of the extraordinarily popular *Indar Sabha*, was not written by a playwright hoping to sell tickets. We overhear a man in the audience explaining to his companion that it was commissioned in the early 1850s by the last of the Muslim rulers of the state of Awadh, Wajid Ali Shah, who before the British East India Company annexed his domain in 1856 was as famous for his voluptuous ways as for his lavish patronage of the performing arts. But Wajid's dispensation has been gone for a good decade, and the artists, poets, and performers who once relied on his munificence have scattered far and wide in search of other sources of remuneration. Some of them have joined the new traveling Parsi theater to help put together commercial productions like the one we see before us now.

And yet what confronts us on the stage, like a visual quotation, is both oddly familiar and strangely changed. There is Indra with his banner staff, and there are the dancing girls, more enchanting than ever. During the ages that have passed since Bharata's first show, Indra's mode of presiding over his performative domain has become more markedly princely, exchanging some of his Vedic authority for a more temporal gravitas—as if he, now, is keeping alive the flame of courtly performative patronage at a time when it is rapidly dying in the real world. Evidently gratified by the sensuous pleasures of the dance and, as such, still operating as a kind of exemplary spectator, Indra is surrounded on stage by a large retinue comprising representatives of all stations of society, each of them occupying clearly defined positions of supplication or support vis-à-vis the central authority of Indra's throne.

As onstage participants in a tightly organized performative order in which everyone has a place, the players are thus enacting, for the paying general public on the other side of the proscenium arch, a relation between performance, patronage, and participation that, in this emergent age of generalized commercial entertainment, already appears outmoded. The mythical resonance of Indra and his banner staff, divine patron of the theater, could, until only a few years before, unproblematically be imagined as continuous with present-day performative contexts. To be sure, at the sight of this delectably staged tableau, many audience members in the theater tonight feel a welling of devotional attunement.[3] But their devotion is interleaved with the impression that the splendor of Indra's performative order belongs to a historical time that is at once irrevocably past and yet now also available, in a vaguely nostalgic mode, as a commodity.

SCENE 3

A Cabaret Show at the British Cinema in the
Military Station of Secunderabad, Hyderabad State, 1926

The scene opens as a scantily clad chorus line of British dancing girls, performing as the Cabaret Company, are shimmying their way across the stage of the former Laik-ud-Daula Theatre, now the British Cinema.[4] The audience is largely composed of appreciative British soldiers from the Secunderabad Cantonment, along with a sprinkling of officers and their wives. Although the British think of the theater as a morale-boosting facility for their troops, the *nizam*, the Muslim ruler of Hyderabad (the largest and wealthiest of the Indian princely states), owns the building and likes to attend movies and shows there with his entourage.

Normally, the British resident in Hyderabad prefers to stay away, feeling that, as the top local representative of the British Government of India, there is something unseemly about going to entertainments over which the nizam appears to think he is presiding—and on a British military base at that. But on this occasion, the resident has decided to show up and is absolutely appalled at what he finds. At the best of times the nizam, although theoretically the colonizers' ally, is an embarrassment to the British. He shows up noisy and unshaven, wearing a moth-eaten fez and an old flannel *sherwani*, and insists on seating himself and his retinue, for all the world like sponsoring deities, in special seats on either side of the stage. Not only does the nizam ignore the proper division between the space of the performers and the space of the audience, placing his disgrace in full view of the public, but he also refuses to observe the self-discipline appropriate to a spectator. On one recent occasion, the resident recalls with a small wince, the nizam shouted stridently across the stage during a performance, demanding that his *nawab*, seated on the opposite side, bring him a glass of lemonade. Ignoring the soldiers' exasperated cries of "Shut up!" and "Sit down!," the nizam has even been known to take strolls across the stage in the middle of the action.

All of this would just be another symptom of the outmoded, arrogant despotism that tinges every aspect of the nizam's administration, a theater state of sorts preserved in a state of suspended (and occasionally picturesque) historical animation by the deal the British have struck with those princely states that agreed to cooperate. But on this night, watching the nizam and his stubbly sons sitting there leering at the white female flesh on display, close enough to reach out and touch the dancers, the resident feels an altogether more intimate humiliation prickling his scalp. The nizam has brought along his senior wife, seating her behind a muslin curtain so as to shield her modesty from the gaze of the British soldiers. But what devices will protect the prestige of the British in the eyes of the Indians, a prestige whose vulnerability is suddenly made horrifyingly palpable in the dancing girls' every seductive step? The resident's foot, which until that moment has been marking the beat of the band, freezes.

SCENE 4

An Imaginary Play Dramatizing Events Taking Place in
Mumbai and Delhi between November 1998 and February
1999 in Connection with the Violent Attacks on Theaters
Screening Deepa Mehta's Feature Film Fire.

The scene opens on a modernist-minimalist stage set in which the seats that, in previous scenes, might have been occupied by Indra, the nizam, or some other patron, have been replaced with three risers, one at each side of the stage and one in the middle near the back wall.[5] On each riser is an overstuffed armchair and each armchair dwarfs an actor, facing stiffly forward. In place of the actors' faces we see three large video screens, suspended from the rafters. The video screens each display a face in tight close-up, magnified so as to be entirely out of proportion with the bodies of the actors sitting in the armchairs. The faces belong to other actors representing, in turn, Prime Minister A. B. Vajpayee of the ruling Bharatiya Janata Party (BJP); Censor Board chief and erstwhile screen siren Asha Parekh; and Bal Thackeray, leader of the Shiv Sena.

The faces of "Vajpayee" and "Thackeray" look straight ahead from either side of the stage, blandly and blankly, like television panelists caught in downtime, waiting for the red transmission light to come on. "Parekh," on the screen in the middle, is blindfolded. Beneath and in front of the video screens, the center of the stage is empty but illuminated by two spotlights. This area, which will be animated by the gestures of successive groups of actors enacting the public outrage of protest groups, represents the public space of the street. The spatial relation between the three actors elevated in the armchairs and the "public space" in front of them is arranged so as to suggest discontinuity: the giant faces preside over this (as yet empty) public space while appearing to gaze over and past it, into a nonspecific distance. The stage is flanked by large banners advertising corporate sponsors. No one is holding the banner staffs.

The voice of a narrator is heard: "In 1996–97, Indo-Canadian film director Deepa Mehta premieres her film *Fire* at film festivals all over the world, including India. The film focuses on the increasingly intimate relationship between Radha and Sita, two sisters-in-law in a middle-class New Delhi household, both neglected by their husbands. Their emergent solidarity gradually takes on erotic overtones. Championed in some quarters as 'the first lesbian film from India,' *Fire* is given an 'A' (adult) certificate by the Indian Censor Board and passed with no cuts in November 1998."

The video image of "Bal Thackeray" blinks. The actor playing Asha Parekh goes into a continuous loop, which will last until the final moments of the performance: signing off on the censor certificate, again and again, impervious to the mounting agitation around her. The narrator continues: "No sooner is the film released in Indian cinemas than the Shiv Sena starts a violent campaign to get it banned, mainly on the grounds that its depiction of a 'lesbian' relationship is 'against Indian culture.' The fact that Radha is played by Shabana Azmi, a Muslim and an activist for progressive causes, is repeatedly emphasized."

A group of actors playing activists from the Shiv Sena's women's wing rush into the center of the stage, shouting slogans and hurling stones. We hear sounds of shattering glass and crunching wood. Immediately, another group of actors, this time portraying young men from the militant Hindu vigilante organization the Bajrang Dal, bustles into the center of the stage from the other direction, joining the fray, shouting and brandishing sticks. A third group of actors, dressed in the garb of the progressive intelligentsia, marches past silently, bearing candles, placards, and a petition for the Supreme Court. The Shiv Sena women and the Bajrang Dal boys run off the stage, to be replaced in short order by a group of male Shiv Sena activists dressed only in underpants, grabbing their crotches and shouting anti-Muslim slogans.

As the noise dies down, the narrator continues: "Despite the censors' approval, the protestors' threats close down screenings of Fire in several Indian cities, even as audiences in other cities, titillated by the controversy, find tickets only on the black market. In a controversial move, the Ministry of Information and Broadcasting sends the film back for re-censoring at the CBFC which, once more, passes it without any cuts." The actor playing Parekh continues, over and over, to certify Fire. "Thackeray" thunders from his screen about how the BJP has gone soft on its promises to uphold Hindu values, gloating: "I added petrol to Fire!" "Vajpayee" objects in dignified tones to the hooliganism and lawlessness of his former coalition partners' boot boys. The underwear protest crew yells: "We are the law!!" A jerkily juxta-posed sequence of clips featuring disclaimers by Fire director Deepa Mehta fills the screen suspended over "Parekh's" body: "Fire is not a lesbian film . . . it's about human desire. . . . If anything, the film is about choices. Hindu concepts like tolerance, nonjudgmentalism, compassion. The incredible loneliness of being that's often the lot of women in India. . . . My film is about love. . . . Fire is a film about tolerance and choice."

The actors at stage center, who have been maintaining frozen poses of protest during these utterances, unfreeze and collapse in a tangled pile of bodies. The stage lights go down. Only the three giant video screens remain illuminated. A scene from Fire plays on all three simultaneously, but the audience, which is already shuffling out of the auditorium, pausing only to pick up product samples from the sponsors, pays no notice:

> The young male servant Mundu, who spends long portions of his days in the family apartment looking after Biji, the aged, bed-ridden mother-in-law, has been instructed by Radha to take the old lady upstairs and show her a video of the televised Ramayana. "Biji really likes religious movies, and the Ramayana is her favourite." Mundu appears to oblige but evidently has another kind of devotional

viewing in mind, for we soon see him energetically masturbating to a porn flick in full view of the old lady who, because she is not only immobile but also speechless, can only flap her hand and whine in ineffectual protest. When the younger sister-in-law, Sita, enters the room unexpectedly, Mundu manages to switch back to the Ramayana *just in time. He attempts to explain his perspiration and Biji's inarticulate agitation as a result of the emotional power of the famous scene in the epic when Ram, lord of his own performative order, demands that Sita demonstrate her purity by undergoing a trial by fire.*

The screens fade to black and a caption appears over the image of a now empty auditorium:

> "Fire is as dangerous to human beings as it is to animals;
> it is the strongest and oldest symbol of the crowd."
> —Elias Canetti, *Crowds and Power*

■ ■ ■

PERFORMATIVE DISPENSATIONS

Mass Publics

What is the historical transition dramatized in the sequence of these four scenes? For my purposes, its most important characteristic is the appearance of what I call the open edge of mass publicity: namely, the element of anonymity that characterizes any public communication in the age of mass publics; the sense that what makes a communication public is not just that "it addresses me" by way of a public channel, but also that "it addresses me insofar as it also, and by the same token, addresses unknown others," others who share my membership in an emergent general public. As Michael Warner suggests,

> In a public, indefinite address and self-organized discourse disclose a lived world whose arbitrary closure both enables that discourse and is contradicted by it. Public discourse, in the nature of its address, abandons the security of its positive, given audience. It promises to address anybody. It commits itself in principle to the possible participation of any stranger. It therefore puts at risk the concrete world that is its given condition of possibility. This is its fruitful perversity. Public discourse postulates a circulatory field of estrangement that it must then struggle to capture as an addressable entity. (2002:81)

In India, as in many other colonial contexts, mass publicity arrived well before the political democratization with which, in mainstream political theory, it is so often associated. As a consequence the British were, as we shall see, often struggling to reconcile the bounded categories through which they sought to understand and manage Indian sociocultural difference with the open edge of mass publicity. But it would, I think, be a mistake to assume that this problem disappeared with the coming of formal mass democracy at the moment of Independence. In other words, while the tension between bounded symbolic orders and the open edge of mass publicity took distinctively colonial forms, it was not an exclusively colonial problem. Nor is its persistence into the postcolonial period to be explained as a pathological survival of colonization. Rather, this struggle, between bounded social orders in which value may be grounded and the infinitely receding horizon of the sovereign people, is a structural feature of mass publics.

We are in many ways used to thinking that mass publics are premised on the kind of abstract idea of citizenship that decisively departs from the personalized publics of patrons, whether clerical or princely. Immanuel Kant made this a condition of enlightenment: the ability publicly to exercise one's critical reason in the face of the "given" authority of ministers and kings. Enlightenment is in this sense also a farewell to idolatry, to *proskynesis*, the self-abasing "kissing-toward" that befits an attitude of prostration before a powerful patron (Freedberg 1989). But as the given authority of a lord or a prince dissolves into the sovereignty of the people, the performative and affective intensity previously focused on the image and person of the ruler is not simply "overcome" by reason. Rather it finds a restless home in the transient, mobile energies of the modern crowds that become the bearers and the addressees of the new mass publicity (Mazzarella 2010c; Santner 2011; Schnapp and Tiews, eds., 2006).

These performative energies remain fundamental to how public cultural value is generated, although since the nineteenth century (in India, at other times elsewhere) they have grappled with the peculiar indeterminacies generated by the open edge of mass publicity. The symbolically ordering and prestige-producing functions of patronage have by no means disappeared in the time of mass publicity. We need only think of how the "by the grace of" of courtly patronage has morphed into the "brought to you by" formula of consumer brand sponsorship. Branded environments seek to construct not only the pomp of dedicated performative spaces but also the exclusive authority to police both the uses of their insignia and the intrusion onto their territory of competitors. Nor is the phenomenon nowadays restricted to the sphere of marketing, although this is perhaps where it is most unabashed. Political rallies and mobilizations similarly seek to forge crowd energies into symbolically dedicated containers of identification and purpose; the "magnetizing" ability of the skilled rhetorician is to create the impression that it is only within the domain of the speaker's discourse that their audience's desires and inclinations can be desirably and purposefully organized.

As I have already suggested, the transition to Independence may have marked the end of the imperial sovereign. But it did not abolish the discontinuity between empirical crowds and open-ended publics. Nor did it do away with the persistent dream of a social order that could morally ground the *mana* (force) of mass society.

The Mana of Mass Society

This is, in a sense, an old anthropological problem. Emile Durkheim's classic analysis of ritual as the foundation of social order in *The Elementary Forms of Religious Life* (2008 [1912]) already grapples with it. Durkheim proposed, through an analysis of societies organized by totemic orders of classification, that one of the basic functions of ritual is to integrate sensuous excitement (the famous "collective effervescence") with symbolic order. This ritual mediation of excitement through order is, for Durkheim, what gives the ways of being in the world that we sometimes call "culture" their sense of compulsion, their moral gravitas. Through ritual, societies harness a fundamental sense of cosmic efficacy or force (mana) to collectively intelligible and binding systems of value. This is how we get not just meaning, but meaning that matters.

Durkheim formulated these thoughts around the turn of the twentieth century. *The Elementary Forms* was, despite superficial appearances, an intervention into the then-live debate about how best to harness the volatile energies of urban crowds in an emergent mass society (Mazzarella 2010c). And yet, of course, Durkheim's expository mise-en-scène was the small-scale, "primitive" society, the face-to-face social order. As in his first major work, *The Division of Labour in Society* (1893), the question that haunted *The Elementary Forms* was whether an understanding of "primitive" social forms might assist us moderns, living under very different conditions, on the path to social solidarity.

Durkheim suggested that in a small-scale society, the proper observance of ritual prescriptions and prohibitions (what he called positive and negative rites) would ensure a relatively stable mediation of excitement and order, of force and value. A regular ritual calendar was imperative to "top up the tank" of collective social commitment. More suggestively for my purposes here, Durkheim noted that mana was always a volatile force, always at risk of leaking, shocking, infecting, and injuring if rituals were not done just right. Like an electrical current, it had to be handled with great care.

All this raises the question of whether we might be able to transpose the problem of how collective energy (mana) gets mediated through symbolic orders onto modern mass-mediated societies. Claude Lévi-Strauss (1987), drunk on totalizing structuralist ambition, famously dismissed the category of mana in his *Introduction to the Work of Marcel Mauss* as nothing but an empty symbol, a placeholder for those areas of social life that science had yet to explain. But this is too intellectualist a solution; here Durkheim's emphasis on the intensely embodied and sensuous quality of the manifestation of mana in collective action is an important corrective, particularly in light of the recent concern in cultural and critical theory with "affect" (Gregg and Seigworth, eds., 2010; Mazzarella 2009).

Four propositions need to be spelled out at this point. First, in mass-mediated societies, the relation between excitement and symbolic order—a relation that, as Durkheim pointed out, is always volatile—becomes chronically and palpably problematic. Second, as a result, in mass-mediated societies various fantasies of face-to-face (ideologically framed as immediate) community coexist with the acknowledgment of their impossibility. Third, this impossibility is what brings modern state censorship into being, since there is no longer—if there ever was—any overall "built-in" mechanism of regulating the relation between sensuous provocation and social meaning. But this impossibility is also what constantly thwarts modern state censorship, since the absence of any built-in social mechanism also leaves it without any obvious grounds for its own judgments. Fourth, it may be useful to use the term "public affect" to describe not some (dubiously ontologized) presocial or presymbolic domain of sensory intensity but rather the sense of "liveness" and emergent potential that arises in the chronic gap between the sensuous resonances of mass-mediated images and the competing ways in which they get partially harnessed to social and political projects of value. Here, again, is the mobile space in which the potentiated reality of the cinema appears. Here is, as it were, the mana of mass society.

Patron/Police: Performative Dispensations

How does the concept of performative dispensations help us adapt Durkheim's insights about the ritual mediation of force and value to our present concerns? Durkheim posited a fundamental distinction between the sacred and the profane. Ritual was sacred timespace; the lifeworld of work and quotidian concerns was profane. But to stress the performative does not just mean pointing out that the making and remaking of social order relies on enactment. Following theorists as diverse as Erving Goffman, Pierre Bourdieu, Jacques Derrida, and Judith Butler, it also points us beyond the formally marked timespaces of ritual and toward performative enactment on stages; screens; street corners; and even in the most intimate, apparently informal, transactions. Across these settings, the performative is not just a matter of adhering to social scripts or adequately playing roles. Rather, it involves a constant multisensory activation of gesture, bodily comportment, and aesthetic potentialities within and against such scripted expectations. As Durkheim remarked of the ritual mediation of sensuous force and symbolic order, the relation between such bodily activation and role expectations is always mobile and, to an extent, unpredictable.

Durkheim has often been dismissed as an essentially reactionary thinker who naturalizes hegemonic ideology as social solidarity. But I do think that his argument in *The Elementary Forms* provides a fruitful starting point for a critical analysis of the performative consolidation of ideology—as well as its fragility. This is where the term *dispensation* becomes useful. A dispensation suggests not just an order of things but one that appears to have been handed down from above—as in "a system of revealed promises and commands regulating human affairs."[6] Handed down, then, from a transcendent authority and overseen in its earthly enactment by a sovereign person/power who is ambiguously at once patron and police, whose banner staff is at once the umbrella under which the performance may take place and the weapon that crushes those who challenge its integrity. A dispensation combines two kinds of claims to sovereign authority: the sovereignty that opens and maintains a protected space in which a form of life can be performed, that is, lived, and the sovereignty that, as Carl Schmitt (2005 [1922]) famously remarked, decides on the exception, on what falls outside the symbolic order of the law.

To speak of a performative dispensation, then, means both to emphasize the fact that our worlds exist only insofar as they are physically enacted —with greater or lesser degrees of ritualized explicitness—and that the authority underpinning these worlds, qua dispensations, appears both in the naturalized mode of "the way things are" and, in moments of rupture or challenge, as being possible only by the more or less exceptional patron/police-grace/violence of a sovereign authority. One of the central claims of this book is that the condition of mass publicity makes this state of exception palpably chronic. As a result, it invites constant invocations of emergency authority and crisis and at the same time renders all such attempts to assert emergency authority problematic.

Can the patron/police unity of Indra's banner staff have any meaning in a democratic age? Who is the patron of the democratic mass public? Is it not the public itself—self-constituting, self-legislating? Does not the sovereign as patron/police belong to another, pre-democratic or "feudal" social order? Does not the finite crowd that gathers under Indra's banner staff open up to the infinity of modern publics? But if a singular, embodied sovereign is an archaism in mass democracies, then what kinds of objects, places, or symbols take over the function of focusing meaning that matters?

In performative dispensations historically preceding the era of mass publicity, patron and police functions could appear integrated in the singular body of a sovereign. This was, of course, always an ideological fiction. The embodied sovereignty of the ruler—king, lord, chief, master—was based on a fetish-effect, a projection of socially generated value onto a singular body. But the claim that the legitimacy of the ruler, as patron and police, was continuous with the local performative space of the community could plausibly be made, more or less successfully as the times might allow. In the age of mass publicity, however, the plausibility of this claim comes undone. A performative dispensation can no longer be imagined as only local, and the nascent sovereignty of the spectator-citizen, in all its intimate anonymity, rubs up against the vestiges of the kind of singularized authority embodied in an auratic emperor.

Four Scenes Revisited

Let me, then, revisit the four scenes I sketched at the beginning of this chapter in order to suggest, in a preliminary way, the kinds of possibilities that thinking through performative dispensations might disclose. Already in scene 1, Bharata's play, we see how the first performative dispensation brings the troublesome lower orders into the fold by means of enjoyment. Indra, prominently seated as the sovereign patron of the first play, is very much a visible player in the ritual. The stage itself is a sacred space to which appropriate offerings must be made. The play takes place by Indra's grace, and whatever gratification it gives to the audience redounds to his greater glory. The audience members are not so much spectators or members of a public as they are participants in a cosmic order, hierarchical but also reciprocal, in which their supplication to Indra's sovereignty is rewarded with incorporation and protection.

By scene 2, the Parsi theater performance of the *Inder Sabha*, all this is being enacted as a fiction on a theatrical stage separated by the invisible fourth wall of the proscenium arch from the "real world" of the audience and its extra-theatrical concerns (Egginton 2003). In the *Inder Sabha*, Inder (Indra) is no longer "really" on the stage, overseeing the players. Rather, he has been folded into the fictional space of the play. And the play is quite self-consciously a dramatic re-presentation of an archaic performative dispensation, staged in a theater that survives by means of the anonymous and "invisible" (because not manifested in the body of a particular person) patronage of the market. The spectators, for their part, are no longer "really" supplicants at the court of a prince-deity. Instead, they are members of an emergent general public—mediated by a new commercial mass market in publicity and performance—a public that is, in principle if not quite in practice, premised on the intimate anonymity of the modern urban crowd. The Indra of the *Inder Sabha*, suggests Kathryn Hansen, represents the moment when the performative dispensations of the court and of the market begin to overlap: "His position in the drama as focus of desire and his royal status as pre-eminent consumer or *mahabhogi*, constructed an imagined self for the emerging spectator" (2001:88). This is not to say, of course, that the relation of the consumer-spectator to what unfolds on this modern stage (or later, in the Indian cinema's mythologicals and the televised epics of the 1980s) cannot still also be devotional just because the ritual is now "fictional" and commodified.

In scene 3, the nizam of Hyderabad's attempts to occupy a place of courtly sovereignty vis-à-vis the Cabaret Company's performance strike the British resident as entirely inappropriate. In a theatrical context understood by the British soldiers who make up most of the audience as one of pure entertainment, the nizam's desire to "lord it" over the space of the stage represents not only an unacceptable breaching of the boundary separating the fictional space of the stage from real life and a failure on the part of an anachronistic potentate to recognize the modern commercial basis of the performance, but also an embarrassing reminder of the "emptiness" of the performative dispensations to which British India had consigned those rulers of princely states who were prepared to play the parts assigned them in the everyday dramatics of the British Empire. In whose domain, under whose protection, is this performance really taking place?

Scene 4 takes place in a postcolonial India in which sovereignty formally belongs to the people. And yet multiple pretenders to symbolic authority compete to speak for and to this people and to forge their performative energies into durable symbolic orders. Indra's banner staff has apparently been retired for good, thrown out as an artifact of an archaic dispensation. But where has his power gone? Technically, it resides in the people and the state that is their political expression. But who articulates it in practice? Who gives the energy that is palpable in the streets a legitimate expression? Politicians? Activist groups? Movie stars? Corporations? Courts? Censors? Through what kinds of language can the provocations of performance—on stage, screen, or street—be measured and judged? Through immemorialist claims to the ancient heritage and moral community? Or through modern norms of progress, rationality, decency, and taste?

Scene 1 establishes from the very beginning that the relation between stage and life is deeply ambiguous. Brahma instructs the assembled to understand the play as a kind of fictional space set apart. And yet its reality is offensively palpable to the demons, who see the play as an objectionably aestheticized reenactment of their own struggle with the constituted authority embodied by the lord and patron, Indra. The affective power of performance is thus confusing; dependent for its effect on the mobilization of real affect grounded in real experience, it nevertheless asks of its spectators to treat this mobilization as both set apart from everyday experience and implicated in it.

The conventional anthropological gesture would be to interpret the movement from scene 1 to scene 2 as a movement from myth to modernity, from ritual to theater (see Schechner 2003a [1974] for a useful critique of this paradigm). Or perhaps more precisely in this case, it would be to read the Parsi theater production of the *Inder Sabha* in the 1860s as marking a transitional moment when essentially religious or devotional content helps a secular-commercial theatrical form to emerge. We might interpret the show as a mythologically themed performance by a theatrical company whose name draws on a repertoire that attempts to index the prestige of the colonizer's grandeur: the Corinthian, the Victoria, and the New Alfred (Hansen 1989). In either case, the implication is that we are witnessing a movement from a "traditional" or "mythical" performative context in which the audience is participating in a ritual where they believe that the Indra on stage is "really" a god to a "modern" or "theatrical" performative situation in which the audience knows that the Indra on stage is "only" an actor.

But it would be a mistake simply to sequentialize these modes of performative consciousness, as if they were markers of a historical development, rather than seeing them as moments in every performative dispensation. So, it is not that "traditional" audiences do not understand that the god depicted in the ritual is not "really" a god—that is, that they are the victims of a performatively induced false consciousness. From the standpoint of ritual efficacy, this distinction between the "representation" and the "reality" is often not in any case epistemologically relevant. Rather, it is "modern" commonsense understandings of performance that tend to enforce a damaging misrecognition: namely, an increasingly rigid distinction between the "fictional" space of the stage or screen and the "reality" of the surrounding world. One might say that the ideological effect of this modern insistence on the fictional character of the performance space is to help shore up the solidity and "givenness" of life beyond the stage, to divert our attention from its essentially performative foundations.

This is an important aspect of the British resident's discomfort at the sight of the nizam of Hyderabad's behavior at the British Theatre in scene 3. Much has been written about the moral panics caused by spicy Hollywood films and European dancing girls in the colonies during the 1920s. Poonam Arora (1995), for example, shows how troubling it was for the British authorities' sense of imperial prestige to see brown men gazing lustfully at scantily clad white women on the colonial screen. Undoubtedly, colonial film spectatorship potentiated a transgression of the sexual and racial hierarchies that were central to imperial legitimation (Jaikumar 2006). But I think the nizam's leering appreciation of the British cabaret dancers has other implications. For one thing, by insisting on seating himself at the side of the stage like a patron of the dance, the nizam is invoking the Mughal performative idiom of the *nautch* in the midst of a commercial European entertainment. It is, in other words, not just the lustfulness of his gaze but also his assertive claim to a patron's sovereignty over the proceedings that challenges the performative pragmatics of imperial authority. The resident's foot freezes not just because of the implicit sexual humiliation of the British rulers offering up their nubile young women for the delectation of a decadent Oriental despot. Its sudden arrest also expresses the resident's recognition that the nizam's insistence on breaching the fourth wall is embarrassing not so much because of its apparently archaic "misunderstanding" of the modern theatrical space but rather because it serves as an uncanny reminder of the performativity not only of colonial entertainments—cabarets, movies—but also of imperial legitimation itself.

By scene 4, and the crisis over the supposed obscenity of Deepa Mehta's *Fire*, the continuity between the performative spaces of stage, screen, life, and street has once again become quite obvious. Indeed, it has become *too* obvious for many, who lament the performative politicization of religion in the BJP's long march to power through the 1980s and 1990s, their rath yatras and Ram shila pujas,[7] the yoking of chauvinist politics to popular entertainment during festivals, and so on (T. B. Hansen 2001; Heuzé 1995; Kaur 2003). Adding another twist to the patron/police dynamic, this performative politicization of popular religion often went hand in hand with violent episodes of public cultural policing, of which the *Fire* furor was only the most widely reported. On the one hand Ramarajya, the legendary polity of the god-king Ram, was the Sangh Parivar's myth model for a performative dispensation in which *dharma* (duty), devotion, and police authority were seamlessly combined. This functioned not only as a rhetorical script for the new Hindu nationalism but also as a dramaturgical playbook for its spectacular rallies and mass actions. On the other hand, modern urban middle-class respectability—the core terrain of the BJP's political appeal—was the space that, at all costs, had to be naturalized as a stable moral space, free of any performative dependence.

Asuric Interruptions

More than once, commentators during the cultural emergency probed the story of Indra's battle with the demons for its allegorical yield. Typically, the goon gangs of the Shiv Sena—or the Bajrang Dal or the VHP or one of their affiliates—were cast as the disruptive and resentful *asuras* (demons). But who in this democratic day and age could claim the unified patron/ police functions of Indra and his banner staff? Perhaps the Hindu nationalists aspired to an updated version of this kind of authority. Not just the sovereignty of secular law, but the moral legitimacy of a new Ramarajya, a new kingdom of Ram. A state that was not just an engine of economic growth but also the sponsor and protector of a new dharmic order. Not for nothing did BJP hardliner and Gujarat chief minister Narendra Modi appear on stage in a gigantic mechanical lotus when he addressed an adoring Mumbai crowd in 2002.[8] But if the Sangh Parivar wanted to reinstall Indra's banner staff, then who were the asuras? Culturally alienated secular liberals trying to wedge Brechtian moments of salutary estrangement[9] into the myth-machinery of Hindu nationalist spectacle?

Cultural critic and dramaturge Rustom Bharucha revisited the story of the first play in 1992, just as Shiv Sena–style "extraconstitutional" street censorship was waxing. (I discuss the formal/informal censorship struggle more extensively in chapter 3.) If we read the new goons as the asuras of old, Bharucha pointed out, then is not their target the secular law that regulates performance—censorship law, licensing law, and so on? "Even if we don't uphold a religious conception of theater today, it is significant that we continue to endorse the idea of protection in our concepts of performance. In the secular world, the regimentation of laws, licenses, and codes (performative and social) have replaced the sanctity of *pujas* (devotional rituals). . . . Unlike the *asuras*, we have to behave ourselves" (Bharucha 1992).[10]

For Bharucha, the point about an asuric interruption is that it is an attack from outside—from a standpoint external to a performative tradition. Much like Shyam Benegal's distinction between spoken and unspoken rules (see the introduction), Bharucha argues that it is precisely in those indigenous Indian performance practices—the very practices that state curatorial and preservationist authorities dismiss as mired in the rigidity of "timeless" tradition—that we find the supple ability to incorporate emergent developments and narrative ambiguity.[11] We moderns, in turn, project our own passive absorption in spectacle onto rustic audiences that in fact "continue to respond to narratives with numerous digressions, juxtapositions, flashbacks, jumps, and abstractions that constitute a most intricate blending of ruptures which one would be tempted to describe as 'interruptions.'"[12] We are the ones who have placed a taboo on rupturing tradition, when living tradition "itself invites interruption, though never arbitrarily." Bharucha's point is that performance traditions grounded in a continuity of local practice reject asuric interruptions, that is, attacks from outside. "But there is always room within its 'protected space' for a basic questioning of its norms and even assertion of irreverence."[13] What Bharucha calls "basic questioning" here is obviously rather different from a modernist notion of ideology critique, even of the immanent variety (Eagleton 1991). It takes place within a moral order that may be expansive but is still hegemonic; it does not open onto the infinity of things being utterly otherwise. But the reason it looks attractive, compared to the "externality" of modern state censorship, is that it is both grounded in the vital moral sentiments of a community and, because of that grounding, unafraid of ambiguity and emergence.[14]

I find the undialectical opposition between tradition and modernity—with all the good stuff on one side, as it were—unsatisfying (just as is it unsatisfying when the valorized side is the modern). And for the purposes of making his argument, Bharucha also rather elides the central role of patronage—and the sovereign authority it helps to constitute—in "traditional" performance settings. A certain local performative dispensation, grounded in the (certainly sometimes oppressive) pragmatics of coexistence, allows the kind of village drama that Bharucha describes to absorb and even encourage what he calls "basic questioning" and "interruption." But the cinema, being a mass medium, presents a very different kind of regulatory problem. In its mode of address, it is at once sensuous and impersonal. A cinema audience is always at once an empirical *crowd*—a particular group of people physically co-present at a particular time and place—and part of a virtual mass *public* that is in principle infinite. My proposition, then, is that the endlessly reiterated assertion of the cinema's "immense power" is linked to this open edge, this intimate anonymity, this corporeal and yet disembodied address.

So is there a performative dispensation that is adequate to a mass public rather than a face-to-face community? This is the basic question that haunts film censorship.

THE CRUCIBLE OF REGULATION

Print and Performance: A Nineteenth-Century Field

So far I have outlined the impasses of mass performative dispensations in general terms. I now want to give a somewhat more specific sense of how the coming of Indian film censorship represented a response to the proximate challenge of the cinema—and how, in turn, the challenge of the cinema pulled into sharp focus a series of regulatory anxieties that had arisen out of an emergent field of Indian public culture during the nineteenth century.

The first Indian Cinematograph Act became law in March 1918,[15] and by the spring of 1920 the amendments that established censor boards with regional jurisdiction had also come into force. On the model of the film censorship laws that had recently been introduced in Britain, the Indian Cinematograph Act took aim at the risk of both physical and moral inflammation. Flammable celluloid was dangerous, especially in crowded, closed spaces.[16] But the specter of such literal conflagrations also served as a metaphor for another kind of fire hazard, requiring "the protection of the public from indecent or otherwise objectionable representations" (Government of India 1918). These were certainly flammable times in India. World War I was in its final months when the Cinematograph Act came into force. In many ways the Act was an anticipatory solution to the problem of how to manage the movies when emergency wartime powers of censorship and information management could no longer be applied.[17] In response to Indian claims to democratic representation, the British were playing a two-fisted game. On the one hand, in 1919 the Government of India (Montagu-Chelmsford) Act significantly expanded political participation for Indians.[18] On the other, March of that year saw the passage of the Rowlatt Act. If the Government of India Act represented the ideal of a sober, gradual incorporation of Indians into deliberative democratic forms under a benign colonial umbrella, then the Rowlatt Act, which provocatively extended some wartime emergency measures on an indefinite basis, expressed a zero-tolerance line toward militant crowd protest. On April 13, General Reginald Dyer's infamously indiscriminate slaughter of hundreds of unarmed Indian civilians at Jallianwala Bagh in Amritsar caused a major embarrassment for liberal British opinion and seriously undercut what little political credibility the British still retained in India. If the cinema was the medium of the crowd, then the closing decades of the Raj saw a continuous struggle between the prospect of gradualist political reform and direct (whether violent or nonviolent) crowd action.[19]

As an object of regulation, the cinema brought together concerns coming out of two earlier public media: print and theatrical performance. Like print, the cinema was a medium of mechanical mass reproduction. Like theater, it mobilized the performative-mimetic energies of bodily action. Of course, the cinema lacked the hot liveness of the theater; its actors could not directly respond to and build on the emergent energies of their audience. But its mass duplication meant that, like print, it could be everywhere at the same time, and its provocation could always be replayed. It was, then, in the cinema that the anonymous intimacy that characterizes mass publicity really came into its own.

In Indian urban centers, a new middle class was emerging during the second half of the nineteenth century. Sections of the upper and intermediate castes found avenues of training and employment in new English-language schools, colleges, and libraries, as well as in the legal institutions that arose around the newly standardized system of criminal law.[20] The upper echelons of the new intelligentsia debated identity and progress in English-language pamphlets and periodicals, but a larger section found its collective voice in Indian-language media. Newspapers and periodicals were being printed in Calcutta from the late eighteenth century onward, and Indian-language publications started appearing in the 1810s, but for political and technical reasons a vigorous Hindi print culture did not really take off across North India until the 1830s and 1840s (Bayly 1996).[21] During these years, newspapers became a central feature of everyday life. Illiterate villagers attended public readings. In the 1820s, only wealthy princes could afford to print; by the 1870s virtually every small town had its own press. Magazines and pamphlets allowed a vast range of associations and interest groups to go public, from the social and religious reformers of the early nineteenth century to the caste associations of its closing decades.[22]

As long as the Indian press operated primarily in English, the government could easily understand both its audience and its content. But the booming Indian-language press was an entirely different matter, bringing the potentials of publicity right up against the limits of colonial liberalism. As the then-governor of Madras, Sir Thomas Munro, noted, "A free press and the dominion of strangers are things that are quite incompatible, and which cannot long exist together; for what is the first duty of a free press? It is to deliver the country from a foreign yoke and to sacrifice to this one great object every measure and consideration; and if we make the press really free to the native as well as to Europeans, it must inevitably lead to this result" (quoted in Gleig 1830:27). In press censorship, as in most matters, British policy in India oscillated between tolerance and clampdowns.[23] Press censors policed what could and could not be said in colonial public spheres. But they were also expected to track emergent trends in Indian lifeworlds.[24]

The conditions of Indian performance were also radically transformed in the mid-nineteenth century. The British were busy annexing territories whose Indian rulers had often, as in the case of Awadh (Oudh, annexed in

1856), been crucial patrons of the performing arts.[25] The performers whose livelihood had thus been interrupted often sought out a commercial living in up-and-coming urban centers, sometimes, as Kathryn Hansen (2001) points out, retailing a kind of "post-feudal aesthetic" to aspirant middle classes hungry for the romance of an outmoded royal order.[26] At the same time, Philip Lutgendorf notes, the slow decline of Mughal power and its Indo-Persian Islamicate cultural idiom opened an opportunity for rising Hindu princes and businessmen to sponsor plays and recitations celebrating the virtues of Ram, "whose myth had retained a strong, martial, imperial, and sociopolitical dimension . . . [with an] emphasis on social and political hierarchy, and on the properly deferential behaviour of subjects and subordinates" (1989:41). By the second half of the nineteenth century, then, Indian performance styles ranged all the way from the broad, corporeally emphatic ribaldry of "folk" forms to the deliberately desensualized, neoclassical Hindi drama of Bharatendu Harischandra (K. Hansen 1989). Seizing the commercial middle ground, the Parsi theater, which appeared around 1850, blended British-derived proscenium staging and the latest special effects with content suitably adapted from North Indian mythological traditions (K. Hansen 2004; A. Kapur 2004). A native product of the new mass publics, the Parsi theater was also aesthetically the most proximate ancestor to the Indian cinema.

Systematic state regulation of the theater was, however, in the first instance triggered by urban middle-class Calcutta productions like Dinabandhu Mitra's anti-indigo play *Nil Darpan* (The mirror of indigo), which put colonial exploitation on the stage during the 1860s and 1870s. Leaning heavily on the sedition and obscenity sections of the Indian Penal Code of 1860 (secs. 124A and 292–94), the Dramatic Performances Act of 1876 took aim at shows that were "likely to excite feelings of disaffection to the government established by law in India" or "likely to deprave and corrupt persons present at the performance" (Government of India 1876).

It is of course interesting that the term *disaffection* is used here and elsewhere to describe a breakdown of the people's loyalty to the state. Sec. 124A of the Indian Penal Code, which deals with sedition, defines *disaffection* as "disloyalty and all feelings of enmity." Legally acceptable public speech, according to this section, consists of "comments expressing disapprobation of the Government with a view to obtain their alteration by lawful means" (or, in other words, what Ranajit Guha has identified as the British ideal of "rightful dissent" [1997:55]). Unacceptable public speech, by contrast, is marked by an intentional affective provocation, by "exciting or attempting to excite hatred, contempt, or disaffection" (Indian Penal Code 2003:41).[27]

Many of the justifications for censoring the theater strongly prefigured later claims about the peculiar power of the cinema. Arthur Hobhouse, law member of the Viceroy's Council, defended the draft Dramatic Performances Bill as follows:

> In all times and countries, the drama has been found to be one of the strongest stimulants that can be applied to the passions of men—"*Segnius irritant animos demissa per aures quam quae sunt oculis subjecta fidelibus*" [What we hear, with weaker passion will affect the heart, than when the faithful eye beholds the part]—said an acute man of the world who knew human nature well.[28] . . . Certain it is that we accept conduct and language on the stage which if we read the same things in a book, we should at once reject as false, absurd and incredible, so powerful is the effect produced by the actual living representation before our eyes. And in times of excitement no surer mode has been found of directing public feeling against an individual, a class or a Government than to bring them on stage in an odious light. It is doubtless for these reasons that the laws of civilized countries give to their government great controlling power over the stage.[29] (quoted in Bhattacharyya 1989:59–60)

Hobhouse's reference to the theater's "actual living representation" invokes not only realistic verisimilitude but also, it would seem, something like the emergent corporeal potentials that, as we shall shortly see, would later be attributed to the cinema. These were potentials that went beyond the referential meaning of a play's "content" to include the more elusive but no less "present" registers of gesture, tone, and bodily attitude. Press censorship certainly involved its own interpretive complications, and colonial censors often had to rely on official Oriental Translators to help them distinguish innocent discourse from politically explosive allegory. But the stage added all the performative insinuations of "liveness" to the problem of interpretation. As playwright Shanta Gokhale put it to me, "The script is censored; the performance cannot be. Suppose an actor is saying something extremely pious and holy and makes a farting sound. He is saying something to the audience at that time which the censor has absolutely no control over."[30] The theater thus presented the colonial censors with a double challenge. There was the problem of distinguishing manifest meaning from latent meaning. But the censors also found themselves confronted with an impression of affective potentiality that seemed irreducible to any particular meaning and, for that reason, all the more frightening.

Inevitably, colonial censorship of the theater grew ever more paranoid, detecting hidden political significance in every other innocent entertainment. Famously, in 1907 the play *Kichaka Vadha* dramatized episodes from the Mahabharata in such a way that "'everyone in the theater knows that Kichaka is really intended to be [Viceroy] Lord Curzon, that Draupadi is India, and Yudhistira is the Moderate and Bhima the Extremist Party'" (quoted in Pinney 1999:217). A few years later, Government of Bombay officials were convinced that a reference to a "Bal Raja" in *Dhanurbhang*, a dramatic adaptation of the *Ramayana*, was a seditious reference to nationalist leader Bal Gangadhar Tilak, barely disguised under "a very thin veneer of religious mythology,"[31] until their Oriental Translator explained that "when Ramchandra [Ram] went to Mithila to wed Sita, Dasharatha, his father, was still living and he [Ram] was therefore a 'Bal Raja' (literally, an infant king), the heir apparent."[32] The possibilities were endless. As an Indian member of the Legislative Council remarked during the debates on the Cinematograph Bill in March 1918, "We should understand that any episode in ancient or modern literature may, if a man is ingenious enough, be squeezed to give some allegorical meaning."[33] Even many British officials grew impatient with the infinite fecundity of their own censors' hermeneutics of suspicion.

Again, plays like *Kichaka Vadha* or *Dhanurbhang* did not seem dangerous only because of the seditious meanings they might encode, but also because of the volatile performative intensity that seemed to emerge between the players and their audience, an intensity that could not be regulated according to content-based prohibitions. The *Times* correspondent's review of a performance of *Kichaka Vadha* vividly illustrates this impression of what I would call *content beyond content*: "It may be said that all this [attribution of political content] is mere fooling. But no Englishman who has seen the play acted would agree. All his life he will remember the *tense, scowling faces* of the men as they watch Kichaka's outrageous acts, the *glistening eyes* of the Brahmin ladies as they listen to Draupadi's entreaties, their *scorn* of Yudhistira's tameness, their *admiration* of Bhima's *passionate* protests, and the *deep hum of satisfaction* which approves the slaughter of the tyrant" (quoted in Pinney 1999:218; emphasis added).

As early as the 1870s, it was clear to some colonial officials that something unnamable yet fully palpable inhabited theatrical performance and, furthermore, that it threatened to undermine colonial authority by slow degrees. Sir Richard Temple, lieutenant-governor of Bengal, wrote during the debates on the Dramatic Performances Bill, "The manner in which all the most revered institutions under which we lived had been brought into contempt by public exhibitions might not amount to treason, and not even to sedition, yet nevertheless, everything which politically ought to be treated as sacred in the eyes, not only of Europeans, but more especially of natives, might be brought day after day, month after month, into greater and greater contempt" (quoted in Bhattacharyya 1989:88).

Noninterference, Custom, and Mass Publicity

This anxious recognition of an emergent performative power that exceeded any particular thematic content would be carried over from theater to cinema censorship. And yet a great deal had also changed between the 1870s and the time of the first Cinematograph Act in 1918. One of the first things that the Government of India set out to discover when cinema censorship came up for serious discussion in 1915 was whether the Dramatic Performances Act could be expanded so as to include the movies or whether they needed laws of their own.[34] Ostensibly, the issue was the difference between the theater and the cinema as media. But the anxieties generated by the cinema were also inextricable from the regulatory challenges presented by the mass image publics that had emerged during the intervening four decades.

Since the 1870s, the exploding market in mass-produced images transformed print publics from a domain of literate elites to a space where "high" and "low" cultural idioms intertwined. The enormous commercial success of vernacular almanacs brought print-industrial standardization to bear on sacred images (Roy 1995; cf. Jain 2007). Commercial presses thrived on picture prints and book illustrations that, to European eyes, hovered indeterminately somewhere between "fine," "popular," and "devotional" art (Guha-Thakurta 1992; Jain 2007; Pinney 2004). Printed texts were incorporated as performative aids at religious recitals (Lutgendorf 1989). Commercial theatrical ventures were quick to exploit the promotional possibilities of print publicity, evolving a visual repertoire in tandem with the emergent craze for "god poster" lithographs (Jain 2007; Seizer 2005).

Vernacular cultural activists, also drawing on the new mass print culture, led regional movements of revitalization around popular festivals (Freitag 1989, 2001; T. B. Hansen 1999, 2001; Kaur 2003; Pinney 2004). In their dramatic enactment and processional traversal of city streets, these mobilizations hovered, with productive ambiguity, between the invocation of "traditional" principles of community authority and an assertive claim to the "modern" public space of generalized citizenship. In short, the whole rambunctious field of what we would recognize today as "Indian public culture" was emerging during these decades (Appadurai and Breckenridge 1995; Mazzarella 2005b; Mazzarella and Kaur 2009; Pinney 2001).

Even as what Partha Chatterjee (1993) has identified as the "inner" domain of Indian cultural identities was increasingly moving into the "outer" domain of publicness, the British, during these same years, were busy detaching themselves from what C. A. Bayly has called an "affective knowledge" of Indian lifeworlds. Starting in the early nineteenth century and gathering speed after the shock of the Great Rebellion (aka the Mutiny) of 1857–58, the Raj was "slowly retreating from that almost tactile feeling for popular mood that came from participation in Indian worship" (Bayly 1996:166). The aggressive-defensive reaction that characterized British policy after the rebellion brought a heightened physical demarcation of British cantonments and civil lines from "native towns," a jealous policing of the sexual integrity of the white women who were arriving in India in ever greater numbers, and a growing ideological investment in determinist theories of racial difference (Cohn 1996; Collingham 2001; Legg 2007; Metcalf 1995; Procida 2002; cf. Stoler 2002).

Despite their more or less clumsy attempts to adapt Indian rituals of incorporation such as *darbars* to their own purposes, and notwithstanding their elaborate projects of anthropological and archaeological classification, the British were, by the second half of the nineteenth century, "weakest in regard to music and dance, the popular poetry of sacred erotics, dress, and food, though such concerns are near the heart of any civilization" (Bayly 1996:55; cf. Cohn 1983; Mazzarella 2010a). Drifting ever further from the inner worlds of its subjects, the Raj was, in Sudipta Kaviraj's terms, an "external" or "suspended" state (1997:150). It was, writes Ranajit Guha, a "doubly alienated" state: not only formally removed from its subjects but unmediated even in its inception by their forms of life (1997:64). Whereas national rituals in modern European states had attempted to emphasize (mediated) continuity between popular and official culture, the rituals of the Raj objectified the multitudinous diversity of India so as to stand apart from it in an attitude of impartial arbitration (Chatterjee 1993; Freitag 1989).

A key aspect of this stance of impartial arbitration was the colonial principle of "noninterference" in the domain of Indian custom. The policy of noninterference was of course in practice constantly breached in cases such as *sati* or hook-swinging, where the British felt that the demands of decency, morality, or hygiene outweighed the dangers of meddling in matters the natives held dear (Dirks 1997; Hawley, ed., 1994; Mani 1998). But its basic assumption—that one could, as Christopher Pinney (2009) suggests, "titrate" an apolitical and traditional realm of custom from a properly political and modern domain of public life—was a cornerstone of colonial administration. Noninterference was by the same token a key feature of the Raj considered as a performative dispensation: an imperial authority under whose benevolently protective banner staff indigenous customary authorities—what the British called "natural leaders"—enjoyed a kind of delegated sovereignty within their respective "traditional" community jurisdictions.

The principle of noninterference in Indian custom also informed the Dramatic Performances Act, which applied only to what it defined as "public dramatic performances"—that is, shows taking place inside "any building or enclosure to which the public are admitted to witness a performance on payment of money" (Government of India 1876).[35] In practice this meant that the Act covered only the kind of market-based, ticketed, urban, middle-class proscenium theater that had at that time been a significant presence in India for no more than a couple of decades. The Act specifically exempted "any jatras[36] or performances of a like kind at religious festivals"—in other words, performances that the colonial optic classified as traditional. Considered purely as a descriptive taxonomy of Indian performative dispensations, the distinction between "public" and "religious" performances was of course always flawed—as the colonial authorities were well aware. Even when the draft version of the Dramatic Performances Bill was being circulated for comment, the secretary of the British Indian Association remarked that "the manner of giving entertainments in this country is peculiar. A private individual gives an entertainment in his own house, to which he invites friends and neighbours; but very little restriction is placed against the admission of persons not invited. Indeed, as such entertainments are frequently given in connection with some religious ceremony or other, it is held unbecoming and uncourteous to exclude persons who wish to join it though they may not be invited" (quoted in Bhattacharyya 1989:59).

Still, a simple opposition between "public" and "religious" performances suited the basic social ontology of colonial administration and could be sustained with some measure of plausibility as long as custom looked like it might stay in its supposedly apolitical place, under the patronage and policing of the banner staff of custom.

The fact that the progressive withdrawal of the British from any intimate engagement with Indian lifeworlds coincided, during the second half of the nineteenth century, with the rise of overtly politicized performative mobilizations of tradition was, of course, a recipe for intense regulatory anxiety. The great irony of colonial legitimation during these years was that the British retreat from the "inner world" of the Indian quotidian happened at precisely the same time that the booming field of vernacular performative publicness was giving this inner world an "outer"—that is to say a properly public—stage. By the time the cinema came up for sustained discussion, the old division between public and religious performance was in tatters. Everywhere they looked, the British saw "revolutionary propaganda" being broadcast "under the cloak of religion."[37] Precisely the so-called traditional domain now seemed likely to be the most treacherously seditious. In a 1910 letter to the Government of Eastern Bengal and Assam, W. J. Reid, the commissioner of Dacca Division, voiced what had become a standard concern: "These 'Jatra' performances are in some ways the most mischievous weapon that the [anti-imperial nationalist] agitators can use. The language is colloquial and the jests while coarse are precisely of the kind that appeal to a rustic audience; while nearly every [jatra] party contains one or two ready-witted individuals whose comments on the political situation reach people entirely or almost entirely unaffected by public meetings or printed matter" (quoted in Bhattacharyya 1989:187).

Cinema and the Impossibility of Public Opinion
As an object of regulation, then, the cinema was in some ways continuous with the theater; in both cases, there was an anxiety about the mischief the potentiated reality of performance might achieve. At the same time, theatrical performative dispensations were imaginable as bounded by, and built on, localizable symbolic orders, even if the logic of those "native" orders often remained frustratingly opaque to regulators. By contrast, the cinema was everywhere at once and nowhere in particular. Plays had their

particular crowds, gathering at particular times in particular places. But at the cinema, a particular audience-crowd was always imagined as metonymic of a larger cinema-public, viewing elsewhere and at the same time. Theatrical performances seemed often to threaten colonial prestige from vernacular recesses deep "within" British India. But the cinema, especially during Hollywood's dominance on Indian screens between the end of the Great War in 1918 and the coming of sound around 1930, seemed to set up an alarming resonance between Indian affects and foreign scenes.

Scholars like Poonam Arora (1995), Priya Jaikumar (2006), and Brian Larkin (2010) have shown how troubling and how transgressively exciting the cinema was in colonial times: a vast, darkened hall in which Europeans breathed the same air and became absorbed in the same images as their brown subjects. The late nineteenth and early twentieth centuries were the heyday of crowd theory in European social science (Mazzarella 2010c). Crowd theory quite routinely metaphorically linked the apparent suggestibility of volatile urban crowds to variously conceived states of savagery. Meanwhile, early European film theorists—Epstein, Benjamin, Balazs, Eisenstein, Lindsay, and others—posited a radical and often romantic connection between the cinema image and "savage" thought (Moore 2000). In the colonies, the metaphor ran right up against its limit as emerging mass publics—not least cinema audiences—were substantially comprised of individuals whom British colonial thought quite literally classified as childlike savages.

Colonial officials during the 1910s and 1920s certainly often believed that Hollywood had managed to develop a hypermodern communications technology that resonated provocatively with savage sensoria. By the same token, the apparent affinity between U.S. films and Indians tended to confirm long-held British suspicions regarding the fundamental childishness of American civilization.[38] The cinema troubled colonial rule in India, then, not only because it brought into close proximity populations that the authorities had, since at least the mid-nineteenth century, struggled to keep apart. Nor was it only a matter of the cinema's power to stir up the senses. Beyond this, the cinema served as a constant reminder of the coming-into-being of a general Indian public, unknowable in its contours—not necessarily nationalist, not necessarily activist, but certainly straining against the culturalist taxonomies of the "ethnographic state" (Dirks 2001).

The coming of the cinema, then, represented a crisis in terms of the imagined foundation of regulatory authority while at the same time radicalizing some of the most disturbing potentials of the press (technological reproducibility) and the theater (performative intensity). Until the cinema, the infinity of mass publicity and the corporeal intensity of performance had remained separate. Now, for the first time, they were palpably juxtaposed in the experience of the spectator. Moreover, the coupling of patron/police functions that could still be envisioned in the theater as a kind of ritual space came undone at the cinema. Again, the general public as patron was not wholly new; as I have suggested, it emerged in tandem with press publics and the commercial theater. But the cinema foregrounded the problem of what kind of moral order would be capable of mediating the collective effervescence of the cinema audience—its noises, its gestures, its agitation—into a workable performative dispensation.

The distinguishing mark of the debate on film censorship is a crack that runs right down the middle of the Durkheimian ritual scenario. Once the cinema is at issue, collective effervescence appears chronically refractory to symbolic order. And this disjuncture is expressed as a split on both the side of the (spectator-)subject and the side of the (film-)object.

On the side of the subject, any discussion of the cinema in India will, as we have seen, include some mention of its intense affective resonance. Everyday talk most often frames this as a function of an inherently "Indian" disposition toward adornment, expressivity, and melodrama. As Anupam Kher told me, "We are larger-than-life people . . . with a large heart." In the 1870s, the "romantic medievalist" viceroy Lord Lytton famously noted, apropos Indians' apparent susceptibility to spectacle, that "the further East you go, the greater becomes the importance of a bit of bunting" (Cohn 1983; Metcalf 1995). Some 130-odd years later, Vijay Anand suggested to me that Indians' love of *tamasha* (spectacle) could be traced all the way back to the full-bore opulence required by Bharata's ancient Natyashastra.

By the 1920s, Indians' supposed predilection for spectacle had been integrated, in the minds of many British, with a racialized theory of difference. E. Villiers of the European Association in Calcutta, giving testimony before the Indian Cinematograph Committee (ICC), argued that this made them particularly susceptible—for better or for worse—to the seduction of the cinema: "You have got a peculiarly constituted people, they are intensely dramatic in thought and action. When you see a cooly [*sic*] and talk to him you realize how intensely dramatic he is. Their language is a very graphic language, much more than the Western, and that is a material which could be made very much better use of" (ICC 1928a, 2:957).[39]

When the ICC published its report in 1928, the committee concluded that while much of the moral panic around what Hollywood spice might do to Indian audiences was exaggerated, Indians did seem preternaturally pre-adapted, if not porous, to the cinema's peculiar mode of address: "Despite some evidence to the contrary we are fully satisfied that Indians gain *the cinema sense* very quickly—the uneducated sometimes more quickly than the educated" (ICC 1928b:112; emphasis added).

Ostensibly, the potential volatility of the "intensely dramatic" Indian character was in the late twentieth century recuperated by means of a celebratory postcolonial discourse of popular pleasure. The "pit class" that whistles and jeers during spicy scenes—in a manner largely undistinguishable from the audiences observed by anxious British witnesses in the 1920s—finds its redemption in the figure of interactive, adoring Bollywood fandom. Film writer Anupama Chopra remarked, "I lived in the States, and I've never seen audiences reacting to cinema in the way they do here. I've never heard people cheering when the hero walks on screen for the first time. [In India] every single time the star walks on screen, you have people whistling, they clap, so it's an interactive experience. It's not passive viewing at all."[40] The susceptibility to affect-intensive spectacle is the same as it always was, but now it powers both a fear of what the pissing man might do and a fondly patriotic celebration of Indian public exuberance.

On the side of the object, the cinema was, from the very earliest days of its global career, credited with peculiar and peculiarly vital powers. Censors regarded these powers with intense suspicion, even as propagandists lionized them. As Hollywood embarked on its path to global domination (although once Indian filmmakers switched to sound around 1930, the mass popularity of U.S. films in India slumped), its boosters as well as its critics linked the vitality of the cinema to the world-historical destiny of the youthful civilization that stood poised to take over the world. Will Hays, who in the 1930s would lend his name to the infamous Production Code by which Hollywood would regulate the content of its films until well into the 1960s, remarked in the late 1920s: "Motion pictures are not dead things, to be regulated like commodities such as freight and good. They are not wares, to be monopolized and traded in by tickets and statues, or marked like iron and soap. They contain a *potency of life* in them to be as active as the soul whose progeny they are" (ICC 1928a, 4:309; emphasis added).

Visual anthropologist and filmmaker David MacDougall suggests that cinema images address us on a nonconceptual level, where "thought is still undifferentiated and bound up with matter and feeling in a complex relation that it often later loses in abstraction" (2006:1). I would resist the implication that cinematic experience travels only in one direction, from sensory concretion to conceptual abstraction and, by extension, the suggestion that the public life of concepts is not also "bound up with matter and feeling." But I do think that this imbrication of cinematic narrative with our bodily and affective being-in-the-world is an important key to the cinema's ability publicly to mediate the energetic potential of what Walter Benjamin called the optical unconscious (Benjamin 1999a [1931]; cf. Sobchack 2004; Williams 1995).

From a censor's standpoint, this same relation of the cinema to the fleshier side of thought and feeling tends to link its potency of life with the apparently regressive unreason of crowds. The 1969 *Report of the Enquiry Committee on Film Censorship* (aka the Khosla Report), the canonical text of Indian liberal-reformist censorship discourse, abjures the conservative-alarmist language of moral panic. But it does linger on the phenomenal experience of spectatorship, emphasizing both the cinema's peculiar intensity of sensory immersion and the cumulative weight of its continuous duration:

> A communication medium which involves the visual and aural senses in a single coordinated process must make an immediate and vivid impact upon the recipient. A modern sound film, [e]specially the version in vivid realistic colours, is unique among all art forms and media for its evocative potential. The viewer is apt to forget the real world around him, because it is completely hidden from him by the impenetrable curtain of darkness which surrounds him and envelopes [sic] him. The device of photographing faces and expressions from extremely close quarters accentuates the realism of what happens on the screen, and not only facilitates but compels a sense of identification with the characters in the film. A book is usually read in an environment which discourages make-belief [sic]. The presence of real [sic], the actual world, cannot be shut out or forgotten. Also the reading is spread over many days, or many hours, and the very passage of time, [e]specially if there are frequent

interruptions, is a reminder of the unreal and the fictional in the book. A film, on the other hand, lasts for two or three hours and runs without interruption. The continuous concentration on the subjects, the feeling of isolation in the darkened cinema hall and the vividness of the moving and speaking pictures conjure up an atmosphere of reality about the whole experience. (Khosla et al. 1969:60)

What is particularly striking about this paragraph, aside from the emphasis on the cinema's "immediate and vivid impact" and "evocative potential," is the manner in which it wrestles with the problem of the cinema as a "realistic" medium. Its hypnotic power (facilitated by the cinema hall's "impenetrable curtain of darkness" and the audience's uninterrupted immersion) cuts viewers off from "the actual world" and draws them into the "accentuate[d] . . . realism" of the diegesis, in which ordinary objects and situations are transformed by extreme close-ups and other cinematographic devices. This is a reality that is not quite real—an "atmosphere of reality about the whole experience"; or, perhaps better, a reality that, qua accentuated reality, is something *more* than real.

At issue here is not a "hyperreality" à la Umberto Eco (1986), although, of course, the screen world does often conjure a hyperreal mise-en-scène in which contingencies and irregularities have been airbrushed out so as to produce an environment whose claim to realism is to be "even better than the real thing." Rather, the Khosla report is pointing toward what I would like to call a *potentiated reality*, a reality that, to recall McDougall's phrase, returns us cognitively to that place where "thought is still undifferentiated and bound up with matter and feeling in a complex relation that it often later loses in abstraction." If hyperreality describes a fiction that invites us to believe that the world as carefully perfected cliché is an improvement on everyday life, then potentiated reality is the opposite: a fiction that, through a peculiarly intensive mode of immersion, pulls us back from the clichés that sustain a normative order and *opens up* everyday life to embedded/emergent sensuous potentials whose destinations are unknowable in advance.

There is, of course, the temptation to associate the hyperreal mode with Hollywood ideology and the kind of semiotic overdetermination that Roland Barthes (1972) called "mythology." Conversely, we might want to place potentiated reality on the side of the (modernist) angels—the cinema of salutary estrangement. But it seems to me that this would be an over-simplification and that most cinema involves a generative oscillation between these two modes. This oscillation is, in turn, partly a function of the way a film is made: the semiotic structure of the film as text, to be sure, but also the mode of engagement that it solicits from the viewer. The ideological "pull" of mainstream commercial cinema, then, is not so much a matter of presenting the audience with a watertight ideological mise-en-scène that does whatever it can to discourage counter-hegemonic interpretations. It is rather a result of the play, within a film, within a single image even, of an emergent potential that hovers uncertainly between sentimental affirmation and sensuous provocation (cf. Vasudevan 2010; see my discussion of "potentiated cliché" in chapter 3).

The authors of the Khosla report seemed to be anxious that the potentiated reality of the film world might escape the moderating influence of "the actual world"—that is, the world in which we experience ourselves as guided and grounded by an everyday sense of proportion, the world which ensures that our practices of viewing will be well-tempered. But the potentiating power of the cinema is at the same time often recognized as a force for progress—*if* the potentials thus unleashed can be harnessed by a socially acceptable symbolic order. Sometimes (usually by conservatives) called culture, sometimes (usually by liberals) called taste, such symbolic orders hover without a given grounding in the transitional moment of the present.

Present-day censorship discourse is as closely related to nineteenth-century Indian bourgeois attempts to carve out aesthetic and moral grounds of judgment in the face of mass publicity as it is to any imported British Victorianism. In response to the lively traffic between "high" and "low" that was characteristic of Indian mass publicity in the latter part of the nineteenth century, elite fractions of the new Indian bourgeoisie developed a politics of distinction that pitted respectable cultural forms "predicated on values of control, order, and refinement" against the vulgarity of popular pleasures with their "public display[s] of eroticism, . . . [their] extremes of pathos and melodrama, . . . [their reliance on] the latest gimmicks and spectacles" (K. Hansen 1989:77; cf. C. Gupta 2001).[41] Time and time again, the target of bourgeois censure was the excessive sensuousness, the unrestrained corporeality of both florid aristocrats and unlettered subalterns. And this sensuousness was, in turn, most often literalized as a concern with sexual morality as a concrete index of civic virtue. As I will show in chapter 5, "obscenity," which as a regulatory term took on its modern form in the 1850s and 1860s, marks the spot where this fixation on sexual morality at once encodes and elides a much larger anxiety about the potentiated reality of mass communication.

This Indian bourgeois discourse was not merely a mimetic copy of colonial norms. Rather, it arose out of longer-term internal shifts in relations of patronage and publicity that were conditioned, but not wholly determined by, colonial policy. And indeed it was precisely *because* it was not a wholly derivative discourse that it was so useful to the British, who were sorely in need of regulatory standards that would be suitable to the new field of mass publicity and not reliant on the old distinction between traditional and public forms of cultural production. Tapti Roy shows, for example, that the Bengali elite of the mid-nineteenth century defined itself in part by asserting aesthetic and regulatory authority over the emergent space of print publicity. But as a result, its authority was bought at the price of an unintended alignment with the censorious imperatives of the colonial state. On the one hand, this new Indian intelligentsia adopted a proto-nationalist standpoint of autonomy vis-à-vis the British. On the other, "the new intellectuals can be seen to be demanding controls not unlike those sought by the [colonial] government; indeed, they often demanded state intervention" (1995:53; cf. Heath 2010). This "native" call for regulation was, of course, altogether convenient for the British in their efforts to police the new public culture. It was convenient because its parameters looked as if they were the organic products of Indian needs. But it was also convenient because it was formally well suited to the new public culture. As a bourgeois discourse, it made its claims in the delocalized idiom of the "public interest" rather than in reference to particular community traditions.

The moralism of the discourse of the new Indian intelligentsia—its preoccupation with decency and so on—also served the British well when the time came to regulate the cinema. By 1915–16, as film censorship moved onto the administrative agenda, the British were, as I have shown, hyperconscious of the fugitive seditious potential of everything that the Dramatic Performances Act did not cover. But the politics of revoking the exemption for "jatras" were too sensitive, as was the prospect of justifying film censorship on political grounds alone. As A. P. Muddiman, an officer of the Government of India, noted in 1916, while clamping down on sedition might have been a pressing administrative concern, a law framed in terms of public morality was likely to win more Indian support: "In so far as the legislation is devised to protect the safety of those who visit the exhibitions, and in so far as it aims at immoral or indecent exhibitions, the legislation is likely to commend itself to all classes."[42] We should not, I think, take these sentiments as evidence that the British used a concern with sexual morality as a cynical fig leaf for their "real" concern with sedition; indeed, I would argue that such terms as "indecency" and "sedition"—which, to be sure, saturate the colonial state's regulatory discourse —are secondary constructs that help to organize a fundamentally uncanny encounter with the potentiated reality of the cinema in such a way as to enable regulation. As we shall see, however, the gap between the sensuous potential of the medium and these regulatory terms remained palpable, not least for the censors themselves.

RECUPERATIONS

Drawing a Line: Liberal Anxiety

Most of the public sound and fury surrounding Deepa Mehta's *Fire* had to do with its purportedly "lesbian" desecration of respectable, middle-class Hindu life. But perhaps the servant Mundu's masturbation scene was actually the most obscene violation of the prevailing performative dispensation. Mundu achieves his febrile jouissance not just as a subaltern male in the feminine interior spaces of the middle-class home, but also under the mute gaze of the very embodiment of the middle-class moral order, the Indian mother-in-law. Mehta's decision to have Mundu masturbating to porn while supposedly facilitating the mother-in-law's pious enjoyment of the televised *Ramayana* is inspired in its understanding of the radical tension between the publicly permitted performative affect of the new *Ramarajya* and the emergent obscenity that constantly haunts the supposedly stable moral world of the middle-class interior. Tellingly, contemporary journalistic commentaries on the *Fire* controversy bemoaned the illiberality and intolerance of the Hindu right's attacks on the film but saved their most vivid expressions of disgusted condescension for Mundu, called variously "a gnomelike servant boy [who] masturbates in frenzied fifth gear" (Mehra 1998), the "onanistic domestic" (Banerji 1998), and "penis jerking Mundu" (Ramesh and Nambisan 1999).

It is not surprising that conservative elements should have voiced their shock over Mundu's masturbation scene. There he is, after all, impugning the dignity of one of India's great epics by watching porn under its protection. Mundu's subaltern lust is a direct affront to the middle-class modesty of the mute mother-in-law, Bibiji, who—as woman and widow—iconizes the integrity of Indian identity.[43] From a cultural-nationalist standpoint, Mundu's lusty abandon in front of the porn video represents a total loss of *swaraj* (self-rule), both of the individual body and its desires and of the symbolic order of the nation, now flooded with loose foreign affect (cf. Mazzarella 2010b). He is the subaltern male whose unacknowledged sexuality erupts in the intimate heart of the middle-class home. And he is a traitor to the symbolic order and decency of the (Hindu) nation: exploiting the devotional alibi of the Ramayana, with its story of female chastity and self-sacrifice, to lose himself in profanity. As a viewer helplessly lost to the mimetic commandment of the image, Mundu is the quintessential pissing man.

More notable were the cracks that Mundu's masturbation scene caused in the liberal defense of *Fire*. Most of the commentators who were prepared to defend Radha and Sita's intimacy against an oppressive patriarchal law—to defend, above all, their "right to choose"—drew the line at "penis-jerking Mundu." I was particularly struck by the fact that even the film's lead actresses, Shabana Azmi (Radha) and Nandita Das (Sita), who had staunchly defended the film on numerous public occasions, placed Mundu beyond the pale. Das told a journalist, "Do you know that people come up to me and say that I should have run away with Mundu, the servant boy in the film [instead of running away with Radha]? Can you imagine? Running away with a stupid, insensitive chap like him?" (quoted in Manjula 1999). And Shabana Azmi, veteran of the Indian "art" cinema and longtime progressive social activist, told me, "Once I went ahead [with the decision to act in *Fire*], I had *no* confusion, *ever*. I was not uncomfortable about anything—except the Mundu bit which continues to bother me even today. What I have *never* accepted is Mundu's masturbation scene. That really, really upset me."[44]

Mary John and Tejaswini Niranjana (1999) argue that there is a tight structural relation between the liberal celebration of Radha and Sita's intimacy and the rejection of Mundu's sexuality, that the disavowal of subaltern desire is the condition of possibility for the flourishing of (queer) middle-class freedom. In the first instance, Azmi herself located her discomfort at Mundu's masturbation scene in its implausibility: "I didn't find it believable that the old woman [Bibiji], being as strong as she is, would not make *such a ruckus* about it that the family would not . . . she was a strong woman and she would have done something. Just because she couldn't speak I don't think she would have let things pass like that." But

Azmi was also quite clear on how the disavowal of subaltern sexuality helps to maintain the performative continuity of middle-class domestic decency:

> I think that it definitely raises an issue which we don't want to deal with, which is that when we live in small homes, then we deal with our staff members and young boys as if there is no sexuality requirement in them. It's something that we all—middle class, upper middle class—it's something that we all deal with, never taking it into account. In our view it's fine if they have a wife, if they go back [to their home villages] once a year for one month, and that should be enough. . . . I find it very strange that in a lot of [middle-class] households, for instance, women have young males looking after their clothes. Which means that they're also dealing with the underclothes of the lady of the house. And you accept it because you *absolutely* behave as if the class difference is so great that in no way can it arouse *any* sexual feelings! . . . You completely behave as if you are *so* far removed from them in status that they can never desire anything of that kind.

Two aspects of the conversation were particularly interesting in this regard. One was that Azmi stressed the importance of not doing anything as an actress that might undermine her public credibility as an activist working with slum women. Here, she was able to defend the so-called lesbian content of *Fire* as a question of defending the rights of a vulnerable minority, of upholding women's rights to self-determination, and so on. But Mundu's masturbation remained an embarrassment, perhaps in part because, as a servant, his character was socioeconomically close to many of the women with whom Azmi worked as a social activist. As such, his extravagant desire was not just a reminder of the subaltern sexuality that every middle-class home disavowed but also a thorn in the side of the essentially desexualized politics of "decency" through which subaltern recipients of social development and "uplift" could be made worthy of middle-class sympathy.

The second notable theme in Azmi's reflections on *Fire* had to do with the conditions of her comfort or discomfort both in enacting Radha's physical intimacy with Sita for Deepa Mehta's cameras and in the subsequent public exhibition of these scenes. Azmi praised Mehta for the tactful way in which she had handled the shooting of Radha and Sita's bedroom scene, allowing them to workshop it in rehearsal well before the cameras rolled and cutting down the crew at the shoot to the absolute minimum. The fact that the key members of the crew were non-Indians also helped

Azmi to relax, trusting in their connection to a more cosmopolitan aesthetic than that of Bollywood. Similarly, she had been proud and unembarrassed to appear in person at screenings of the film on the international festival and campus circuit. Friends had warned Azmi that seeing the film in a regular Indian movie theater would expose her to the embarrassment of catcalls and salacious remarks from the audience, and so she had stayed away (cf. Naim 1999). But one day, during Azmi's term as a nominated member of the Rajya Sabha, "there were some male friends of mine, parliamentarians, who told me that '*Fire* is coming on TV and we are watching it'—and after that, *nothing*. They didn't mention it and I didn't have the courage, honestly, to ask them what they thought. But I distinctly felt uncomfortable watching it."

Azmi's discomfort here had nothing to do with the content of her performance per se; indeed, she emphasized to me that although she was normally extremely critical of her own screen work, *Fire* "is the film in which I have made the least number of mistakes as a performer." More pertinent is the fact that the intimacy of the scene on the screen—a scene that, within a cosmopolitan context of production and reproduction, felt comfortable—was now being exhibited in the far more ambiguous intimacy of Indian homes all over the country, where real-life domestic servant, like the fictional Mundu, might well be watching. But the film had already screened to all kinds of audiences in cinemas across the nation and beyond. So what was the problem? Reaching for an explanation, Azmi hinted that it might have had something to do with the *distracted* intimacy of television viewing as compared to the *focused* intimacy of the cinema: "There is something about the intimacy of it being in your home and seeing it in circumstances where your concentration is not totally there. You could also be doing five other things, and so the magic of the dark theater enveloping you into a world which takes you away from any interaction with reality . . . *lifts* you in a way that television doesn't."

This is a striking comment in part because at first sight it seems counterintuitive. One might imagine that the television audience, with one eye on the screen and one on the newspaper, would be imagined as more grounded, as less likely to get "carried away" by the fiction. But instead it is precisely the cinema audience, because it is *lifted* "away from any interaction with reality" that feels safer to Azmi. It is as if the old difference between theater and cinema is here being reimagined as a difference between cinema and television. The cinema might be provocative, but its audience is still, as it were, more enclosed within the ritually heightened performative dispensation of the fiction. The discomfort of television is that its publicity is *casual*, its on-screen intimacies are not in the same way contained by the totality of the fiction, but rather cross-connect, in unpredictable ways, with the viewer's everyday life (Rajagopal 2001). Whether the object of anxiety is cinema vis-à-vis the theater, or television vis-à-vis the cinema, the worry is the same: that the open edge of mass publicity will render the intimate provocations of performance uncontainable within an authoritative performative dispensation.

Taken together, the irreducible indecency of Mundu's masturbation and the creeping discomfort of the televised *Fire* demarcate the structural impasse of publicity after the cinema. Mundu is the pissing man, the affectively incontinent spectator, unconstrained by tradition and incapable of mature self-control. The queasy prospect of Sita and Radha's intimacy in millions of Indian homes expresses the open edge of mass publicity, the tendency for obscenity to emerge at the place where the moral and aesthetic assurances of a performative dispensation are no longer reliable.

Claiming a World: Conservative Desire

The liberal press typically caricatured the men and women who smashed theaters screening *Fire* as nothing but rampaging mobs, self-appointed moral police forces taking the law into their own hands. But although the right wing certainly quite consciously mobilized the volatile energies of lumpen elements for these demonstrations, the cultural logic of its activism was very much addressed to the urban middle class. The right was just as interested in reinventing the "patron" aspect of Indra's banner staff as enacting its demon-smashing "police" side. Its fantasy was that the two functions of Indra's banner staff—patron and police—could once again be seamlessly integrated in the age of mass publicity. In Mumbai, the Shiv Sena's public cultural interventions in the late 1990s consistently—and very performatively—manifested this desire.

In November 2003, I interviewed Pramod Navalkar, veteran journalist and politician and minister of cultural affairs in the BJP–Shiv Sena state government of 1995–99.[45] Navalkar knew that I came to our encounter with an interest in censorship and correctly presumed that I had imbibed the English-language press's depiction of him as a prudish moral crusader.[46] With a great deal of charm, he blended arms-spread-wide appeals to the reasonableness of his positions—"We have been talking for the last half an hour;

you see now that my views are certainly liberal"—with rhetorically striking, often witty summations of the cultural emergency as he diagnosed it:

> This is a transit period: we are gradually changing. It's an operation, surgery which is taking place. This cultural surgery—slight pains are going to be there. And you have to bear with these pains. After that, whether we come out healthy or we die—we don't know [laughs]! I am a very forward person. If you want to drink, you drink. Don't get drunk. My objection is to drink at the cost of somebody else. If I become the minister again, the first rule that I will make is, if you want to drink, you should drink on your own money, not someone else's money [laughs]! When you drink on someone else's money, then there's no limit—one, two, three, four, five![47]

Much of Navalkar's rhetoric took the familiar form of patriarchal cultural nationalism presented as a gallant defense of the moral integrity of Indian women: "Woman in our culture is respected. Everywhere they're trying to exploit women. We cannot degrade our sisters and mothers to that extent. *Respect* a woman. You must keep the respect—please do." But what struck me most forcefully in the course of our conversation was not so much the well-worn metonymy of national and female integrity. Rather it was Navalkar's tendency to describe his public cultural struggle as an attempt to carve out a protected space of cultural thriving, a space in which the Shiv Sena could exercise the unchallenged authority of the patron and thus ensure the enjoyment and incorporation of a native public (Indian or Maharashtrian, depending on the context). In short, Navalkar aspired to a performative dispensation.

The elementary form of his argument was a distinction between "respecting" and "accepting" foreign cultural influences. Navalkar's ideal of respecting without accepting meant holding on to a strong core of cultural identity in the face of seductive appeals to indiscriminate immodesty: "Earlier we were just respecting [Western culture] but now we are accepting it. What happens now? Our girls used to wear saris. Now they are going in shorts. And in bikini on the stage for dancing!" The important point to note is that Navalkar's discourse was not simply about policing lines of cultural difference; he was also articulating a critique of illegitimate cultural patronage.

The biggest culprit was the post-liberalization commercial media which, entranced by advertising rupees, could be corrupted into sponsoring events and performances that were directly injurious to Indian cultural integrity. Liberal critics would often complain that a trivial tabloid celebrity culture had displaced "serious," socially engaged journalism. But Navalkar's primary objection seemed to be that it represented a highly influential competing center of spectacular (because lavishly capitalized) cultural patronage:

> *Times of India, Bombay Times* today. *Maharashtra Times*. They are promoting all kinds of competitions. Artists are there, journalists are there, celebrities are there. So gradually they are developing. Even for movies. *Maharashtra Times* has awards for Marathi movies. The award function takes place in a very big way. So not only are they sharing it, they are *initiating* certain cultural activities. That is ridiculous. And editors have become more powerful. They decide. They decide. A paper decides to harm any party? They can do that. They can do that. Normally at the higher level they don't do it, but at the lower level, some of these journalists, they are purchased. Money, money.

Against this kind of apparently unprincipled exertion of political power in the guise of cultural patronage, Navalkar saw himself and the Shiv Sena as holding the line in the name of national integrity. Again, it is no accident that the following anecdote, delivered in jocular tones, describes a struggle over a performance space:

> Another thing that I did: we have only one government theater [in Mumbai], the Rangbhavan. Government open-air theater is only one. Now the fifteenth of August is our Independence Day. Fifteenth of August. So that should be celebrated in a manner where you see the reflection of our culture. Do you agree? Indian culture, Indian thing— ABCD the whole day.[48] On that day they wanted the theater for a rock show. I said "don't take it on *that* day. Take it on any other day. Not on our Independence Day." But then there was a hue and cry: "Pramod Navalkar is opposing rock shows!" I was not opposed. How can I oppose rock shows? Once you have a theater, you can show anything. Once you have a shop down below, you can sell cola, you can sell gold. I can't do anything. But on Independence Day, for five continuous years before I became the minister: rock shows. They called it "independent rock." *Arré*, what is "independent rock" [laughs]?!

On one level, then, Navalkar portrayed himself as helping to protect, as it were, a minimal performative place for the nation in an age of globalization. But the Shiv Sena's ambition to be both patron and police was also more expansive than that. I had been asking Navalkar about the importance of performance, whether on the street, in a theater, or at the movies, and whether there was not something about the "charge" of a performative context that made it particularly powerful and dangerous. Misinterpreting me as suggesting that only Western media and performance style contained that kind of "charge," Navalkar responded with an illustration of the Shiv Sena's desire to preside over a performative dispensation that could draw on the earthy potency of indigenous traditions while mediating it through the trappings of a decent middle-class publicness:

> I'll tell you. When you talk about "charging," I don't agree that for charging a certain type of music is required, a certain type of sex is required, this-thing. It's not that. If you see a *lavani*, that will charge you to any extent [laughs]! Lavani and *tamasha* [boisterous Maharashtrian "folk" performance idioms]. We [that is, the Shiv Sena] accepted it. When I was the culture minister, I was the first to organize a lavani and tamasha *mahautsav*. A festival. For two long days! And all those artist girls, who were totally neglected and ignored by the society, they were only in that dirty area; I brought them here to the Yashwantrao Chavan air-conditioned theatre. Two days' performance was there. And all those girls gave performances, dressed up, to respectable people like Naushad [Ali, legendary Hindi film music composer]. Now there are shows going on all over Maharashtra. [Lavani singer] Surekha Punekar, if you have heard of her, she is on top of the world now. She said, "On that day, I was introduced to a real audience, and now my life has changed."

The attempt to render the erotics of indigenous entertainments respectable as objects of middle-class consumption is, as I suggested above, rooted in the emergence of a bourgeois politics of cultural distinction that was itself a response to the rise of an Indian mass public culture in the latter half of the nineteenth century. But we should mark Navalkar's insistence on the continued performative potency of these shows ("that will charge you to any extent!"), a potency now mediated through a performative dispensation that set itself up as a morally (because culturally) grounded alternative to the corrupt and deracinated cultural patronage of the mainstream media.

We should also not be too distracted by the cultural nativism of this example. To be sure, as a Mumbai-based movement, the Shiv Sena could claim a particular kind of cultural authority, qua patron, vis-à-vis entertainments that were recognizably "Maharashtrian."[49] But as scholars like Thomas Blom Hansen (2001), Raminder Kaur (2003), and Tarini Bedi (2009) have shown, Shiv Sena–funded celebrations, from the neighborhood level of Ganpati (Ganesh) festivals and beauty pageants all the way up to the city's theaters and stadia, attempted to fold the performative potency of any and all public cultural signifiers, local or global, into their dispensation. In a certain sense, the (anachronistic) performative dream of the Shiv Sena at its height was seamlessly to fuse political and theatrical spectacle, somewhat in the manner of the nineteenth-century *rajas* of Banaras who on occasion themselves would play the part of Ram in the spectacular festival enactment of the Ramlila that literally overlaid the mythical landscape of the *Ramayana* onto the physical spaces of the royal Ramnagar Fort by using them as stages for the play (Freitag 1989). As Kajri Jain notes, "If the procession of sacred images or symbols through the streets established a direct connection between the symbols of a community and a physical territory, it also simultaneously mapped onto human territory and human bodies the orders of sacred time and space—those of a mythological diegesis and of an abstract, eternal, cosmic divinity" (2007:111).

By the 1990s, however, political community was inevitably mediated as much by electronic media as by localized gatherings. The Thackeray family, which has led the Sena since its inception in the 1960s, has close ties to Bollywood. And most notably, at the height of Shiv Sena founder Bal Thackeray's prestige and power in the mid-1990s, even the crotch-grabbing global mega-celebrity of Michael Jackson became fair game for attempted incorporation. Presumably unaware of the complex cultural politics of their collaboration, Jackson's people had tied up with a wing of the Shiv Sena to stage his concert at the Andheri Sports Complex in Mumbai in November 1996.[50] The most telling detail in the publicity that followed was the pride with which Bal Thackeray announced not only that Michael Jackson had visited his home (and thus allowed himself to be incorporated as a kind of supplicant at Thackeray's court) but also that the King of Pop had used his toilet. (Little squares of the bedsheets that Jackson had used during his stay at the Oberoi Hotel were later sold off as indexical relics of his visit.) A couple of months after Jackson's visit, I asked a Mumbai street vendor, whose stall was plastered with images of Thackeray, to tell me to whom this ubiquitous face, with its jet-black dyed hair and sunglasses, belonged. His reply came in English: "He's the King of Bombay."

Present-day critics of Indian film censorship often imply that the distance which persists between empirical audience pleasures (effervescence) and the moralizing discourse of regulation arises in part out of the colonial origins of Indian film censorship—specifically, out of the colonial state's distance from the affective textures of Indian lifeworlds. But I think that at the very least we need to take into account the relation between the colonial state's affective deficit and the structural challenge presented by the cinema as a medium; the way then, as now, it has made palpable the open edge of mass publicity. This also means that if the sense of distance between popular pleasures and censorial moralism has persisted into the present, then its recent forms need to be understood not only as inert colonial survivals but as evidence that the struggle to reconcile state legitimation with the open edge has also persisted, even though, as I will show in chapter 3, its content and its possibilities have changed.

Bal Thackeray may well have been able, during the Shiv Sena's heyday, to claim the title King of Bombay. But the members of the Censor Board can of course not claim to be kings—or queens—of anything. As servants of a democratically elected government, they are supposed to represent the interests of the general public (even though they themselves are not democratically elected). But from very early in the story of Indian film censorship, this has been a problematic claim—and not just because it is regularly challenged by "extraconstitutional," self-styled censors who do not shrink from proclaiming quasi-regal performative dispensations (see chapter 3).

In 1928, after almost a decade of formal film censorship, the *Report of the Indian Cinematograph Committee* noted that the role of the censor was to be "the interpreter of public opinion, and ultimately his decisions derive their sanction from public opinion" (ICC 1928b:111). But the ideological loop of censorship was apparently already in effect, because the report also noted, much earlier on, that "public opinion is not sufficiently organized or articulate to make it possible to dispense with censorship" (ICC 1928b:2).

One might be tempted to conclude that this was a classic colonial symptom: professing liberal principles while practicing authoritarian pragmatics. But the problem did not disappear with Independence because, as I hope to have shown in this chapter, the problem was not only a function of a nondemocratic political order but also a structural symptom of the condition of mass publicity. Responding to protests from the film industry in the late 1940s, the Ministry of Information and Broadcasting let it be known that "in the absence of strong public opinion to lay down this standard [for the moral orientation of the cinema] it is being laid down by the censors" (quoted in Vasudev 1978:85). The difference between colonial and post-Independence Indian governments has largely been in the relative emphasis that they have given to different ideological explanations for the persistence of the problem. If, in the colonial period, it was common to blame the dilemma on the racial and cultural gaps that separated Indians from Europeans, then post-Independence Indian governments have tended to opt for an indigenized version of the white man's burden: a kind of permanently institutionalized discourse of historical crisis according to which censorship becomes necessary because India is (always) in a time of transition. This, then, is the subject of the next chapter: the problem of legitimating the censors' judgment as something other than arbitrary in a time that is always exceptional.

CHAPTER 2

WHO THE HELL DO THE CENSORS

THINK THEY ARE?

GROUNDS OF THE CENSOR'S JUDGMENT

Censorship of every kind is always difficult to administer with promptitude and effi-
ciency, with due regard to the susceptibilities of the public, to the objects which the
censorship itself propounds, to the interests of industries which may be involved, and to
an infinity of considerations of that kind. Indeed I may say that of all bodies exercising
public functions there is hardly one which is more exposed and more subjected to
censure than the [*sic*] censorship. I have had too much to do with censorship of many
kinds for my own comfort and peace of mind. I have realized in a very hard school what
its difficulties are.

—J. Crerar, Home Member, addressing the Indian Council of State, 1925

Why does censorship become necessary? Because, it seems, we are living in exceptional times. We need censorship because we cannot govern ourselves. We have lost track of the unspoken rules, the traditions that once constrained us. And we have not yet achieved a set of spoken rules that would be reliable and capacious enough to mediate all the many interests and sentiments of our complex, modern societies. We are stuck in between. Our time, the present, is a transitional phase of uncertain duration where tattered survivals of the past struggle with emergent intimations of the future.[1]

Something like this diagnosis, interestingly enough, is just as likely to come from liberals as from conservatives. Liberals are more likely to project the fullness of a stable social order onto a mature, enlightened future that never quite arrives. Conservatives are more likely to want to bring back a refunctioned version of a long-gone golden age. Either way the present is an ocean full of treacherous currents, between an old country that is rapidly fading from view and a new world that always remains just out of reach. The Hindu cosmic calendar says that we are living in *kaliyuga*, the age of strife, the fourth and darkest age, 432,000 years long, the time that Saleem Sinai, the hero of *Midnight's Children*, calls "the losing throw in our national dice game; the worst of everything" (Rushdie 1980:233).

Whether we think in *yugas* or in decades, the appearance of being in a transitional moment tends to produce the kind of institutionalized anxiety where energetic enthusiasm appears dangerously uncoupled from good judgment. It also tends to produce binary oppositions like the one on which the enunciator's exception (see the introduction) is based: the opposition between the pissing man who cannot control himself in the presence of a provocative image and the coolly continent viewer who is ultimately the model for the ideal spectator-citizen, the person in whom enthusiasm is exquisitely attuned to judgment. Linked to this opposition between different kinds of imagined viewers are other binaries that work as shorthand for an assumed trajectory of social development—for example, the opposition between feudal/traditional and democratic/modern social orders. Vis-à-vis these oppositions, the in-between society is understood to be neither/nor, yet also both. Because it is assumed to be at best "on its way" and at worst "stuck," exceptional measures—for example, official film censorship—become necessary to nudge it down the teleological track.

This chapter focuses on the grounds of the censors' judgment. By what right do they judge on behalf of others? How is this right expressed vis-à-vis particular kinds of image-objects? And what are we to make of the peculiar, even incredible opposition that lies at the heart of the censors' discourse: the opposition between the pissing man and the censor, that is to say, between a form of subjectivity that is utterly porous to image-objects and one that is utterly imperturbable?

Censorship involves both policing and pedagogy. It aims both to keep the peace and to help move society from incontinence to temperance, from "feudal mindsets" to enlightenment. And yet the relation between the pissing man and the censor, on one level absolutely intimate, also seems absolutely discontinuous. Their relation looks something like Slavoj Žižek's "parallax view," a "constantly shifting perspective between two points between which no synthesis or mediation is possible. Thus, there is no rapport between the two levels, no shared space—although they are closely connected, even identical in a way, they are, as it were, on the opposed sides of a Moebius strip . . . although they are linked, they are *two sides* of the same phenomenon which, precisely as two sides, can never meet" (2006:4). The road from the pissing man to the continent viewer, from past to future, is Moebius-warped; just when you think you are going to switch tracks, a sudden curve swings you back to where you started. And so the ideological loop of censorship thrives on the failure of its own stated aim. We remain in a blocked time, the time in between.

On the basis of my argument in chapter 1, I want to suggest that we need to put aside the teleological assumption that underlies both the censors' discourse and that of most of their critics—that is, the assumption that censorship is either helping or hurting a movement along a path of social progress. Once we suspend that idea, we are in a better position to move beyond the repetitive re-presentation of censorship as an exceptional response to a social condition of lack and failure, a situation of being stuck in what Dipesh Chakrabarty (2000) calls the waiting room of history. Instead, we might begin to think about the ways that censorship at once registers the structural condition of the open edge of mass publicity and helps to avert a more radical engagement with it. My basic proposition in this chapter, then, is that the temporal discourse of being "in between" both expresses and disavows the deep challenge of mass publicity by displacing it onto a story of perennially thwarted progress.

They themselves think they are a superior class. They can see a woman's
breasts. But not the ordinary man. It's a sex-caste system.
—B. K. Karanjia, November 2003

Roman Polanski once spat: "Fuck the censors. They're preposterous; an imposition on society. Who the hell do they think they are telling me what I can read or see?" (1997:172). This, indeed, is one of the mysteries of censorship: in a democratic society, where the people are supposed to be sovereign, what is the ground from which the censor claims superior judgment? Is the censor's talent built in or does it somehow come with the job? As former CBFC member Kishore Valicha puts it, "The moment you are on the Censor Board, you become righteous. You feel the weight of society's morals on your shoulders. You stop shrugging" (Mishra 2001).

What protects the censors? What amulet keeps these people from being damaged by frequent exposure to the image-objects that they deem unacceptable for public circulation? Polanski resumed his tirade: "Who are these people who are allowed to watch all this? What do you do with them at the end? Lock them up in an insane asylum? Put them in prison because they've become a danger to society or themselves? Or should we give them compensation for exposing themselves to images, like we do to people who get exposed to radiation?" Apropos the British *Lady Chatterley's Lover* obscenity trial, literary scholar Rachel Bowlby remarks that "the jury are supposed to decide, on behalf of the populace at large, whether this is an obscene book, whether it has this 'tendency to deprave or corrupt.' . . . If they *have* been depraved or corrupted then . . . they are no longer in a position to judge the book: they have become depraved and corrupted. But they will not know this, because a depraved person is no judge of depravity. There could thus never . . . be such a thing as a fair trial for obscenity" (quoted in Steiner 1997:34; ellipses in original).

By what logic can the censors claim to be both representative of the people at large—a "cross-section of society," as the CBFC puts it—and immune to the same images that would damage the people they apparently represent? Documentary filmmaker and anticensorship activist Rakesh Sharma paints a heavily sarcastic picture of the "representative" sample of polite society that comprised the CBFC's Advisory Panels:

They usually represent a wide cross-section of society—a Minister's girlfriend or his unemployed nephew, a local corporator's convent-educated wife, some M[ember of the] L[egislative] A[ssembly]'s campaign accountant who helped him hoodwink [the] E[lection] C[omission]'s regulations, a Jai Shri Ram chant-enthused party worker from the BJB/VHP/Bajrang Dal/Hindu Jagran Manch/Durga Vahini or one of Soniaji's [Sonia Gandhi's] Congressmen. As associates or chamchas [literally, spoons; colloquially, toadies] of some politician, they have a rare intellectual depth, a deep understanding of culture and aesthetics and an even deeper understanding of the dark sides of the human soul. Since they also happen to possess expertise in constitutional matters, they can swiftly figure out whether a dialogue will cause a law & order problem and breach peace, faster than any court of law as they only have 3–4 hours to do so while any court can drag on a case for years! (R. Sharma 2005)

In the course of our interviews, the censors themselves suggested two main foundations for their judgment: professional expertise and cultural grounding. For Vijay Anand, professional expertise and the aesthetic judgment that flowed from it, rather than any fixed conception of "Indian culture," came first. As a director during the 1960s, Anand had himself battled the Censor Board, and the memory still rankled:

It's too ridiculous! You have to remember, the man sitting in the chair of the censor chief, he didn't know the language. He didn't know cinema. He didn't know films at all. He didn't know what he was talking about! He had a *moral* code in his mind and he wanted to say "no—this is vulgar, you cut it out. This is not done. This is not Indian culture." *Ut*-ter nonsense! I say if you have a dance festival and you have judges, you can't have a musician sitting there. He must be a man of dance. If it's a music festival you can't have dancers. And if it's a film thing you can't have people who don't understand what cinema is about.[2]

In line with the Khosla Committee's recommendations, Anand insisted that a certain kind of cosmopolitan aesthetic training and experience were basic requirements for the job:

I said no, there has to be a training course. Any man who comes into the Censor Board, he must be strong, he must be educated, he must be a lover of cinema, he must understand aesthetics. He must understand international cinema. Regional officers, of course the Government pays them, you have them. But they should have a certain qualification. It's not that because [the regional Censor Board at] Guwahati doesn't have a chairman, you'll get the railway officer to come and sit on the chair.

Anupam Kher, for his part, agreed that the chairman of the CBFC needed to have a cosmopolitan understanding of cinema:

> I have grown up to be a certain kind of person. I came from a lower-middle-class family. I am an educated theatre person. I have been a teacher in acting. I'm a fairly progressive person. I understand world cinema. I am part of an international cinema now, as an actor, after *Bend It Like Beckham* [in which Kher played Jesminder's father, Mr. Bhamra], also many other films. As a student of cinema, I know world cinema. As a student of theatre, I understand Arthur Miller. I understand Tennessee Williams. I know Chekhov. I know Grotowski. So it's not *some guy* who has been given the job of a chief. I understand the network, the vastness of cinema.[3]

At the same time, for Kher this kind of cosmopolitan knowledge could easily turn into another kind of provinciality if it remained detached from the lifeworlds of the Indian masses. Joining the Censor Board meant, precisely, *not* imposing some abstract, global set of standards on an Indian reality but rather being able to connect with the cultural particularity of Indian audiences. In a clear dig at Anand's proposal for X-rated theaters, Kher told me that

> it's the easiest thing to be the popular guy among so-called media people. You have to say the right things. But I think that will be damaging the rest of the country. The easiest thing for me would be to make some very fantastic statements—that "with liberalization, everything should be allowed. Cinema has to have creativity." Of *course*. That's a statement that's very good for metropolitan cities. But when you go to the interiors of India, the censorship laws do work there.

Between them, then, Vijay Anand and Anupam Kher articulated the censor's two key qualifications: aesthetic judgment and cultural grounding. The relative emphasis given to each varied with the speaker. But taken together, they defined censorship as an activity that must at once be open to cosmopolitan creative provocation and modulated by the moral order of an imagined community. This was the self-image of Indian censorship after the 1960s. But things were not always thus.

FROM THE ETHNOGRAPHIC STATE
TO THE CITIZEN-SPECTATOR

The most important shift in the grounds of censorship before the 1960s happened not at the moment of Independence in 1947 but during the 1920s and 1930s. This was the time that the last vestiges of the colonial ethnographic state—a form of governmentality based on the management of essentialized Indian differences—gave way to a prospective version of the film spectator as consumer-citizen.

During the 1920s, provincial governments assembled regional censor boards so as to balance "official" (which at that time still generally meant British) members with "nonofficial" representatives of local Indian communities.[4] So, for example, in Bombay a Hindu, a Muslim, and a Parsi member joined the official contingent (the commissioner of police as ex officio president, the provost marshal of the Bombay Brigade, and the principal of Elphinstone College). In Madras, the nonofficial numbers consisted of two Hindus and a Muslim. Things were a bit different again in Calcutta, where the commissioner of police, a military officer, and members nominated by business associations were joined by an educational representative who had to be Indian and two government appointees, one of whom had to be a woman. Until the end of the colonial period, however, most of the actual examining work was not done by the members of the censor boards but rather by one or more inspectors, relatively lowly government employees who reported directly to the president.[5]

One of the recommendations of the Indian Cinematograph Committee's 1928 report was that the censor boards either formally incorporate or informally consult with a wider range of experts and interest groups. And indeed, by the 1930s, the earlier logic of proportional community representation was coming under pressure from, on the one hand, a vast range of social reform, moral hygiene, and community associations collectively comprising an emergent civil society and, on the other hand, new professional organizations claiming to represent the interests of the cinema industry. In other words, while it was not until the post-Independence invention of the CBFC in the 1950s that advisory boards designed to embody a "cross-section of society and interests" were actually constituted, the shift toward something like a general public as the referent of the censor's judgment was already well under way by the 1930s.

At the same time, what we see during these years is not simply a transition from a relatively "closed" logic of community representation in the 1920s to a more "open" conception of a generalized public in the 1930s, but also a shift in the relation between the censor's judgment and a transcendent notion of progress. Already in the 1920s, the censor board members who were chosen as representatives of their communities were envisioned as "gentlemen of culture, of various communities."[6] "Culture," here, meant two things at once: that these gentlemen should be "cultured" in a general cosmopolitan sense, but also that they should be specifically representative of their respective cultures. We see here, then, the roots of the conception of culture as a relay between universality and particularity that still survives in the censor's discourse today. To be a "gentleman of culture," then as now, means being in touch with the needs and susceptibilities of particular audiences while at the same time being able to take the broader view that allows the censor, more or less subtly, to take on the work of guiding those audiences toward a transcendent horizon of "good taste."

Thomas Metcalf (1995) argues that British colonial policy in India was driven by a constant tension between universalizing ideals (the liberal-utilitarian civilizing mission, standardized education, and such) and particularizing practices (Orientalism, government on the basis of Indian cultural differences, and so on). Film censorship during the 1920s manifested this same doubling. As patron/police, or rather *maa-baap* (mother and father), the colonial government represented both an auratic exemplar/agency of civilization and a supposedly impartial guarantor of the separate rights of India's communities. Cinema spoke directly to both of these impulses.

Insofar as the visceral appeal of the medium was often construed as a kind of universal language, the cinema could be imagined as offering a sensuous transcendence of local particularity. But at the same time, precisely its sensuously performative quality connected it with the deeply ingrained, affective particularities of local lifeways.[7] Both of these takes on the cinema suggested promise as well as panic. Its transcendent potential promised to lift Indian audiences out of the inertial slough of custom, to give them a feel for the ways of the world, and to overcome the affective deficit of empire. And yet Hollywood, in particular, also threatened a pleasurable short-circuit between American and Indian mass sensoria that might challenge the imperial banner staff. The cinema's apparent ability to resonate with the everyday foundations of Indian lifeworlds seemed the most promising way to communicate, on a mass level, in the "very graphic language" that was taken to be a native trait. And yet precisely this potential also raised the specter of a hotly "corpothetic" public sphere (Pinney 2001, 2004), shot through with loose affect, uncontained by either the strictures of tradition or the sobriety of reason.[8]

The tension that characterized film censorship in the 1920s—between a universalizing notion of progress and a particularizing notion of cultural differences—started to give way in the 1930s to a prototype of the generalized Indian spectator-citizen whose interests might be expressed as those of a general public. If the ICC's report in the late 1920s had complained that censorship was necessary because there was, in effect, no such thing as properly developed public opinion in India (see chapter 1), then the debate on film censorship in the 1930s shifted toward the parallel question of whether the membership of the censor boards accurately reflected a public opinion that was assumed to exist. This newly confident invocation of public opinion was, of course, in some respects connected to the progressive democratization of Indian administration during these years—most notably as a result of the August 1935 Government of India Act.[9] As an article that November in the *Bombay Sentinel* noted, "In these days of democracy, it is necessary that the public opinion should have some hold on the Censor Board."[10]

Then, as now, the dubious credentials of the censors as suitably expert representatives of the public interest were mercilessly mocked. Baburao Patel, pioneering film journalist and editor of *Filmindia*, tore into the Bombay film censors in 1936, starting with Inspector Cursetji and moving on to the community representatives N. V. Mandlik (Hindu), S. K. Barodawala (Muslim), and Sir Byramji Jeejibhoy (Parsi):

> Why does Inspector Cursetji carry with him a dozen ladies from his family to view the picture whilst he is censoring it? Does he not know that unless a picture is passed it should not be shown to the public? Do not the ladies in his family constitute part of the public? . . . Is the Censor Board a family concern in which all the members of Cursetji's family have shares? . . . Who is this man Mandlik? He is practically unknown in the city. What have been his public activities to recommend him to the Board of Censors? Take a census of men in the city

knowing Mandlik and you will hardly find a hundred. And this man without any record of public services, without any special distinction, and with very little right to dictate morals to the Presidency is on the Board of Censors. Why? And that chap S K Barodawala who had contested the recent elections as a candidate and is reported to have got only four votes in a constituency having several thousand voters. And out of these four votes, two must have been his and two his wife's. . . . That man represents Mahomedans on the Board? . . . Sir Byramji Jeejibhoy's only qualification is that he has money and that he goes to clubs regularly. What he knows of censoring films is probably not worth knowing. He is the tailor's dummy on the Board.[11]

This kind of scurrilous indictment of the old "gentlemen of culture" formula had become quite commonplace by the mid-1930s.[12] But what had taken its place as a ground for the censor's judgment? In short, a newly discovered mass subject at once motivated by the pursuit of discerning pleasure/good taste (as such, a consumer) and morally anchored by a rather vaguely defined conception of the "national interest" (as such, a proto-citizen).

Unsurprisingly, the regional censor boards largely resisted outside pressures to expand, but they did become somewhat more inclusive during the 1930s and 1940s.[13] All this changed in the 1950s with the post-Independence rethinking of the censorship process.[14] Under the apex authority of CBFC headquarters in Mumbai, a regional officer now oversees each regional center and constitutes examining committees (and, if necessary, revising committees) for each film by drawing on a relatively large pool of respectable citizens collectively known as an advisory panel. At the time I write this, the CBFC comprises eight regional centers in addition to its Mumbai head office.[15] If, in colonial times, nonofficial (albeit officially appointed) censor board members were supposed to be "influential members of leading communities,"[16] then the post-Independence specification did away with such explicitly identitarian thinking, relying instead on the vaguer notion of a "cross-section of society and interests."[17] Today, the central government continues to control appointments at every level, from the members of the Central Board down to the advisory panels.[18]

Most of the ICC's concrete recommendations were carefully sidelined or ignored by the colonial administration in the years immediately following their publication in 1928.[19] But its exhortation that "timely steps should be taken to create a national atmosphere" through film (ICC 1928b:61) was taken up *rhetorically* by the increasingly organized film industry of the 1930s.[20] Industry representation on the censor boards had been discussed for years before the All-India Motion Picture Convention adopted the demand as a formal resolution in February 1935.[21] One might say that a discourse of nationalism enabled the film industry to appear to conform to the needs of the government while at the same time subtly shifting the legitimate grounds of censorial judgment. By July 1946, a year before Independence, the same Baburao Patel who ten years earlier had lambasted the members of the Bombay Censor Board was editorializing in *Filmindia*: "Patriotism demands that our film industry should be planned on national lines and an immediate beginning should be made by controlling the producers through official censorship. Though censorship is a negation of democracy, wise censorship is most essential in a country debauched by two centuries of slavery, now trying to find its ancient soul and self-respect."[22] The question of precisely how such "national lines" were to be discovered and defined was largely left open. The professional standing of the film industry was less grounded in a discourse of patriotism per se than in the more consumerist-populist claim that the success of its products demonstrated its unrivaled understanding of Indian values and needs. The spectator-citizen's moral right to exercise informed choice through the consumption and appreciation of "good" films was, the industry argued, to be nurtured as the foundation of a truly popular and thus authentic public opinion. M. K. Gandhi may have awakened the masses to their national destiny. But the films were, so the industry argued, not far behind (even if the Mahatma himself famously and tersely dismissed their social relevance in his three-sentence response to the ICC's questionnaire[23]). In its combination of visceral address and mass reach, cinema seemed to promise the mediation of inarticulate, sensuous inclinations into something resembling a general will. In those times of cresting nationalism, the industry sought official recognition of its ability to harness mass desire in the name of nation building.

The search for official recognition was not only a matter of trying to secure the financial regularization of formal industry status for the film business (which would not happen until 1998), but also of "professionalizing" censorship under the sign of industry expertise. This figure of a citizen spectator, morally grounded by means of the invocation of a public interest defined as national was, one might say, invented in the 1930s and has remained a basic referent of film censorship ever since (Rajadhyaksha

2009). At the same time, a conservative culturalist discourse has also persisted from the earliest days of Indian film censorship to the present. Then, as now, cultural conservatives may be found bemoaning the inappropriateness of provocative imported images in the context of Indian "values" or "culture." But whereas in the 1920s, the moral panic over Hollywood in India revolved around the question of whether racy films "misrepresented" life in the West in such a way as to injure white prestige, the emergent citizen-spectator of the 1930s made it possible to couple a discourse of entertainment to one of social progress in the name of nationalism.

Perhaps the peculiarity of this phase, which lasted from the 1930s to the early 1960s, was that a genuinely vibrant popular nationalism managed to bring aesthetic discernment and cultural order into relatively smooth alignment. Historians of the Hindi cinema often refer to the 1950s as a golden age when films by Raj Kapoor and Guru Dutt potentiated the nation-building project through epic melodrama. And conversely, the epic melodrama of nation building could during these years be figured as one big movie. In February 1955, the chair at a film seminar of the Sangeet Natak Akademi (the National Academy for Music, Dance, and Drama) welcomed Prime Minister Nehru to the proceedings in terms that would have seemed implausible in any other period: "I welcome you, Sir, as the Director of one of the greatest films in history—the film of New India's destiny. Politicians and statesmen, capitalists and workmen, scientists and technicians, artists and poets and millions of common men and women are participating in this great film of which you are the supreme director" (quoted in Roy 2007:40).

By the same token, during this period film censorship operated within what looked like a functioning performative dispensation. Before the 1930s, this was not the case; as I have suggested, film censorship during the 1920s was still marked by a tension between what it meant to be "cultured" in a general sense and what it meant to belong to a particular "culture." And in the 1960s, this compact came undone again as the high-water mark of popular nationalism started giving way to a plethora of more specific claims to cultural and national recognition. The new angry-young-man film hero of the 1970s—iconized by Amitabh Bachchan—embodied insatiable drive rather than patriotic pathos. Once again, the censor's twin qualifications—cosmopolitan aesthetic judgment and cultural-moral grounding—cohabited uneasily.

Nehru died in 1964, a couple of years after a humiliating war with China.

As the popular nationalist consensus started to unravel, India entered into a period of political fragmentation and violence, shortages, economic stagnation, currency devaluation, and failed monsoons. At the same time, film censorship discourse shifted into a mode of what one might call "tempered liberalism." New positions on obscenity in the United States (*Roth v. United States*) and the United Kingdom (the Obscene Publications Act) during the late 1950s[24] inspired seminal statements in India—among them, Justice Hidayatullah's Supreme Court judgment on *Lady Chatterley's Lover* (1928) in 1964 and Justice Khosla's Film Enquiry Committee report in 1969. The distinctively liberal aspect of these statements was that they tended to argue that disturbing or provocative image-objects might be justifiable "in context"—which, in principle, generally meant within the overall aesthetic framework of a film, book, or other work. In practice, however—and this is where the "tempered" part comes in—the "context" often turned out to be the apparently volatile state of Indian society and culture as a whole. Which led to the familiar formula: in (formal) principle this object is probably not problematic, but in (Indian) practice it probably is. Subtext: because we are in a time between. Thus, in turn, the enunciator's exception: it may be OK for us cultured, cosmopolitan folk, but not for the pissing man.

I discuss the problem of obscenity in much greater depth in chapters 4 and 5. For now, I want to turn to a couple of examples that illustrate how this tempered liberalism has played itself out at different moments when faced with actual cinematic image-objects. I begin with a film, Shyam Benegal's *Nishant* (1975), which had the historical misfortune of running into the great exception itself: Indira Gandhi's Emergency. And yet it was, paradoxically, precisely during the Emergency that the censors felt the need to deny that Indian society was in a state of exception.

EXCEPTION AND EMERGENCY: *NISHANT*

When they killed the youngest brother, it was sunset.
Fresh from the acclamation and controversy surrounding his plays *Ghashiram Kotwal* and *Sakharam Binder* (both 1972), Vijay Tendulkar was feeling uninspired. A group of theater people, trying to enthuse him about a possible collaboration, had offered him a series of scenarios, but nothing quite caught his fancy. Until, some time after the meeting, Tendulkar felt this one line still reverberating in his imagination. *When they killed the youngest brother, it was sunset.*

The line came from an old newspaper clipping about the Telengana peasant revolt of the late 1940s and early 1950s. In this particular incident, the peasants of one village had risen up against the local landowners and wiped out the whole family. Tendulkar had adapted the Maharashtrian "folk" theater style of tamasha for *Ghashiram Kotwal*, a scathing attack on the then-rising Shiv Sena told in the form of episodes from the life of the eighteenth-century Peshwa minister Nana Phadnavis, and thought that this new germ of an idea might also benefit from a treatment that was more "ritualistic" than "naturalistic."[25] So he traveled to rural Andhra Pradesh to explore local forms, but again nothing quite inspired him. Some friends to whom he had mentioned the idea passed it on to Shyam Benegal, then basking in the success of his first feature film, *Ankur* (1974), which had been widely hailed as marking the consolidation of a new, "serious" Hindi cinema. Benegal in turn contacted Tendulkar and asked him to turn the story into a screenplay.

In the resulting film, *Nishant*, a lower-middle-class Brahmin schoolteacher and his wife arrive in a village. We realize soon enough that no local authority, whether secular or spiritual, whether police or priest, is any match for the iron fist with which the landowning family, a group of four brothers, asserts its dominance in all matters. The two middle brothers are violent drunks, only too happy to roar in the shadow of their truly leonine oldest sibling. The youngest brother is the odd one out: timid, sensitive, and the constant butt of his brothers' jokes. Noticing that the youngest brother seems to have taken a mute shine to the schoolteacher's wife, the two middle brothers abduct her from the house she shares with her husband and imprison her in the manorial compound where she becomes fair game for the brothers' appetites.

An acute tension develops. Outside the compound we see the schoolteacher, rights-bearing citizen of a modern democratic state, utterly failing to mobilize the formal forces of law and order to get his wife released. Inside the compound, a volatile and unexpected intimacy develops between the youngest brother and the schoolteacher's wife, an intimacy in which brutal violence and sexual tenderness seem inextricably entwined. During a chance encounter between the schoolteacher and his wife at the village temple, she berates him for his ineffectual lack of manliness and returns to the place where she has now become a kind of manorial property. The twin resonances of Sita's abduction by Ravana in the *Ramayana* and the relatively recent memory of the abduction and tortured repatriation of women abducted during Pakistan's partition from India hang heavy over these scenes.

At his wits' end, the schoolteacher joins forces with his fellow Brahmin and spiritual counterpart, the village priest, in a plan to incite the peasants of the village to rise up in revolt against the oppressive rule of the landlords. Seizing the occasion of a festival day on which the landlords' blessings would normally be sought, the peasants storm the compound in blind anger, indiscriminately killing anyone who falls in their path. The youngest brother manages to escape from the building with the schoolteacher's wife, but the crowd eventually catches up with them amidst some nearby boulders and finishes them off. Having fallen behind the mob whose fury he released, the schoolteacher is left to survey the devastation wrought by his attempt to bring progressive revolutionary consciousness to the peasants.

As minister for information and broadcasting, Indira Gandhi had been behind the push toward a new breed of state-sponsored "good" films in the mid-1960s.[26] Good films needed good censorship, and in the wake of the Khosla Committee's recommendations, I. K. Gujral (Mrs. Gandhi's successor as information and broadcasting minister and fellow future prime minister) attempted, during the mid-1970s, to infuse some Khosla-approved sophistication into the censorship process:[27]

> The Censors must possess suitable educational qualifications and cultural background. They should be persons commanding public respect; they should have a broad outlook on life. They should know something about the arts and the cultural values of this country. They should have traveled widely and should be persons who can be expected to deal with the problem of censorship without the handicaps of unreasonable inhibitions or an obsession with petrified moral values or with the glamour of so-called advanced groups. (Khosla et al. 1969:100)

Anil Dharker was one of a small group of "supercensors"—formally, advisors to the chair of the CFBC—that Gujral invited to bring their judgment to bear on the "new wave films" which were "more sophisticated than a normal Hindi film" (the other advisor from Bombay was the celebrated Urdu writer Qurratulain Hyder). Dharker remembers the regular film censors of that time as "true blue government servants" who "would never go out on a limb. It was always safer to chop."[28] And this was the mode of censorship to which mainstream filmmakers had pragmatically adapted; knowing that the censors were likely to demand a certain proportion of sex and violence to be cut out, they would simply shoot twice as much as they needed. But censors habituated to operating in this crudely quantitative mode—cut so-and-so many feet here, 40 percent there—were simply not equipped for the new era, where, as Justice Hidayatullah had ruled in the Supreme Court, provocative image-objects might be permissible "subject either to their artistic merit or their social value over-weighing their offending character" (*K. A. Abbas v. Union of India* [1970]).[29]

As it happened, *Nishant*'s arrival at the CBFC coincided with the declaration of Mrs. Gandhi's Emergency in the summer of 1975. How are we to make sense of the apparent contradiction embodied in the figure of the prime minister? As information and broadcasting minister in the early 1960s, she had been at the forefront of promoting the production of socially engaged Indian films.[30] But in declaring the Emergency, she came to preside over the most repressive and intolerant phase in the annals of Indian censorship. Films were banned outright or simply destroyed, as in the infamous case of Amrit Nahata's *Kissa Kursi Ka*. The government's arbitrary flouting of court orders found its corollary in a more personalized regime of approval in which Mrs. Gandhi's younger son and heir apparent, Sanjay Gandhi, would take "donations" to his party in return for permitting the release of new films in Delhi.[31]

With the declaration of the Emergency, V. C. Shukla replaced I. K. Gujral as minister of information and broadcasting. Here, again, were the two faces of Mrs. Gandhi's regime. Gujral represented the awakening of government to Khosla-style aesthetic liberalism; Shukla, by contrast, played the dictator's philistine yes-man. As chairman of the Film Finance Corporation, the government-backed body with a mandate to nurture "good" films, B. K. Karanjia dealt with Shukla directly and remembered him, almost thirty years later, as being "as ignorant as he was arrogant."[32] Sociologist Shiv Visvanathan describes him as "a trifle sinister, a trifle silly with a touch of the illiterate, another satrap still not successful in deparochializing himself" (1998:59). Although Shukla replaced Gujral, Gujral's supercensors lingered on into the summer of 1976, that is to say, for more than half of the Emergency. The censorship situation that *Nishant* encountered, then, was an apparently peculiar blend of liberalism, courtesy of the supercensors, and authoritarianism, courtesy of the new regime at the ministry.

Although *Nishant*'s plot was based on events that had taken place in the late 1940s, that is, during the very earliest years of Indian independence, its depiction of peasant uprising resonated directly, in the mid-1970s, with the then-surging militant Maoism of the Naxalite movement. According to Vijay Tendulkar, someone from the Ministry of Information and Broadcasting informally warned Shyam Benegal that the film was likely to run into trouble. Anil Dharker recalled that Benegal, uneasy about the film's prospects, invited him and his fellow Bombay supercensor, Hyder, to a special screening ahead of the formal screening for the CBFC's Examining Committee. (Benegal did not remember Dharker being involved at this stage.)

During his work with the Censor Board, Dharker had observed that, when potentially controversial films were shown to an examining committee, the CBFC's regional officer would invariably preempt debate by insisting on certain cuts as soon as the end credits were rolling. The committee members, not wanting to lose their perks,[33] would fall into line. So when the time came for *Nishant* to be examined, Dharker and Hyder showed up, pretending not to have seen the film before. Dharker figured that he could play the regional officer at his own game:

> He would make sure he got his say right in the beginning. So I used that tactic. I positioned myself in front so that I could turn around and face them all. The moment the end came, I said "wow! What a film! One of the best films I've ever seen!" I really launched into, you know, "we should pass it without a cut" and I gave a little speech [laughs]! So after that the Regional Officer was stunned. He couldn't contradict me because in the hierarchy I was higher than him.

Initially, *Nishant* did get its censor certificate in October 1975, although Benegal was required to insert introductory disclaimers to play down any implication of contemporary relevance: not only the usual "All characters and names in this film are fictitious and bear no resemblance to any person living or dead," but also the more temporally specific, "In a feudal state . . . the year 1945." Even then, as we shall see, V. C. Shukla would revoke the certificate before Mrs. Gandhi personally made sure it was reinstated.

The eyes of the world.

At one level, it would appear that the Bombay regional officer of the CBFC, frustrated by Dharker seizing the initiative at the screening, referred the matter upward to the ministry in Delhi, where Shukla reasserted official authority by ordering a ban. But as it turns out, both Shukla's ban and Mrs.

Gandhi's objection to it were not only expressions of a local attempt to manage the terms of an authoritarian political order but also, in a fundamental way, mediated by the kind of anxiety that thrives at the open edge of mass publicity.

Both V. C. Shukla and Mrs. Gandhi were, in their different ways, responding to a sense of shame arising from a sudden shift in perspective: seeing their own dispensation as if from outside. According to Benegal, Shukla got cold feet abroad while attending a screening of *Nishant* as the head of the Indian delegation at a film festival in Vancouver. Benegal was determined to fight Shukla's revocation of his censor certificate and assembled a stellar group of Indian auteurs (including Satyajit Ray, Mrinal Sen, and Hrishikesh Mukherjee) to petition Mrs. Gandhi on his behalf. As a well-known enthusiast of "good" Indian cinema, Mrs. Gandhi was perhaps predisposed to a favorable response. Benegal recalled, "She had asked to see the film. She'd seen *Ankur*, she'd liked it, and she'd got her friends and so on for a couple of shows. She was following my work. She was following Satyajit Ray's work earlier."[34] But the clincher here, too, seems to have been the potential for international embarrassment. Banned at home thanks to Shukla, *Nishant* was busily picking up prizes at prestigious international festivals, including an audience award at Cannes in May 1976. Benegal again: "She called V C Shukla—which I heard later—and said 'do you want to make us a laughingstock by doing this? How can you ban a film like this? Because sooner or later it will come out, and it'll be a slap in our face.' She said 'you solve this problem.'"

Seeing themselves, as it were, through the eyes of the world, both Shukla's and the prime minister's responses expressed classic authoritarian insecurities. Shukla's discomfort was that of a potentate shamed on foreign shores by cultural producers who were supposed to be tightly folded into his patron/police power. Mrs. Gandhi's anxiety stemmed from a desire to insist to the world that her dictatorship was not just some crude power grab but rather an intensified commitment to national progress that was by no means incompatible with world-class aesthetics. In an obvious way, the Emergency was an attempt to concentrate total patron/police powers in the hands of the state and to achieve complete control over the field of mass publicity. It is significant, then, that both V. C. Shukla and Mrs. Gandhi—while coming to opposite conclusions regarding what should be done about *Nishant*—felt intimations of the film's potentiating power as it circulated through an international public field that they could not control and which, as such, functioned as an open edge vis-à-vis the performative dispensation of their regime.[35]

According to Benegal, Shukla objected to *Nishant* because he interpreted the film as a treasonous incitement to violent rebellion against the state. But as Madhava Prasad (1998) has argued, *Nishant* is provocative precisely because of its political ambiguity. While it conforms to the dictates of "statist realism" by staging a confrontation between "feudal" and "modern" social forms, it refuses to reassure the viewer that a middle-class leadership will successfully be able to harness the energy of popular frustration to a state-led project of national development. Prasad notes that the soundtrack of the scene in which the priest and the schoolteacher first try to mobilize a crowd of peasants to rise up against the landlords gives us not their words but rather an overwhelming density of bells and drums. He interprets this absence of language as marking the impossibility of a discourse that, from within the generic space of statist realism, would manifest the peasants as both the natural enemies of feudal oppression and as "an obedient army" (208).[36] And, of course, once the peasants do rise, their rage and violence is indiscriminate, leveling everything and everyone in their path.

Girish Karnad, who played the schoolteacher in *Nishant*, felt that the film was not so much politically ambiguous as both idiomatically unrealistic in its use of language[37] and politically implausible. The idea that two Brahmins—the schoolteacher and the priest—should succeed in convincing the villagers to rise up against landlords of the Reddy caste when the film seemed to suggest that the peasants themselves were Reddys (rather than, say, [landholding] Kammas or [formerly untouchable] Dalits) was simply unbelievable in a place where "it's a question of caste loyalty before law, logic, justice—anything." Karnad attributed this political misreading of the situation in rural Andhra Pradesh to the Maharashtrian Vijay Tendulkar's unfamiliarity with the local context.[38] At a fundamental level, Karnad felt that *Nishant* was incoherent because it had failed to reconcile the opposing aesthetic impulses of Tendulkar, whom he characterized as a socially conservative writer, and Benegal, who "wanted a progressive film."

Certainly, even the optimistic connotations of the film's titular "dawn" seem diametrically opposed to the tenor of the line that originally inspired Tendulkar: *When they killed the youngest brother, it was sunset.* To the extent that *Nishant* conveys a political "message," there is, again, room for both views. Either the mob's indiscriminate violence can be interpreted as a conservative, cautionary tale about the need to keep a tight lid on popular uprisings that will only lead to death and destruction. Or it can be interpreted as a radical critique of the middle-class statist presumption that the revolution can be directed from above. But the relation between Tendulkar and Benegal in the making of *Nishant* deserves to be considered more carefully. Things become more interesting once we move our sights beyond the most overtly "political" dimensions of the film.

Cuts and Complicities

The problem of a "modern" overcoming of "feudal" social forms is, as noted, a characteristic theme in what Madhava Prasad calls the statist realist genre of filmmaking. On that level, *Nishant* conforms to generic requirements while offering no easy solutions. But it also raises a subtler and perhaps more subversive question about forms of agency and desire that become possible *within* the space marked "feudal"; forms of agency and desire that are inextricable from degradation and violence.

I have in mind here the relationship between the imprisoned schoolteacher's wife, played by Shabana Azmi, and the landlord's hapless youngest brother, played by Naseeruddin Shah. A sexually charged intimacy develops between them, a relation in which genuine gentleness is blended with physical brutality after she has scorned her husband's ineffectual attempts to get her released from the landlord's compound. The relationship is not simply, as Prasad argues, a conventional instance of the middle-class cinema's fetishistic fascination with an "untamed" sexuality that is supposed to be characteristic of the feudal order. Certainly, the more boorish elder brothers' behavior might be understood that way. But the youngest brother's mixture of awkwardness, effeminacy, gentleness, and violence, coupled with the schoolteacher's wife's forthright way of offering herself to his approach, suggests a more complex erotics.

We see the youngest son alone one evening, drinking himself into a state of volatility, whipping the ground with a length of rope in a rather stilted imitation of the easy aggression of his older brothers. Thus fortified, he enters the room in which the schoolteacher's wife is being kept, brandishing the rope as if to use it on her. Rather than cowering in a corner—and certainly not manifesting the "mute submission" that Prasad (1998:206) attributes to her—the schoolteacher's wife rises and approaches the youngest brother in an attitude that subtly blends an element of submission with more than a hint of provocative, level-eyed desire. As if overcome by the power of her presence, the youngest brother roughly pulls her to him, and for a few seconds we see them embrace in a standing position, his face expressing nothing so much as bewilderment. The image then abruptly cuts to the following morning, as the camera pans down and to the side from the brightly lit wall of the room to reveal their two bodies, side by side, on a mattress on the floor. We do not see their faces; she is fully clothed, he wears pajamas. Within seconds there is another sudden edit, and we find ourselves in the outdoor crowd scene where the teacher's and priest's "impossible" voices will be drowned by drums and bells.

The first few times I watched this sequence, I was sure that the abrupt cuts were traces of the censors' scissors. But Shyam Benegal insisted that, whatever other obstructions officialdom may have devised for *Nishant* (of which more in a moment), neither the CBFC nor the Ministry of Information and Broadcasting had pushed through any cuts. As it turned out, the cuts were his own. Vijay Tendulkar remarked,

> You know, there is something missing in the film. I don't know whether you have noticed? Violence of sorts is at the base of the film. It's something basic to the film. Yet you don't see a single drop of blood in the film. You will be surprised to know how it happened. There was blood in the film, and the film was ready when the Emergency came. And this probably would have been the first film to go to the censors. And Shyam Benegal became jittery. He felt that, well, this will be banned. That was again the general mood at the time. So on his own he voluntarily drew out all the blood from the film.

As for the jumpy cuts in the highly charged scene between the schoolteacher's wife and the landlord's youngest brother, Tendulkar told me that Benegal was persuaded to chop it by the visceral revulsion of a female acquaintance for whom he had screened a rough edit of the film. In Tendulkar's version of the scene, as it was originally shot the landlord's brother had in fact started beating the schoolteacher's wife, but his approach, rather than resolving itself peacefully in an embrace, had spiraled into frenziedly eroticized, and thus libidinally heightened, violence: "When he is indulging in violence with her she says something. He is hotheaded and starts beating her. He beats her *severely* and, in that, suddenly he becomes erotic. And that is the point that he gets involved with that woman."

Benegal confirmed that he had cut several scenes, not because of any outside pressure or anticipated objections but because they seemed to him gratuitously literal in a film already highly charged with "implied violence."[39] But in its diluted form, this particular scene manifests an abrupt discontinuity between the eroticized violence that drives the characters' approach to each other and the apparently pacific resolution of the embrace, which quickly transitions into a placid few seconds of apparently postcoital recumbence. If the bells and drums both emphasize and disavow the "impossibility" of a middle-class mobilization of the peasants, then equally this sudden edit both foregrounds and represses the discontinuity between the "feudal" brutality of the violent approach and the "modern" placidity of their companionship.

What lurks in this cut is the traumatic corollary to the schoolteacher's dutiful but vain attempts to get his wife released by going through the proper modern channels. This is not just the implication that the systems of the modern state are corrupt, which is, as we have seen, the standard theme of thwarted progress. It is something much more unsettling, something implied in the provocative blend of meek surrender and defiant desire that Shabana Azmi brings to her performance: namely, that (feudal) domination and (modern) empowerment are not incompatible.

Tendulkar's story about the woman who was repelled by the unedited version of this scene rings true to me. But then so does Benegal's claim that he felt the violence was gratuitous. He may well subjectively have experienced the jitters that Tendulkar attributed to him as an affront to good taste rather than as a more tactical anticipation of what the censors would permit.[40] But to allow these aspects of the situation to speak to the central question of this chapter—the grounds of the censors' judgment—I need to turn to the final act in the story of *Nishant* and the censors: how the three-way impasse between Shyam Benegal, V. C. Shukla, and Indira Gandhi was finally resolved.

The Infamous Intertitles

Benegal remembers that Shukla, having been reprimanded by Mrs. Gandhi, ordered him to submit *Nishant* for recertification, knowing that the CBFC could then demand various cuts. Alternatively, according to Aruna Vasudev's 1978 account, the next installment of the drama took place after the film's producers, having been invited to screen the film at the Chicago Film Festival in November 1976, applied to the Ministry of Information and Broadcasting to release the foreign exchange they would need to have English subtitles added in Brussels.[41] According to Benegal, the film faced further cuts at the hands of a humiliated Shukla, but a joint secretary at the Ministry of Information and Broadcasting who was one of the victims of Shukla's purges used his very last day in office to offer Benegal a compromise. In Vasudev's telling, the ministry agreed to release the foreign exchange in return for one more alteration. The original October 1975 certificate could stand if Benegal would only agree to insert a new set of much more declarative intertitles at the beginning and end of the film.

In the beginning: *This film is a fictionalized recreation of a story of the past when the feudal system was prevalent in British India. It has no bearing with* [sic] *the present day India where feudalism has been abolished and no section of the people suffer from any oppression from another section.*

And at the end: *The scenes depicted in this film relate to a period when India was not independent. Citizens of India today enjoy equal rights and status, and working together are moving ever forward.*

In Vasudev's version of the story, Benegal accepted the intertitles but the ministry still managed to prevent *Nishant* from going to Chicago (Benegal's first film, *Ankur*, was shown instead). According to Benegal, the joint secretary at the Ministry of Information and Broadcasting knew full well that the new intertitles would, through their performative excess, have exactly the opposite effect to what the minister intended. "People will laugh," he told Benegal. "Let them know what this [the Emergency] is all about." By accepting the deal, Benegal got his certificate back and audiences rolled in the aisles. "And *then*, as soon as the Emergency was over [in 1977], I got a letter from the Censor Board saying 'you can remove those things!' "

I started this chapter by arguing that the censors justify their actions by claiming that society is in a state of exception, an in-between time. When it came to film censorship, the peculiarity of the Emergency was that as a regime that made the state of exception absolutely explicit, it was nevertheless also more committed than any other regime in Indian post-Independence history to the constant assertion that the political situation was absolutely "normal." Before and after the Emergency, censorship was premised on the idea that image-objects have to be managed by a specially qualified cadre of individuals because society at large is in too much of a state of instability to handle it. But the joint secretary's intertitles were a masterstroke because they perfectly expressed the official ideology of the Emergency while performatively underlining its absurdity. By the official logic of the Emergency, whatever instability *Nishant* insinuated could not possibly be relevant to the present, since the present was, by definition, modern and progressive compared to a feudal and oppressive past. And yet if the present was so stable, then why did the absolute distinction between the past and the present have to be so strenuously and so repeatedly asserted?

Madhava Prasad assumes that Shyam Benegal added the original disclaimers spontaneously because "the pastness of feudalism is a necessary protocol of realist representation" (1998:196). Benegal's own version of events would seem to require a somewhat different interpretation. The pastness of feudalism was certainly a necessary protocol of official Emergency ideology. And it does seem to have guided Benegal's decision to exsanguinate *Nishant* so as to distance it from Vijay Tendulkar's more visceral but also more provocative vision, leaving just a trace of something emergent in Azmi's insinuating performance, around the edges of the cuts. Benegal's commitment to a certain conception of cinematic "taste" may have led him to those edits anyway, Emergency or no. But the story of *Nishant* does suggest that, ironically enough, censorship during the Emergency relied on denying the ideology of exception—the claim that we are in a liminal time where unspoken rules have failed—which has otherwise been the consistent justification for the censors' work. Film censorship has, as I have shown, generally rested on a concern about the potentiated reality of mass-mediated image-objects. The peculiarity of Emergency-period censorship was perhaps after all not so much its intensification, still less its arbitrariness. More fundamentally, its distinguishing abnormality was its desperate attempt to banish the problem of potentiated reality altogether by asserting a state of absolute normality.

FORCE AND MEANING IN THE MASS-MEDIATED IMAGE-OBJECT

Indian cinema censorship since the 1960s has, as I argued above, generally referred films to the judgment of censors who are supposed to combine, in varying proportion, aesthetic discrimination and cultural responsibility. But these conventional grounds of the censors' judgment are, in turn, premised on a persistent anxiety about the instability of mass-mediated image-objects. The anxiety revolves around a basic question: can the visceral *force* of image-objects be judged as a function of their contextual *meaning* (within a film, vis-à-vis an interpretive community, and so on) or is force quasi-autonomous of meaning? Kajri Jain neatly characterizes the contending standpoints in her analysis of Indian calendar art: "the idea that the efficacy of an image stems from the effects of its work of representation on a viewing subject" versus an approach that sees the image "as preinvested, as inherently or immanently powerful, its effects in the public arena emanating from its very presence like a contagion, or by remote control" (2007:299).

In the annals of film censorship, the question came up early. One of the things the Indian Cinematograph Committee set out to determine in 1927–28 was whether films were harming audiences. The ICC began by assuming that if films contained a kind of force that might harm audiences, then this force only did its work if audiences understood the meaning of the films they were watching. At the same time, the ICC assumed—as would censors in later decades—that audiences could be divided up into what I have called continent and incontinent groups. Finally, the films that were considered most harmful were the spicy American social dramas that were a staple of cinemas frequented by more educated (that is, continent) audiences.

Taken together, this set of assumptions quickly led to the conclusion that the cinema could not be doing much harm, since the audiences that were likely to understand the meaning of such films were composed of the kind of continent spectators who were shielded by their education from any corrosive force that might emanate from the cinematic image. As ICC member A. M. Green stated, "If the illiterate do not understand it and the literate do not mind it or are not affected by it, there does not seem to be very much reason to object to it" (ICC 1928a, 2:273). In its own terms, Green's logic was impeccable. The problem was that the sense of an unsettling mobile intensity coming off the screen persisted. And it has persisted into the present, reappearing as a constant oscillation in the censor's discourse between the meaningful image and the forceful image.

Shekhar Kapur's *Bandit Queen* (1994) is a gritty biopic about the real-life female outlaw Phoolan Devi, lifelong victim of caste and sexual violence turned ruthless avenger and, later, member of Parliament. A short analysis of the film sets the scene in chapter 3 for my discussion of how competing performative dispensations claimed censorial authority inside and outside the law during the 1990s. But *Bandit Queen*'s travels and travails—from Examining Committee to Revising Committee to Appellate Tribunal to High Court to Division Bench and finally to the Supreme

Court—also amount to an excellent object lesson in how the force/meaning conundrum has played itself out across the various formal arenas of film censorship.

Bandit Queen contains plenty of disturbing sequences: multiple scenes of rape, public humiliation, and retaliatory violence. The question from the beginning, then, was whether these scenes were inherently unacceptable because of their provocative character or whether they could be justified in terms of some higher purpose. In return for granting Kapur an A (adult) certificate,[42] the CBFC's Revising Committee asked that many of the expletives that peppered the script be deleted, that a scene showing a policeman beating Phoolan Devi with the butt of a gun be taken out, that a sequence in which Phoolan Devi is shown beating up her first husband be reduced by 70 percent, and that a scene that depicts the naked buttocks of the character Babu Gujjar as he rapes Phoolan Devi be shortened.

Bandit Queen's producer, Bobby Art International, took the case to the Film Certification Appellate Tribunal (FCAT), which reduced the Revising Committee's list of cuts but also, more important, issued a ruling that explicitly sought to apply an affectively distancing, "contextualist" yardstick of judgment to its evaluation of the film's more troubling scenes. On the question of the language used in the film, the FCAT effectively argued that the dramatic criterion of realism trumped whatever upsetting force the expletives might emanate if "taken literally": "The tone and tenor of the dialogues in the film reflect the nuances locally and habitually used and spoken in the villages and in the ravines of the Chambal, not bereft of expletives used for force and effect by way of normal and common parlance in those parts; these expletives are not intended to be taken literally" (Bobby Art International v. Om Pal Singh Hoon [1996]).[43]

When it came to one of the most controversial scenes in the film, a sequence in which Phoolan Devi is publicly humiliated by being stripped naked in front of a crowd of villagers and forced to fetch water from a well, the FCAT acknowledged the affective intensity of the scene. But comparing the contested scenes of nakedness in *Bandit Queen* to frontal shots of naked Holocaust victims in *Schindler's List* (1993), it argued that the larger narrative structure of the film would ensure that this intensity would eventuate not in gratuitous prurience but rather in a suitably moral indignation at Phoolan Devi's victimization through a performative mobilization of "sympathy": "Much emphasis was laid before us on the fact that Phoolan Devi is shown naked being paraded in the village after being humiliated.

The Tribunal observed that these visuals could not but create sympathy towards the unfortunate woman in particular and revulsion against the perpetrators of crimes against women in general. The sequence was an integral part of the story. It was not sensual or sexual, and was intended to, as indeed it did, create revulsion in the minds of the average audience towards the tormentors and oppressors of women" (Bobby Art International v. Om Pal Singh Hoon [1996]).

After several months of festival screenings, punctuated by a case brought against the film's producers by Phoolan Devi herself that was settled out of court,[44] *Bandit Queen* opened in Indian theaters in January 1996. After only two days, however, one Om Pal Singh Hoon, claiming to represent the Gujjar community, filed suit against the film in the Delhi High Court, complaining that the character of the brutal rapist Babu Gujjar was offensive to Gujjars, that the depiction of Phoolan Devi "lowered the prestige" of her Mahalla community, and that the film in general was "abhorrent and unconscionable and a slur on the womanhood of India."

Quashing the FCAT's certification of *Bandit Queen* in March 1996, the Delhi High Court directly reversed the reasoning of the tribunal, with its insistence on placing controversial sequences in social and formal context, and upheld the idea that certain images—Phoolan Devi being shown frontally nude during the well scene and the "naked posterior of Babu Gujjar" during the rape—*inherently* transgressed the CBFC's guidelines ("HC Stays Screening of Bandit Queen" 1996). In upholding the High Court's opinion against an appeal by *Bandit Queen*'s distributor, ABCL, a Division Bench of the court affirmed the danger that the film's performative force was liable to trigger in audiences not sympathy but rather unwholesome and overexcited mimicry: "The manner in which [the expletives in the script] are expressed are intended to stir immoral emotions. These words tend to make viewers emulate these persons which is sufficient to say that these words are obscene" ("Ban on *Bandit Queen* to Continue" 1996). As for Babu Gujjar's bare behind, the Division Bench appears to have conducted a kind of time-and-motion study, solemnly noting with the aid of a stopwatch that the Babu's buttocks bounced for twenty seconds. If the Appellate Tribunal had found in these images an indictment of violence against women, then the Division Bench of the Delhi High Court was less inclined toward interpretation: "Rape is crude and its crudity is what the rapist's bouncing bare posterior is meant to illustrate" (Bobby Art International v. Om Pal Singh Hoon [1996]).

The Supreme Court finally settled the matter after two years of wrangling. Its May 1996 judgment reinstated an FCAT-style meaningful-image reading against the CBFC and the Delhi High Court's anxiety about mimetic force. The Supreme Court's central proposition was that "a film that illustrates the consequences of the social evil must also show that social evil. . . . No film that extols the social evil or encourages it is permissible, but a film that carries the message that social evil is evil cannot be made impermissible on the ground that it depicts social evil. At the same time, the depiction must be sufficient for the purpose of the film" (Bobby Art International v. Om Pal Singh Hoon [1996]).

On one level, then, the Supreme Court upheld the idea that a certain performative intensity would be necessary in order to convey the moral horror of a "social evil." On another level, it demanded that the narrative structure of the film ensure that this performative intensity be unambiguously moralized in such a way as to ensure audience indignation. What is interesting about the judgment is not the insistence upon adherence to a moral message per se, but rather the assumption that the performative intensity and mimetic potential of particular provocative images—which it implicitly acknowledges—could be *positively potentiated* (in terms of a normative standard of social progress) by means of the formal and narrative structure of the work as a whole.

Liberals, of course, often complain—in India as elsewhere—that those who seek bans on books or films often have not read or watched the items to which they so vociferously object (see chapter 3). In that light it becomes interesting that the Supreme Court was able to reach its "liberal" judgment as a matter of general principle, that is to say, without having seen the film.[45] To be sure, the Supreme Court was in part quite reasonably insisting that the work of evaluating the singularity of any given film should remain with the CBFC and the FCAT. But it is nevertheless significant that the insistence on interpreting images in context was articulated in general terms, at a principled (or rather a safe) distance from the singular potentials of any particular image.

Public discussion of *Bandit Queen*'s complicated encounters with the Censor Board and the courts tended to affirm the meaningful-image opinions of the FCAT and the Supreme Court as progressive, insofar as they appeared to grant spectators the maturity of autonomous judgment—at least in the presence of a "good" film. By the same token, the Censor Board and the Delhi High Court came off badly, seeming to assume that the image–audience relation is crudely and mechanically mimetic, and that audiences are helplessly porous: what the pissing man sees, the pissing man does. But both positions, we should note, are heavily moralized. The meaningful-image advocates justify provocative images by demanding that they subtend a normative narrative of social uplift and progress, while those who warn of the inherent power of images routinely invoke the specter of moral corruption. In both cases, the underlying anxiety is that the performative force of images might leak out beyond the containment of a moralized symbolic order.

The paradigmatic representation of this possibility is, of course, the pissing man whose liminal position between a shattered traditional culture and an elusive secular enlightenment makes him vulnerable to the screen and unable to judge for himself. I was thus entirely unsurprised to find the then-regional officer of the CBFC in Mumbai, V. K. Singla, invoking a version of the pissing man when I asked him why, say, a taxi driver or a *paanwallah*[46] could not be appointed to the CBFC's examining committees which, after all, were supposed to represent a "cross-section of society and interests." Genuinely horrified, Singla exclaimed: "But he might go out and *do* what he saw in the film!" Such subalterns apparently lacked what the Khosla Committee called an "adult discount"—a mature sensory prophylaxis against the commandment of images (Khosla et al. 1969:119). I was rather more surprised—perhaps naively—to find that Vijay Anand, staunch defender of the contextualist Khosla doctrine, was just as emphatic on this point. When I suggested to Anand that the CBFC represented the general public, he almost cut me off: "It doesn't. It represents the government. . . . You can't have, for example, a milk seller."

But why not? Walter Benjamin, for one, famously argued that the advent of the cinema meant that, for the first time, everyone was in a position to be at once an absorbed enthusiast and a critical expert: "The progressive attitude [made possible by the cinema] is characterized by an immediate, intimate fusion of pleasure—pleasure in seeing and experiencing—with an attitude of expert appraisal" (2008b [1936]:36). But while the censor acknowledges both sides of this equation—pleasure and expert appraisal—he cannot admit their intimate fusion. The discourse of censorship, whether aesthetic or culturalist, insists on the diremption of the subject of immersive pleasure and the subject of critical distance. Between one and the other, there can be no continuous passage; the parallax gap remains ("*two sides* of the same phenomenon which, precisely as two sides, can never meet").

Or rather, the gap appears as a gap—for example, the unbridgeable distance between the judicious subject who can be allowed onto the Censor Board's advisory panels and the pissing man paanwallah who most certainly cannot. And precisely for this reason, the censors cannot help but appeal to various kinds of moralized symbolic orders that are supposed to provide an apparently "objective" way of navigating the gap, of moving from the intensive immersion of spectatorship to critical judgment and back again. Sometimes these moralized symbolic orders are called "good taste," sometimes they appear in the guise of "Indian culture." But whatever shape they take, they are, as it were, the ideological fantasies that attempt to suture the gap between the faces of the subject of censorship: the "hot" pissing man and the "cool" judicious censor.

It would be easy to assume that the pissing man and the censor are simply terms by which a dominant bourgeois class ideologizes the gulf that separates the privileged from the subalterns. But while the parallax gap between the pissing man and the censor certainly does serve this purpose, it is not only a cynical discourse of class domination. Rather, it expresses— in the frozen ideological form of ideal typical subject positions—the predicament of mass publicity as I outlined it in chapter 1: the gap between collective effervescence and symbolic order. The frozen ideological opposition between the two subjects of censorship—the (immediate, helpless) pissing man and the (mediate, composed) censor—is, as it were, the anthropoid form of the endlessly repeated claim that India is in a state of transition, an in-between time, a time of exception. But this repetitive assertion of historical liminality is not only a legitimating tactic. It is also the place in the censors' discourse that at once marks and disavows an awareness of a more structural indeterminacy: that public culture is less a given assemblage of objects to be regulated by suitably authorized subjects than a mobile field out of which the censor's discourse attempts to forge stable subject- and object-effects. And it is the truth of this mobility that, in misrecognized form, survives in the apparently nonsensical (and thus too easily dismissed) claim that certain image-objects may be inherently objectionable, over and above any attempt to contextualize them.

The "good" cinema of the 1960s and 1970s—the statist realist genre of which Shyam Benegal's early films were so exemplary—no longer exists as a living form. In the 1980s, many of the "serious" directors moved into television, which for a few years commissioned quality work. In the 1990s, mainstream Hindi film achieved a new kind of cultural legitimacy under the "Bollywood" rubric, aided in no small part by its global recognition (Gopal and Moorti, eds., 2008; Kaur and Sinha, eds., 2005; Kavoori and Punathambekar, eds., 2008; Rajadhyaksha 2009; Vasudevan 2010). And the rise of multiplex theaters in Indian cities since the turn of the millennium has meant that smaller-budget, more adventurous films have been able to find a market, especially with more affluent urban audiences.

Most of the younger multiplex filmmakers positively abhor the "behalf-ist" moralism that they associate with statist realism. This was filmmaking "inspired by a Brechtian form of engagement, [that spoke] a language of conscientization that [fit] the imperatives of the realist art cinema and documentary film [of the 1970s and 1980s]: to strengthen a civil social discourse of reasoned representation, communication, and debate" (Vasu-devan 2010:318). Against this "socially conscious" version of "good" film-making, Kaizad Gustad, enfant terrible director of *Bombay Boys* (1998) and *Boom* (2003), expressed the irritation of many members of his generation: "Why does every film have to have 'meaning'? Why is every director asked 'what were you trying to say?' Why do I have to address 'problems of the youth,' pray? . . . Respect only seems to come to grey beards with twenty films that never leave the festival circuit" (1999). From this perspective, a "socially engaged" realist film like *Bandit Queen*, although it was made in the 1990s, was decidedly old school. As such it was also, in the end, emi-nently intelligible within the teleological moral matrix of the censorship apparatus.

At first sight, big-budget commercial directors and independent docu-mentarists would seem to occupy entirely different positions vis-à-vis the censors. Bollywood directors enjoy lots of room for negotiation when it comes to sex and violence—such and such a certificate can be given if so and so many percent of given scenes are cut. Officials can be wined and dined or paid off in other ways.[47] Films are submitted with extra sex and fight footage so that some of it can be sacrificed in order to keep other scenes or to secure the larger audiences that "U" (universal) or "U/A" (universal/adult) certificates permit. A moralized narrative structure modulates sexy content; the femme fatale dies in the end or, at the very least, is abandoned by her lover and left to rue her foolishness. Politically critical content, on the other hand, is not so negotiable. Scenes of sex and violence can be cut down without fundamentally changing what they are "saying," whereas political critique does not appear to be "divisible" in the same way. Doyen documentarist Anand Patwardhan's long record with government censorship, for example, would seem to attest to this: constant tussles with the CBFC and the state television network Doordarshan since the mid-1970s, but not a single cut conceded.

The legal judgments arising out of Patwardhan's decades of struggle now amount to a priceless precedent for any filmmaker wishing to challenge political censorship (see http://www.patwardhan.com). His triumphs have built him a profile—internationally as well as in India—as an indefatigable David to the government's Goliath. At the same time, Patwardhan's legal success has not been the product of tenacity alone; it is also a function of the *kind* of political speech his films embody. While they are always directly critical of reigning elites, the political voice of Patwardhan's films also invariably addresses the sort of "big" themes that are expressible in a morally clear-cut fashion and in terms of widely recognized yardsticks of social justice: the oppression and exploitation of subaltern groups, the authoritarian infringement of free speech, the crisis of secularism, ecology and corporate greed, violence versus the rule of law, and so on. In other words, while Patwardhan has been a tireless thorn in the side of the CBFC and the authorities more generally, his films also represent the kind of "loyal opposition" that can appeal to a relatively unambiguous public interest.

But what about films that do not appeal to any kind of moralized public interest? On what grounds can they claim integrity? Consider two examples from around the turn of the millennium: Sunhil Sippy's *Snip!* (2001) and Anurag Kashyap's *Paanch* (2000), both of them debut features from young filmmakers who for various reasons were not in any position to play the game.

... and *that's* when you start shitting yourself.

Sunhil Sippy looked back on his unhappy experience with the censors in November 2003, three years after the fact: "In a sense I really asked for it. I really did. I was young, I was cocky. I said 'fuck everyone, I'm going to go and make a film and I'm going to make it my way, and I'm going to take everybody on.' You know? And I had the kind of guts to do that, and the *ignorance* to do that, really."[48]

The nephew of Ramesh Sippy, director of the Amitabh Bachchan/Dharmendra blockbuster *Sholay* (1975), Sunhil Sippy had grown up in London and studied in the United States before returning to Mumbai in 1995. He was determined to make a film that was neither Bollywood *masala*[49] nor "serious" in the statist realist style of the 1960s and 1970s. But the mainstream film establishment greeted him with ridicule and contempt: "They told me to fuck off straight. With an attitude of, who do you think you are, making a film for a festival? We're Indian—you don't understand our commercial cinema." Only a few years later, in 2001–2, Mira Nair's *Monsoon Wedding* and Gurinder Chadha's *Bend It Like Beckham* would spearhead a "crossover" fad. But in the late 1990s, Sippy's only available reference points were a handful of young directors tentatively trying to carve out a new hip, ironic, and urban cinematic space: the aforementioned Kaizad Gustad, Nagesh Kukunoor (*Hyderabad Blues* [1998]), and especially Dev Benegal (*English, August* [1994] and *Split Wide Open* [1999]).

Once *Snip!* was completed, Sippy thought himself lucky to secure distribution through a powerful diamond merchant who had seen and enjoyed the uncensored version. As a first-time director, Sippy was therefore not about to argue too hard when this gentleman insisted that two song sequences be added. In any case, the audience response at a series of private screenings was highly positive. The next step was to submit the film to the CBFC. Sippy recalled that "there was a lot of swearing [in the film]. *Too* much swearing. I had a pretty fair idea that the word 'fuck' wasn't going to get through but, you know, that wasn't going to affect the film too much. The visuals I never thought for a minute would get chopped. I *never* imagined that a single frame of the film would get cut. There was no tits and ass, there was nothing. I mean there was *nothing* in the film that I felt was provocative. At all. Nothing visually. Nothing titillating, nothing provocative, nothing that could even stir anyone's eyes. I just thought 'no way.' "

On the appointed day, the Examining Committee arrived to view *Snip!* at a small preview theater in the fashionable suburb of Bandra. Sippy recalled the sudden dread that gripped him when he actually came face to face with this "cross-section of society and interests":

> There are these two oldish men, one oldish woman, and two youngish
> women in their thirties, I think. So we go in there and try to be very nice

and all that crap. And *that's* when you start shitting yourself. You're thinking, "oh *fuck*." You're wondering if it's going to come out with a single frame intact [laughs]! To look at them, you know what I mean?! As you look at their faces you're, like, "God, these are the people that are going to decide the fate of the film." You're suddenly really embarrassed. I mean, on a Western level, it's like making a hardcore porn film and then showing it to your best friend's parents. You know?! That's what it felt like—the *shame* when somebody finds it [laughs]! That's what it feels like.

Not allowed into the theater itself during the screening, Sippy sat anxiously in the projection room "looking down into the theater, imagining my fate." Film over, committee deliberations completed, the filmmakers were invited into the theater to hear the verdict and be given an opportunity to respond. Initially, the news seemed good: only five cuts. These five cuts, however, quickly turned out to be about eighty-five cuts: inter alia, every occurrence of the word "fuck," every shot of cleavage, and—fatefully— every shot of a vibrator that played a comic role in the narrative.

This vibrator did not appear in any directly sexual manner. A character played by Saurabh Shukla sneaks into an empty apartment only to be mystified by a strange, long, white object sticking out of a saucepan on the stove. Ignorant as to its function, he picks it up, turns it around in his hands, and finally tries stirring the contents of the saucepan with it. In private screenings, this had been one visual gag that had invariably worked, and Sippy was determined not to lose it.

Then they said the vibrator—they called it a dildo—they said "anywhere where the dildo is seen, that's one cut." At which point I got up off my chair and I said "you can't do that. You *cannot* cut this out." I could have lived with a lot of the other cuts. I felt that the language was too extreme in parts. That was just me being a bit immature and stupid and not being as in control of the film as I should have been while shooting. But *this*, I was livid. I argued and begged and pleaded and they were *on the verge* of letting it go. Even the old men. I said "there's nothing wrong with it, it's totally innocent fun." And the old men were sort of about to let it go. And then there was this thirty-five-year-old woman who just said no. They had to be unanimous about this. And this woman said "no—no way." And that was it.

A personal appeal to Asha Parekh, then chair of the CBFC, yielded nothing. Sippy was stuck. A commercial filmmaker tends to be under financial pressure from backers and cannot afford significant delays. Adding to the pressure, the diamond merchant distributor was furious when he learned of the cuts and made Sippy promise not to make any public statements about *Snip!* having been snipped lest audiences be turned off.

The film bombed. And to add insult to injury, when interviewers on television and in the press asked him about censorship, Sippy had to insist that the film was intact, just as he had made it. All this was, of course, humiliating from an artistic point of view, and with the benefit of hindsight there were many things that Sippy felt he should have done differently. He could have refused to release the film in India and screened it abroad while raising a stink in the foreign media about the Indian censors. But he also knew that no matter how much he might have been able to complain, he would not have been in a position to seek legal satisfaction through the usual channels: to push for a revising committee and, beyond that, a hearing before the FCAT and, ultimately, a fight in the Supreme Court: "Wasn't going to go there. Because I realized what I was doing, it was frivolous. Whatever fun I was having, it was not a *significant* piece of cinema. I had the maturity to see that. I mean, it wasn't like me trying to reflect modern culture or to change the times or say 'this is about India.' It wasn't. It was frivolous."

Wendy Steiner notes that the most "confounding implication of American obscenity legislation is the notion that art advocates ideas . . . and that it can be shielded only on this ground. Entertainment value is not defensible; the promulgation of ideas is" (1995:35–36). Similarly, Sunhil Sippy knew that he had no legal leg to stand on when it came to his splendidly silly vibrator. The fact that his film was not trying to advocate any Big Ideas made any claims about its integrity as a piece of entertainment moot within the discourse that grounded both the censors' decisions and a filmmaker's opportunities to contest them. *Snip!* was, quite literally, insignificant; its provocation was, in terms of the ideology of censorship, unmediated by any adequate meaning.

Your film is neither healthy nor entertainment.
Some might explain Sunhil Sippy's experience as a result of his having grown up abroad and being out of touch with Indian expectations. But no one could make that claim about Anurag Kashyap, born in Gorakhpur; schooled in

Gwalior and Delhi; arriving in Mumbai to pursue filmmaking; and by his own telling, living on the streets until he caught a break as a writer on Ram Gopal Varma's *Satya* (1998). In 2000 Kashyap submitted to the CBFC his own first feature film, *Paanch*, a piece of hard rock Hindi noir about a botched kidnapping that sends five friends into a spiral of betrayal and violence.

As per the usual procedure, Kashyap was called in to hear the Examining Committee's verdict after the screening. No one spoke except the regional officer who cut straight to the chase: "Why have you made this film?" Wrong-footed, Kashyap responded, "because I wanted to." The regional officer tried again: "What does cinema mean to you?" Increasingly baffled by this abstract line of questioning, Kashyap threw the question back: "What does it mean to *you*?"

> And he said "cinema means healthy entertainment. Your film is neither healthy nor entertainment." And I said "I don't get you. What do you mean by that?" He said "your main character has no motive. He's just negative. There's no reason for him being negative." I said "why should there be a reason?" . . . I said "OK fine, you tell me what is objectionable, what you want me to change, so I can argue." He said, "we don't know. Take the film back, change it, and bring it back."[50]

Exasperated, Kashyap did exactly what Sunhil Sippy had not: "I made a lot of noise. I had some two hundred screenings all over. I showed it to anyone who wanted to see it. I said 'make your opinion known.' I didn't tell them anything. I said 'please write about it. I want your opinion on the movie.'"

Under growing public pressure, the CBFC reiterated that the film was not healthy entertainment, that all the characters were "negative," and that it contained no "social message." After Kashyap appealed on the grounds that the CBFC's objections were too vague, the film was reexamined by a revising committee that lurched from the Examining Committee's qualitative but vague complaints all the way over to a very specific but completely quantitative list of cuts: "They said 'delete this word, delete that, delete that'—they had these random things. 'Delete the blood shots by 50 percent.'" Whereas the Examining Committee's blanket rejection of *Paanch* had initially stumped Kashyap, he now found himself unable to engage with a revising committee that was applying guidelines from the CBFC's handbook in an entirely mechanical way, without any consideration of the film "as one integrated piece which must be assessed and judged as a whole and not as a collection of distinct and separable parts."[51]

Sunhil Sippy went on to become a highly successful director of commercials with Highlight Films. Anurag Kashyap eventually hit the jackpot with *Dev D* (2009). After *Paanch*, which never achieved a formal release but has circulated online for several years, he had several other run-ins with the CBFC. First, the release of *Black Friday* (2004), Kashyap's soberly realistic inquiry into the Bombay bombings of 1993, was delayed while the bombings themselves were still *sub judice*; then, under pressure from his producers, he had to acquiesce to cuts. Conversely, his surrealist cri-de-coeur, *No Smoking* (2007), brought him the twin satisfactions of receiving a U/A certificate with no cuts for a rather disturbing film and of being officially felicitated by the Ministry of Health for making a film that, as far as Kashyap was concerned, glamorized smoking. If Kashyap became better at anticipating the workings of the CBFC during the years following *Paanch*, then the Censor Board also formed its own expectations of him. When he submitted *The Girl with the Yellow Boots* to the censors in 2010, the Mumbai regional officer called him to recommend therapy as an alternative to repeatedly subjecting Indian audiences to "your catharsis."[52]

Like Kashyap's *Black Friday*, Mani Ratnam's *Bombay* (1995) dealt with the violence that rocked the city after the destruction of the Babri Mosque in 1992. As we shall see in chapter 3, *Bombay* caused a far greater public stir than *Black Friday*. But because Mani Ratnam's film ultimately amounted to a melodramatic hymn to communal harmony, it was possible for the then–election commissioner T. N. Seshan to defend it by saying "this is a film that every Indian should see" (Radhakrishna et al. 1995).[53]

It is hard to imagine a public figure saying that about *Snip!* or *Paanch*. Sippy's and Kashyap's reactions—judging by their own accounts—are interestingly different. Confronted with the actuality of the Examining Committee, with particular middle-class people, Sippy suddenly felt intense embarrassment. It was as if the anonymously intimate abstract field of mass publicity had suddenly become too concrete for comfort. Kashyap went into the process, characteristically, with youthful idealism, expecting to engage the censors in a principled debate about the aesthetic merits of his film. But both directors discovered that although, by the terms of the Cinematograph Act, they would be granted "an opportunity for representing [their] views," the constitutive presuppositions of censorship guaranteed that they would be unable to defend their work.

I began this chapter by arguing that the censors justify their judgment by claiming a quasi-permanent state of exception. I described the moralized symbolic orders that ground the censors' work today: the twin figures of cosmopolitan taste and cultural location. I traced the emergence, during the late colonial period, of the generalized spectator-citizen out of the dying embers of the ethnographic state. And I suggested that the one exception to the narrative of exception was, paradoxically enough, censorship during the Emergency.

My aim in this chapter has been to suggest that the censors' work—grappling as it must with the open edge of mass publicity—is constantly faced with the prospect of having to make aesthetic judgments for which there cannot be rules. Censorship is, among other things, a response to the persistent phenomenal experience of a tension between the sensuous force and the significant meaning of mass-mediated image objects. But because the censors' political brief is, in the end, to maintain social order, they must constantly duck the challenge of making aesthetic judgments that would respond to this challenge in an open-ended way. They do this by restlessly (many say arbitrarily and incoherently) oscillating back and forth between, on the one hand, trying to force the potentiated reality of the cinema into the straitjacket of a moralized symbolic order (films must be tasteful, films must be meaningful, films must not violate cultural norms) and, on the other, acting as if individual image-objects are somehow so inherently powerful that they cannot be allowed to stand (Sippy's vibrator, Phoolan Devi's nakedness, and such). Thus, the structural antinomies of the censor's parallax gap live on, and the narrative of social crisis that necessitates censorship is reproduced. At the same time—and this will be the subject of chapter 5—the incommensurability marked by this parallax gap also points toward an opening: a tendency or potential in public culture that both triggers and exceeds the censors' moralizing requirements.

If censorship is a form of practical reason with its own recurrent symptoms, then it is also, of course, a claim to official public authority. This authority has been formally challenged from time to time, most famously when K. A. Abbas went to the Supreme Court to question the constitutionality of precensorship for the cinema.[54] But the 1990s also saw a rash of informal, yet often quite spectacular, even violent, challenges to the CBFC's monopoly on film censorship. As self-styled guardians of culture and morality took to the streets to ban films, the battle lines shifted. Suddenly, as we shall see in chapter 3, even some of the staunchest critics of film censorship found themselves upholding the legitimacy of the CBFC as the embodiment of a secular rule of law.

CHAPTER 3

WE ARE THE LAW!

CENSORSHIP TAKES TO THE STREETS

> These days unfortunately some people seem to be perpetually on a short fuse, and are
> willing to protest often violently, about anything under the sun on the ground that a
> book or film or painting etc has "hurt the sentiments" of their community. These
> dangerous tendencies must be curbed. We are one nation and must respect each other
> and should have tolerance.
>
> —Husain v. Pandey 2008; para 117

Reflecting on the derogatory portrait of Richard III enshrined in Shakespeare's eponymous play, Polish filmmaker Andrzej Wajda once noted the
crucial importance of myth to performative efficacy: "It is difficult to change
an established image projected by Shakespeare's 'politically unjust' play, simply by using arguments which may be correct but which have no myth to act
as a vehicle" (1997 [1988]:108). "Myth" here works to potentiate a narrative
claim, to give it an affective force that exceeds its propositional meaning. In a
sense, Wajda is saying that "fiction" is indispensable to the efficacy of "fact."

In my discussion so far, I have chiefly explored performative dispensations in terms of the sociological problems they present. I have asked how authority legitimates itself as political fact to better regulate fiction. But it is only during periods of relative stability that the line between state law and street law, and the distinction between fact and fiction, are so sharp. This chapter explores the so-called cultural emergency of the 1990s as a crisis that, as crises often will, disclosed the kinds of traffic that smoothly functioning performative dispensations obscure: both the ritual traffic between legal authority and quasi-legal activism and the curious way that both formal and informal censors depend for the potency of their authority on the fictions that they presume to regulate. This chapter is thus in part an account of a moment when the grounds of the censors' judgment was challenged by all kinds of competing claimants to public cultural authority. Liberal critics routinely dismissed these often-violent challenges as not properly political—or, what amounted to the same thing, as "just politics." One of my arguments in this chapter is that the hastiness of these dismissals rests on an inaccurate conception of how public culture works. It is also an ideological conception in that it works to deflect sustained analytical attention away from "uncivil" forms of cultural activism—less because of any radical *difference* they might assert than because of the potentially more embarrassing *similarities* between formal and informal, legal and quasi-legal claims to public authority.

The phenomena that this chapter considers—the close relationship between laws and outlaws, the interdependence of regulatory fact and regulated fiction—are often, in India as elsewhere, taken as symptomatic of an incomplete historical transition to full modernity. As in chapter 2, however, I want to resist this normatively teleological assumption, although not simply in order to assert a pluralized conception of modernity. Obviously, the events that populate these pages are the outcomes of particular Indian histories. And yet I want to suggest that these particular histories—because of how they combine mass publicity, mass democracy, and extreme sociocultural diversity—may also yield more general clues to the future of public cultural contestation in an ever more globalized world.

OUT/LAW: BANDIT QUEEN

A gang of lower-caste outlaws has established rough-and-ready patron/police powers over a village in the rustic Chambal region of Uttar Pradesh. When one of its members is unmasked as a woman, the gang leader Vikram Mallah shores up her legitimacy in the eyes of skeptical villagers by proclaiming that her name is Phoolan Devi and that she is an incarnation of Putli Bai, born to protect them.[1] He encourages her to don what will become the visual signature of her ruthless efficacy, a bright red headband that embodies Durga's blessings and prompts the villagers to solemnize her coronation with cries of *Durga mata ki jai!* (Victory to Mother Durga!).

Launched into recognition by the mediation of a man, Phoolan Devi soon comes into her own. Married off to an ignorant and violent man at the age of eleven, abandoning him only to become the target of relentless upper-caste violence, she has been sexually brutalized all her life. But Vikram Mallah, a handsome, roguish Robin Hood figure, helps her to harness and hone the avenging feminine energy that will eventually allow her to wreak a terrible revenge on her oppressors. Guided by Vikram Mallah, Phoolan Devi learns the skills of the outlaw life: shooting, climbing the rugged ravines, and so on. Having thrived under Vikram Mallah's protection, Phoolan Devi falls in love with him. But this is also the moment at which she ceases automatically to submit to his male authority; their sexual union begins with her slapping him several times across the face. Now it is Vikram Mallah who yields to her, arm pinned against a rockface.

Symbolically, Phoolan Devi—as much as her outlaw persona channels the wild female energy of Durga—has become a man of sorts. Returning to her home village, her stride is confident and buoyant, she wears shirt and trousers, her bushy hair waves free. Of course, she sticks out like a sore thumb. Her mother, moved, embraces her, but her father turns away, ashamed and appalled at his daughter's refusal to bow to patriarchal authority.

The ideological discourse of the gang under Vikram Mallah's leadership is egalitarian: among the outlaws, distinctions of caste, religion, and sex are irrelevant. At an intimate level, equality appears as an open question in Phoolan Devi's erotic relation with Vikram Mallah. It is a wrestling match, a game of push and pull in which neither will allow the other to ascend for long. Vikram Mallah's protection may have allowed Phoolan Devi both to thrive and to love. But when he tries to pin her down and take her on the floor of a rented flat in Kanpur, their sexual play soon turns into an entirely serious struggle.

Phoolan Devi's story, as thus depicted in Shekhar Kapur's 1994 film *Bandit Queen*, dramatizes the questions: What is the relation of the outlaw to state law? Is the performative dispensation of an outlaw leader outside state law but nevertheless a kind of parallel law, with its codes of honor and its hierarchies? Is the incipient egalitarianism of outlaw society, despite its internal power struggles, a direct challenge to the institutionalized hierarchies of the state? Or are the outlaw and state law ambiguously complicit with each other, each dependent on the other's tacit but unreliable cooperation (see Comaroff and Comaroff 2006)?

At a more sociological level, Kapur's film suggests a contrast between Vikram Mallah's merry band and the broader, violent hierarchy of the landowning Thakurs, whose feudal domination requires the outlaws not only to submit to their authority but also to do their dirty work. These are nested dispensations: the outlaws find themselves complicit with the Thakurs; the Thakurs are complicit with the state police. With police collusion, the big-man Thakur Sri Ram emerges from a spell in jail determined to bend the increasingly autonomous Vikram Mallah to his will, to "make that monkey dance to my tune."

With finely honed patron/police instincts, Sri Ram knows that the most effective way to tame Vikram Mallah is to assert sovereignty over Phoolan Devi, to domesticate this dangerous woman. Having arrived back in the ravines, Sri Ram allows Vikram Mallah, in a formal gesture of tribute, to present him with a rifle and smear a *tikka* (clay or paste mark) on his forehead. When Sri Ram sniggers that Vikram Mallah seems to have made quite a name for himself in Sri Ram's absence, Vikram Mallah responds with dutiful submissiveness: "*sahib*, it is by your grace." But he is boiling inside at Sri Ram's oily attempts to lay claim to Phoolan Devi, to put her back in a woman's proper place.

Sri Ram recognizes that Vikram Mallah poses a real threat and has him killed. Vikram Mallah's death means that Phoolan Devi, for all her independence, is once again exposed to the limitless brutality of the upper-caste landlords. After being gang raped, Phoolan Devi is subjected to the infamous humiliation of being stripped naked at the village well (see chapter 2). Grabbing her roughly by the hair, Sri Ram publicly reasserts his authority by parading her in front of the villagers, reversing her own defiant assertion of autonomous subjectivity (the very first words we see her utter are: *Main hoon Phoolan Devi, behenchod, main hoon!* [I am Phoolan Devi, sisterfucker, I am!]) by contemptuously reinscribing her as an object subordinated to caste hierarchy (*Yeh hai Phoolan Devi! Chambal ki rani!* [This is Phoolan Devi! Queen of the Chambal!]). In so doing, Sri

Ram is also forcing the wild energy of this "low-caste goddess," this rustic Durga, to flow through his performative dispensation.

But Vikram Mallah has trained her well. Avenging both his murder and her own degradation, Phoolan Devi eventually revisits the site of her humiliation and slaughters her Thakur tormentors, although Sri Ram manages to escape. Even then, however, Phoolan is not acting on her own. By appealing to the grace of another outlaw boss, Baba Mustakim, she is able to mobilize a gang—some of them erstwhile associates of Vikram Mallah's. The gang hails Phoolan Devi's power; Phoolan Devi passes on the tribute to Baba Mustakim, although the Baba will soon be cursing her as a *saali-devi* (bitch goddess) as her exploits bring the heat of police attention onto his men.

Thus far, the story of Phoolan Devi could well be interpreted as an account of the out/law that emerges at the edges of the state law in the zones that resist full incorporation into the state. Outside the formal law, these gangs may be manipulated or eliminated by the police according to the needs of the moment. But now something happens: because of Phoolan Devi's renown among the rural lower castes, the authority that she enjoys within her own performative dispensation is no longer, from the standpoint of the state, dispensable. Knowing that this Chambal-ki-rani has won the hearts of large chunks of the electorate, the central government in Delhi cannot afford simply to dispose of her in a so-called encounter death. The corpses of her less famous associates can be lined up at the feet of the police, decoratively posed for the press in tableaux of hunting prowess. As police pick off her comrades one by one, Phoolan Devi is, within her own domain, increasingly isolated and anxious. Sri Ram, as ever hand in glove with the state police, combs the ravines for her. And yet on the wider stage of public reputation, her fame has never been greater. For her the government will have to devise a more elaborate ceremony.

Knowing that the game is up, and fearful that the power of the goddess has abandoned her, Phoolan mounts a stage set up as a jerry-rigged approximation of the darbars of old and surrenders the insignia of her rebellion, her rifle and her bullets, to the chief minister in a kneeling gesture of obeisance.[2] But even at this moment, when the forces of law and order seem conclusively to have defeated the outlaws, when the state seems to have reaffirmed its monopoly on legitimate violence, when the theatrical staging of Phoolan's surrender seems to position the government as the only true patron and police, the massed audience—that is to say, the physical embodiment of the public—roars: *Phoolan Devi ki jai!* (Victory to Phoolan Devi!) Phoolan turns to face the crowd, awed and moved by their unexpected tribute. Kapur's final edit cuts from this adult Phoolan, humbled by the adulation of her newfound public, back to the child Phoolan, once and once again defiant: *Main hoon Phoolan Devi, behenchod, main hoon!*

■ ■ ■

Shekhar Kapur's film version of the Phoolan Devi story ends ambiguously. Legality triumphs over illegality. The state wins. But the state only wins by collaborating with the feudal-cum-criminal authority of the Thakur Sri Ram and his henchmen. Even within its own sovereign domain, apparently, it still needs to blur the line between legality and illegality simply in order to get by. So does this mean that the Indian state is not fully modern? That it languishes in a liminal zone of arrested development, stuck between a corrupted form of feudal tradition that refuses to die and a modern legal-bureaucratic order that is just out of reach? Once again, an indefinite in-between time that justifies exceptional measures?

Something like this seemed to be the underlying assumption of many commentators as *Bandit Queen*'s tortuous journey to Indian screens (chapter 2) was followed, during the late 1990s and early 2000s, by a spate of news reports about the shocking deterioration of Indian democracy. State assemblies were full of legislators with long criminal records. No wonder they found it hard to sustain rational debates for any length of time and seemed constantly, in the most unseemly way, to be scuffling and breaking chairs over each others' heads. And why were such goons being elected? Because, the argument went, in the absence of successfully functioning impersonal institutions, personalized power was going to win every time. The relation was imagined in strictly zero-sum terms: "Personalized power bears an inverse relationship with institutional law. If there is more of one there will be less of the other. It is, therefore, important to know why institutional law, which is impersonal and impartial, can be so easily bypassed in favour of personalized power in our country. In a society which is inefficient and where the normal rights of citizens are far from being realized, it is almost true by definition that personalized power will triumph" (D. Gupta 2002). If the polity was stuck in an in-between state, then its citizens were bound to develop inconsistent symptoms. Ordinary Indians, commentators complained, would typically disapprove of crime and yet "develop [a] deep and sub-rational appreciation for successful criminals, especially those who create the impression of 'taking on the unjust system'" (Agnivesh 2001).

Bandit Queen could easily be read as a salvo in this critique, as an indictment of the shocking persistence of feudalism in an ostensibly modern polity. But the film also points in a different direction. As I hope to have suggested by my selection of scenes, Phoolan Devi's movements in and out of a series of performative dispensations within the film are not to be reduced to a simple zero-sum opposition between feudal and modern structures of authority.

For starters, there is the exceedingly theatrical manner in which the apparently modern state authorities receive Phoolan Devi at the end of the film. Phoolan Devi's surrender of her rifle at the feet of the chief minister in his high-backed chair in front of a crowd of thousands is a direct quotation of the film's earlier moments of tribute, obeisance, and incorporation exacted by outlaws and feudal lords. The gestures are the same, the performative idiom only marginally adjusted in the direction of "modern" authority. But if we are not going to read this performative continuity as a symptom of an incomplete transition to modernity, then what are we to make of it?

The element that is most crucial to the efficacy of the closing ritual is the spectators' effervescent affirmation/recognition of Phoolan Devi at the moment of her surrender: *Phoolan Devi ki jai!* The cry is ambiguous. On one level it expresses resistance: victory to Phoolan Devi, insofar as she embodies something that remains defiant vis-à-vis any state that would claim her, even as she is laying down her arms. On another level, it expresses sublation in the orthodox Hegelian sense: a synthesis that at once transcends and preserves a preexisting opposition. In other words: victory to Phoolan Devi, whose power has, through this ritual, now been both superseded and revitalized—in the mode of a truly "public" figure. What kind of political collective is expressing itself here? A feudal-devotional crowd? Or a modern-rational public? Does putting the question in those terms—the terms that the zero-sum feudal/modern analytic would require —even make sense?

NOTHING OFFICIAL ABOUT IT

Bandit Queen was a fiction that purported to present something like a factual account of outlaw life in the Chambal ravines. But I started this chapter with an analysis of the film because its staging of the intimate yet fraught relation between state law and the outlaw also operates as a handy allegory of the crisis that, by the time of its release in the mid-1990s, had beset the CBFC's claims to exclusive censorial authority.

Until the rise of Indian television as a vibrant commercial medium in the 1980s, the CBFC had enjoyed a real sense of sovereignty over the exhibition of mass-mediated moving image-objects in India. During the 1990s, satellite television and, in a preliminary way, the Internet joined the Indian media mix. Not only was cinema no longer the only game in town, but the CBFC's centralized, national mode of regulation seemed increasingly obsolete in an age of distributed, transnational media networks. As Vijay Anand noted: "We have opened the skies to the whole world. Even a child can switch on any channel out of the one hundred available. There are blue films coming, gay films coming, films about lesbians coming. The films that we censor, for example, we might give an Adult certificate: children not allowed. In a few months they appear on television without a single cut. Then what happens to censorship?"[3] The performative potentials of this new mediascape had, in other words, begun to elude the CBFC's banner staff.

The cultural emergency was not just a "culture war" between irreconcilable worldviews. More fundamentally, it threw open the question of the legitimate location of public cultural regulatory authority (Hansen and Stepputat, eds., 2001). Rough and ready activist associations, many of them with more or less formal links to established political parties, brought media censorship out of the domain of preview theaters and examining committees and into the streets. At times it looked like a struggle between the agencies of the state, such as the CBFC, and "extraconstitutional" claimants to the censor's job. At other times, the line between legal and illegal action grew altogether murky. Especially between 1995 and 1999, when Bal Thackeray's violently nativist Shiv Sena and the Hindu nationalist Bharatiya Janata Party (BJP) jointly ruled the state government of Maharashtra, the line between the gravitas of the state and the often-violent performativity of street politics grew blurry (T. B. Hansen 2001; Kaur 2003).

The chilling effect of the Shiv Sena's "informal" or "extraconstitutional" censorship—its capacity to issue plausible threats of harm to those who would resist—should not be underestimated. Producers and actors shied away from screenplays that were even mildly critical of the Sena. Printers would only run protest posters anonymously (and thus illegally). And while many of my informants were quite happy to discuss the Sena's cultural politics, several concluded our interviews with a quiet request that I not get them into trouble by publishing their remarks.

Of course, there were longtime veterans of Maharashtrian cultural politics like playwright Vijay Tendulkar and filmmaker Anand Patwardhan who had grown up alongside the Shiv Sena and understood it as a kind of culturally intimate enemy.[4] Such prominent cultural figures enjoyed just the right blend of local credentials and international profile to stand up to Thackeray and his henchmen. But they were the privileged few. The reflection of one executive was more typical: "It's one thing to have an intellectual conversation, quite another to have your house burned down or having the people you care about hurt."

The BJP was not able to form a national government until the spring of 1998, by which time their alliance with the Shiv Sena was growing strained. But although the Shiv Sena itself lost control of the Maharashtra state legislature in 1999, its informal regulatory authority remained strong. This put the CFCB in an ambiguous position. On the one hand, even former CFCB chair Vijay Anand acknowledged, quite pragmatically, that it made sense for a film producer to seek Bal Thackeray's blessing for a major release, simply to avoid trouble. ("His phone call will do the trick. Going through the court may delay the matter for ten years.") On the other hand, there was the somewhat curious phenomenon of activists and filmmakers who in principle were opposed to state censorship strategically insisting on the formal authority of the CBFC's certificates as legal bulwarks against the "lawlessness" of big-man politicians and their ruffian bands.[5] So, for example, the Aanchal Trust, a support group for women's sexuality, organized a protest in June 2004 against attacks by the Shiv Sena's student wing on theaters screening the putatively "lesbian" action drama *Girlfriend* (2004), directed by Karan Razdan. Its press release made it clear that legality rather than content was the primary issue: "Even though we have serious criticisms around the way the film portrays lesbians and gays, we still do not believe that the Shiv Sena can be cultural police and decide what the general public should see and shouldn't, especially since the film has got the certificate of the Censor Board."[6]

Despite all principled claims to the contrary, then, during the second half of the 1990s, the actual locus of regulatory authority vis-à-vis the cinema and other mass media had become uncertain. Mani Ratnam's *Bombay* (1995) and Deepa Mehta's *Fire* (1998) both ran regulatory gauntlets of unprecedented complexity. I will have more to say about the politics of spectator-citizenship evoked by the struggle over *Bombay* below; for now I simply want to give a sense of how contested the *location* of regulatory authority was becoming during these years.

VOLATILE LOCATIONS

Bombay

Bombay is a Hindu–Muslim love story set against the backdrop of historical events that were still very recent at the time the film was made: the Hindu nationalist campaign to storm and destroy the Babri mosque in Ayodhya in December 1992 and the violence that followed in Bombay in 1992–93. For a whole host of reasons, the film was ripe for controversy: its sensitive subject matter, the recency of the events that served as a historical backdrop for its fiction, and its ambiguous realism. Since director Mani Ratnam was based in Chennai, *Bombay* was originally submitted to the CBFC's regional branch office there in late 1994. Reports of what happened next differ. Either Ratnam objected to the Chennai Examining Committee's cuts and asked for a revising committee. Or he agreed to the cuts, but the Chennai office smelled trouble and passed the film on to CBFC headquarters in Mumbai.

In any case, the Mumbai CBFC, having received the film, decided to bring in police officers as expert consultants. Whether this was done before or after its revising committee saw the film is, again, unclear. Either way, the legal standing of this consultation was ambiguous. In one version of the story, the censors brought in Police Commissioner Satish Sawhney because he "must be deemed to be an expert on questions of public order" (Padmanabhan 1995). In another, the Mumbai police, clearly aware that any meddling by the executive branch would look fishy, took pains to affirm the CBFC's sovereignty in the certification of films and emphasized that the police had done nothing more than offer "informal suggestions" (Vijapurkar 1995). According to yet another version, the state government of Maharashtra issued a "no objection certificate" to the CBFC in February 1995 (S. Sinha 1995).

The inevitable impression was that the CBFC was no longer able to act on its own. As the range of bodies involved in approving and modifying *Bombay* multiplied, the Mumbai release date—initially set for January 14, 1995—kept being pushed back, first to March 31, then to April 7. (The film opened in Chennai and Hyderabad-Secunderabad on March 10, although in some districts it was subsequently closed down by local authorities; in London the premiere was held on April 8.) During this time, private screenings were held to secure the approval of all manner of players: not only police officers but also, according to some reports, Home Ministry officials: the then state chief minister, Sharad Pawar; and, most controversially of all, Bal Thackeray.[7]

Despite his undisputed charismatic leadership of the Shiv Sena, Thackeray had himself never been elected to public office and thus had no official standing. This, peculiarly but effectively, remained the case during the Shiv Sena's tenure at the helm of the Maharashtra state government in 1995–99. Back in the 1930s and 1940s, when all kinds of interest groups and self-styled industry organizations inundated the censor boards with demands to be included, the problem for the local authorities had been what kind of voices could reasonably be admitted into the circle of formally constituted authority. By the mid-1990s, the formally constituted authority of the state as arbiter of public communication was itself being called into question.

Once word got out that Thackeray had been consulted, Muslim groups also demanded a say (Prabhu 1995). Muslim leaders were particularly incensed that Thackeray had apparently been allowed to demand his own cuts to *Bombay* after the CBFC had cleared it. The authorities' willingness to comply with Thackeray's demands was an affront on both "communal" and "secular" grounds; it meant that the state was capitulating to Hindu extremist opinion, and it represented a violation of the CBFC's legal sovereignty (Ramanan 1995).[8] By this time the Shiv Sena had formed a state government with the BJP and appointed Manohar Joshi as chief minister. Joshi's response to the outrage was telling: he advised Muslim groups to pursue their grievances through official legal channels. The message could not have been clearer. Thackeray and the Shiv Sena were the new sovereign patron/police power that got to decide on the exception; everyone else had better follow the letter of the law. A special screening was eventually arranged for Muslim leaders on April 6, after which the release date was once again pushed back.[9] Their demand for a total ban gained little public traction and was withdrawn on April 11.[10]

Amid bomb scares and death threats, vitriolic communal discourse, and exceptionally heavy security, *Bombay* finally opened in central Mumbai on April 15, 1995.[11] Ahead of its Mumbai release, director Mani Ratnam brushed off charges that he had given in to goons by saying that the cuts amounted to no more than about two minutes of screen time and that "instead of wasting time and energy on arguing, I'd rather ensure that my film reaches the people" ("Truth or Dare" 1995). A couple of months later, once the furor had died down and the film turned out to be a hit, Ratnam was keen to reassert his artistic integrity as an auteur by insisting that he had in fact refused several of Thackeray's demands for cuts.[12] Even so, in July 1995 Ratnam narrowly escaped being killed when two men—allegedly Muslims—threw a pipe bomb at his house.

Fire

Deepa Mehta's *Fire* depicts the intimacy that emerges between two sisters-in-law in a middle-class Delhi household, an intimacy that some among the film's supporters as well as among its critics interpreted as "lesbian" (Ghosh 2010). The supposed foreignness of lesbianism was a central plank in the Hindu right's attack on the film, with the Shiv Sena again taking the lead. Unlike *Bombay*, *Fire* does not overtly thematize Hindu–Muslim relations. Still, the fact that Shabana Azmi, one of its lead actors, was both a Muslim and a prominent spokesperson for progressive social causes allowed right-wing activists to position woman-to-woman sex as a foreign perversion. The names of *Fire*'s two main characters, Radha and Sita, are within Hindu mythology overdetermined signifiers of wifely devotion, whether the (sometimes sublimated) eroticism of the milkmaid Radha's devotion to the playful Krishna or the more solemn and self-sacrificing devotion of Sita to the god-king Ram. Thackeray seized on this apparently shameless affront to Hindu dignity by demanding that the protagonists be given new, markedly Muslim, names: Shabana and Saira.[13]

Whereas *Bombay*'s engagement with the CBFC was, from the beginning, a rather murky business. *Fire* got an A certificate with a minimum of fuss. The only change required by the censors was that the character Sita be renamed Nita for the Hindi version.[14] Originally passed in May 1998, the film, having already been widely screened abroad, opened in India on November 13.[15] On December 2, the Mahila Aghadi, the Shiv Sena's women's wing, having consulted with the Sena's Minister of Cultural Affairs Pramod Navalkar, initiated a series of violent attacks on theaters exhibiting *Fire*. Since *Fire* had already been passed by the CBFC and released, liberal criticism of the attacks did not in the first instance focus on the state's capitulation to illegitimate pressure but rather on the right-wing activists' refusal to respect the law of the land (which, in the case of *Fire*, conveniently coincided with the enthusiasm of international festival audiences).[16] On this occasion BJP politician Sushma Swaraj, whose conservative moralism earned her the epithet Sushma Scissorhands during her stints as information and broadcasting minister in 1996, 1998, and 2000–2003, also stood firm against the Shiv Sena's rough and ready cultural justice: "I do not agree with the Shiv Sena's way of protesting. If you are not happy with the censor's approval of a film you can go to the Appellate Tribunal" (Jain and Raval 1998).[17]

But this staunch defense of the rule of law did not last. It was perhaps not altogether surprising that Maharashtra chief minister, Manohar Joshi, being a Shiv Sena man, should have publicly congratulated the Mahila Aghadi for its actions. But soon even the central government caved in. Two successive ministers of information and broadcasting—Mukhtar Abbas Naqvi and Pramod Mahajan, both leading lights of the BJP—suspended the screening of *Fire* and sent it back to the CBFC for reexamination. (*Fire* was cleared for a second time on February 12, 1999, without cuts, although in Mumbai the names of the two female protagonists were dropped altogether.[18]) The Shiv Sena's culture supremo, Pramod Navalkar, having originally passed on the Mahila Aghadi's petition against the film to the CBFC, proudly gave public voice to this legally ambiguous state of affairs: "The film has been banned, if not formally then informally" (Jain and Raval 1998).

The reception room at Matoshree, Bal Thackeray's residence in Bandra East, rather than the CBFC's office in Walkeshwar, was now the darbar at which directors and producers had to pay tribute. Faced with such an apparent usurpation of due process—complete with Mahila Aghadi activists proclaiming "We are the law!"—the secular-liberal intelligentsia could only bemoan the "ferociously medieval . . . mindset" that seemed to have undermined all distinctions between government and goons, producing "a hooliganism that had state protection" ("Fire, Burn" 1998; Jain and Raval 1998). On one infamous occasion, a group of Shiv Sainiks turned up outside veteran (Muslim) actor Dilip Kumar's house to taunt him in their underwear. In response to the cinema trashings and harassments, a group of notables including Kumar, scriptwriter-lyricist Javed Akhtar, filmmakers Mahesh Bhatt and Yash Chopra, activists Atul and Teesta Setalvad, and playwright Vijay Tendulkar filed a petition in the Supreme Court demanding a restoration of "the rule of law and the Constitution before the situation slips into complete anarchy" (Jain and Raval 1998).

Azmi observed at the time "it is strange that the government which is providing me security is the same under whose governance *Fire* is being vandalized" ("Shabana Surprised . . ." 1998). To be sure, it was indeed strange from the standpoint of a polity where the legislature and the executive were expected to be separate. But from the standpoint of an organization like the Shiv Sena, whose "cultural inquisition" (Swami 1998) was driven by the dream that the patron and police powers of Indra's banner staff could be reunified in the age of mass publicity, there was nothing strange about it at all.

JUST POLITICS

The mob's never a progressive force in India.
Both defenders and opponents of censorship tried to explain the performative success of Shiv Sena–style cultural activism as a symptom of political immaturity. Vijay Anand told me, quite baldly, "I don't think we are ready for a democratic country. I don't think the voter is intelligent enough to vote. He's being compelled to vote, he's being bribed to vote. The considerations for voting are not political judgment, but some other: he belongs to my caste, he belongs to my religion."

For some of my interlocutors, the apparent immaturity of Indian voters constituted an argument for "benign dictatorship." For others, it pointed to the desperate need for more effective political education in a country that had achieved its political revolution (independence) without completing its social revolution (the transition from feudalism to modern democracy). But the underlying diagnosis stayed the same across the political spectrum.[19] Playwright and actor Girish Karnad lamented the repeated failure of Indians, in times of stress, to rise above the crowd pull of communal loyalties and work toward the kind of generalized public interest worthy of a nation of citizens: "it happens in India very often, as in fact in Gujarat [in 2002], that when there is a major uprising or communal conflict or so on, people just forget about law and order and justice and so on, and you just side with your own group."[20]

Whereas *publics* might be expected to engage in the kind of coolly critical deliberation that would support a principled rule of law, *crowds* were hotheaded and mired in the moment (Mazzarella 2010c). In this figure of the Indian crowd, we encounter the aggregate, collective form of the pissing man. Endlessly porous, helplessly mimetic, the defining characteristic of the crowds that responded to charismatic demagogues like Bal

Thackeray was that they were crying out to be led. As the lawyer P. Sebastian, who during a distinguished career pursuing social justice in the courts has on several occasions defended Anand Patwardhan against censorship, told me: "This is very unfortunate but it is true. People are at a stage where they can be confused and they can be misled by clever manipulators."[21] Vijay Tendulkar, whose plays had routinely been attacked by the Shiv Sena, dismissed such agitations as essentially lacking in proper political content:

> The reasons are psychological mostly. Mostly. Mostly. I'm not saying every time. Yes, because culturally we have been wrongly groomed. We are confused about lots of things. Very erratic about our reactions. Lack consistency, lack thinking. So all controversies in this country, more or less, are childish in a way. They do a lot of damage, but if you look at it the other way, if you put aside the damage, then they are the work of a few children. They neither understand anything, nor *want* to understand anything. But they want to do something. "I'll break something, I'll throw something. That's all—I'm happy." I can understand a controversy which is provoked by some thinking. Maybe I won't agree with the thinking at all. But it makes some sense to me; at least they are serious about it. That hardly ever happens in my country. Destruction for destruction's sake—there is a certain joy in it. And in this country people like to have their joy once in a while. To destroy.[22]

Many of my informants suggested that, for whatever reason (not fully overcoming colonization/not fully overcoming feudalism/the venality of Indian politicians, and so on), India had failed, on a mass level, to nurture citizens who were able to think clearly and critically when it came to public life. Consequently, Indian crowds were constantly failing to manifest a genuine political will. As Karnad put it, "the mob's never a progressive force in India. It's very difficult to project it at any point to the kind that brought the French Revolution along with it." The crowds who stormed stages and cinema lobbies fell short of a genuine politics, then, because they were *too* spontaneous; they were not interested in thinking through their actions, only in the pleasure of action for its own sake. And yet at the same time these demonstrations were also dismissed for not being spontaneous *enough*, for not expressing the authentic will of the people but rather the cynical and manipulative designs of political opportunists.[23]

So, for example, when Shiv Sainiks smashed Mumbai cinemas screening *Fire*, the fact that they waited for the news media to be present before they started rampaging was taken as a sign of the cynical artificiality of the outrage being enacted, as if only a spontaneous and unplanned eruption of indignation could count as politically genuine. Pritish Nandy, himself a Shiv Sena representative in the Rajya Sabha (upper house of the Indian parliament) at the time of the *Fire* fracas, concluded, "It's all about the media ultimately. Your ability to catch the headline, whichever way you can."[24] That these protests seemed to have been carefully orchestrated seemed to signal that they were not authentic expressions of public opinion. As *Fire* director Deepa Mehta demanded, "Does the Shiv Sena constitute public outrage? If a handful of people indulge in lawless behaviour, they don't constitute the public" (Jain and Raval 1998).

During one conversation about the density of protests during the cultural emergency, an advertising executive interrupted me quite emphatically: "I really want to say one thing: I don't know if all these protests are *actual*, genuine guys-off-the-street protests. Or politically motivated protests. And there's a difference. Obviously. A real public uprising? I don't think so." This sense of skepticism about the authenticity of protests against films, plays, and books was pervasive. The actor Saurabh Shukla, who played Phoolan Devi's roly-poly cousin in *Bandit Queen* at an early stage of his film career, suggested that the troublemakers' desire to gain publicity for themselves (on the backs of credulous crowds ready to follow) rendered most of these protests suspect: "There is a tendency that everybody has to pick up an issue, to make their place. It's a human tendency. So suddenly people find an issue and then there are fifty thousand people who get up. There are fifty thousand cases—they can be baseless. You don't know whether they are concerned about that problem or not. Do they genuinely feel? There must be people who are genuinely feeling. But most of them are picking up issues to make their own place."[25] On one level, then, the question was one of political-emotional sincerity. On another, many commentators accused political leaders of whipping up storms over trivial things like films as a way of diverting their constituents' attention away from their inability to solve "real" political issues like poverty, education, and so on (Sanghvi 1995; T. Singh 1995).

A case in point was Shiv Sena cultural affairs minister Pramod Navalkar's obscenity case against the advertising agency Ambiance's 1995 campaign for Tuff Shoes. In these press ads two models, the briefly affianced Madhu Sapre and Milind Soman, appeared naked but for an artfully coiled snake and the titular shoes. An important part of the public affective potency of the situation was that Sapre and Soman belonged to the decadent, sexy world of fashion while also being characterizable as nice middle-class Maharashtrian Brahmin youngsters. The Shiv Sena women's wing massed outside Madhu Sapre's home, burning copies of *Cine Blitz*, one of the publications in which the ads had appeared.[26] By September the state government was threatening Bollywood filmmakers with legal action if they worked with Soman or Sapre. Meanwhile, Navalkar launched a case against as many of the participants as he could, including the agency, the models, and the photographer (Prabuddha Das Gupta, who had photographed the famous KamaSutra campaign in 1991 [Mazzarella 2003]).[27]

In November 2003, Pramod Navalkar remembered the episode, chuckling, "Completely nude! For advertising a shoe?! Immediately I got them arrested. The case is still going on. How can we tolerate such nonsense? We *cannot*. Nudity is not allowed in our culture."[28] At the time of the campaign he told the press, "I was particularly upset about the Madhu-Milind ad because they are going to get married to each other. How can we allow anyone to pose in the nude with his wife? . . . Freedom does not mean the demeaning of one's wife" (Rajadhyaksha et al. 1995). Ashok Kurien, then head of Ambiance, remembered being called to a meeting where Navalkar demanded cash in return for calling off his troops and openly admitted, "'look, I need to do this because I need it for me. For my political stand. But don't worry, I can make sure nothing happens to you. We might have to arrest you, but don't worry, *beta* [son], I'll take care of you.' We spoke to each other in Marathi, because I speak Marathi and grew up on the streets of this city. My name didn't get too much in there, just Madhu and Milind."[29] Not at that moment carrying cash, and certainly not wanting to risk physical harm, Kurien wrote a check to a charitable trust registered in the name of Navalkar's wife.

A carefully staged simulation of legal process followed: "We had a pretend arrest where we went in [to the police station] and had a cup of tea with the cops and they took us out the back and put us in a cop van and took us home. But that was enough for the headlines to say, 'Arrested— Photographs of the guys being taken to jail' and so on and so forth." And yet at the same time, the court case was procedurally real. It dragged on for fourteen years partly because Navalkar had filed it as a public interest litigation. Cases on behalf of the public cannot be settled out of court and yet the prosecutors remained consistently unable to find credible individuals who were prepared to appear as suitably offended representatives of that public. The case bounced inconclusively back and forth between lower and higher courts as a series of starstruck judges kept summoning the defendants while constantly deferring the responsibility of ruling on the notoriously slippery obscenity charge. Pramod Navalkar himself passed away in 2007, before the suit he had launched was finally dismissed. But the case of Tuff Shoes still stands as a paradigmatic example of "playing politics," cultural emergency style.

Under Suspicion: Water

Rabble-rousing politicians were not the only ones whose motives were under suspicion. The documentarist Anand Patwardhan was routinely accused, as I noted in the introduction, of using his confrontations with the cultural right to boost his own public standing rather than sincerely trying to foreground social issues. Many characterized *Bandit Queen* director Shekhar Kapur as a master publicist. As one director remarked, "You're playing politics and you're playing the media game and you're playing all of that. I mean, sure, it is about the integrity of the film, but you also know that if you have a nude woman walking through the thing, the whole country's going to come and see it. And it's going to make your numbers, right?"

When shooting for Deepa Mehta's *Water* was closed down by Hindu nationalist activists in Banaras in 2000, the incident was interpreted by many sympathizers in the media as yet another symptom of the gathering storm of cultural repression. *Water* portrays the treatment of indigent Hindu widows critically and was, as such, guaranteed to rub the right wing the wrong way. Sure enough, trouble descended as soon as Mehta tried to shoot an open-air scene on the Banaras *ghat*s (the steps leading into the Ganges) in which the lead actors—as in *Fire*, Shabana Azmi and Nandita Das[30]—had their heads shaved to signify widowhood. In retrospect, however, several of my informants expressed doubts about the innocence of Mehta's motives. Why did she decide to film a scene she must have known would be controversial in such a public way so early in the shooting schedule? Why did she allow, even encourage, television cameras to cover the event?

Anurag Kashyap, who grew up partly in Banaras, was a writer on the project. He remembered the whole incident as a lesson in political realism. Being young and idealistic, he launched himself wholeheartedly into a defense of the production, only to come to the conclusion that both Mehta and her attackers were engaged in a tactical game:

I was passionately involved. I am from Banaras. I took the forefront. I fought all the battles for Deepa Mehta. Really going out and fighting with the Police Commissioner. I've lived in the city. I know in the city which theatre shows porn movies, which theatre shows what. Because I was an insider I *knew* it, and I wrote pamphlets about it against those people who were protesting against *Water*. I was distributing them on the streets. To get the support. Because I knew there was hardly a bunch of people who were trying to protest and the situation was getting political.[31]

Kashyap felt from the beginning that the protests were entirely cynical:

It was just a platform that they used to form a political party. It was an opportunity. Cinema is the big opportunity in India to get noticed. Because most of the newspapers in the country are fifty percent about cinema. Which is why it becomes an easy platform for anyone to gain any kind of mileage. That Kashi Sanskriti Raksha Sangharsh Samiti [roughly, the Association for the Struggle to Protect Cultural Integrity], that party was formed overnight. That party did not exist before the first day of protest against *Water*. Next day it had a name.

National-level Sangh Parivar organizations like the RSS and the VHP sensed an opportunity and affiliated themselves with the newly created KSRSS, whose leader was in turn able to launch a political career on the back of his newfound visibility. But what really disillusioned Kashyap was his discovery that Mehta herself was apparently being no less calculating— if somewhat less skilled—in her desire for publicity: "I was the one who was fighting and taking it seriously. Until I sat down with an actor and they told me how they wanted some publicity, and they told me things. . . . I was *shocked*. My thing was, I *believed* it. Everybody was playing it but I *believed* it. You feel like your passion and idealism are being used."

It's not even about the film itself.

Anurag Kashyap's experience was particularly acute. But he was expressing a widespread opinion: that controversies which appeared to be about whether or not the content of a particular film was acceptable to Indian audiences were actually driven by political interests and motivations that were entirely external to the film. So, for example, the fuss over *Bandit Queen*, when it was not simply dismissed as the competitive posturing of public intellectuals,[32] was read as a response to the consolidation of Dalit political power vis-à-vis the formerly powerful Thakurs in Uttar Pradesh and, in that connection, to the public reemergence of the real-life Phoolan Devi, this time as a member of Parliament (Raman 1995).[33] The wrangling over *Bombay* in Mumbai was read as inextricable from the Maharashtra State Assembly elections that concluded in March 1995, in which the Shiv Sena–BJP alliance brought a temporary halt to the Congress Party's long-standing dominance. And the release of *Fire* in late 1998 coincided with the Shiv Sena's attempts to hold the BJP to a more hard-line Hindutva politics just as the BJP was tending its national political ambitions by trying to look moderate on communal (that is, religious-identitarian) issues.[34] The pattern was well established. Vijay Tendulkar remembered the Shiv Sena activists who held up his play *Ghashiram Kotwal* in 1972, assuring the actors that the harassment would stop as soon as soon as the long-delayed municipal elections in Pune were over.

Of course, the fact that many of the people who seemed most indignant about these films had not actually seen them only added to the sense that the upset was not really about the film in question. Tendulkar explained, "One has to understand that the creative work ultimately becomes—what shall I say?—the scapegoat in the whole exercise. Or the writer sometimes. Or the artist. So actually that creative work only remains as a pretext to achieve something through a controversy." Commentators loved to wax sardonic over the upstart activists who had not bothered to watch the films they were protesting against: "A gaggle of Muslim leaders who few people had heard of . . . made a Shahabuddin-style objection.[35] They hadn't seen *Bombay*, they said, but they thought that they might be offended if they did" (Sanghvi 1995). A spokesman for a group calling itself the Ulemah Muslim Council, one Maulana Abdul Q. Kashmiri, even went so far as to make it a matter of principle: "I have not seen the film myself. Maulanas do not see films" (Prabhu 1995).

But in fact, this stance of objecting on principle, whether one had seen a film or not, was not confined to the conservative right; indeed, it was just as likely to be found on the liberal-secular side. As director Mahesh Bhatt put it around the time that he was putting his name to the Supreme Court petition calling for the restoration of law and order in the wake of the attacks on *Fire*, "I have not seen the film. But I have an animal sense of repression telling me that this is the sign of an impending cultural emergency" (Nambiar 1998). For his co-petitioner Dilip Kumar, it was in a similar way a matter of defending a principle much larger than any one film: "I haven't seen it. [But] I know the cause. We have to stop this kind of vandalism on our cultural life" (Jain and Raval 1998).[36]

To be sure, for writers, artists, and directors this sense of being strung up as sacrificial victims by people who could not be bothered to pay any attention to the work itself was often infuriating and exhausting. Tendulkar remarked, "It's very . . . disgusting that ultimately what someone has written or what someone is doing rather seriously makes no difference." And in a certain way, one might even argue that this kind of informal censorship was all the more effective precisely because it refused cultural producers the moral dignity of taking a stand on the actual substance of what they had created. What was the point of risking violence and harassment for some principle that was entirely external to the work? Novelist and playwright Kiran Nagarkar, who faced harassment from both official and unofficial censors in the 1970s over his play *Bedtime Story*, observed that "every actor and actress who went in for rehearsals, by the second or third rehearsal they were threatened. Their lives were threatened. The directors were threatened. I was threatened. And you know, ultimately I began to wonder: 'Do I want to write stuff for these guys, who have not read the thing, and are merely utilizing it to get some political mileage out of it? And for *what*? They are not interested.'"[37]

Incite-ful Speech?

The filmmaker's (or writer's, or playwright's) frustration at being attacked by people who are largely ignorant of their work is eminently understandable. And yet at the same time, I think it would be a mistake simply to dismiss these kinds of protest actions as politically empty.

For one thing, the complaint that the protests are not really "about the work itself" implies that we can draw a clear line between what is "in" the work and what is external to it. But from a social standpoint, the "content" of the film includes not only the layers of interpretation and reaction that it generates over time—its interpretive patina, sometimes even its canonicity —but also its continued potency, its ability to potentiate its contexts in unpredictable ways. Of course, authors or directors cannot be held personally responsible for everything that their work may yield. But as Ashish Rajadhyaksha points out, drawing on Lawrence Liang's legal scholarship, both attempts to censor films *and* moves to defend their makers' freedom of expression tend to reinstall the writer-director as responsible author.

Public action against and in support of a movie "cannot . . . easily account for forms of representation that do not yield an ideologically coherent source of speech. . . . The author, then, is the most convenient incarnation of the speaking subject of the cinema, so much so that legal practice has found it difficult to introduce any category of the subject that might reside elsewhere than in an authorial *persona*" (Rajadhyaksha 2009:175, 176). By the same token, the audience-public is imagined as only receiving a message whose meaning has already been established by the author: "the recipient of the speech can and should demonstrate no transgressive capacity to share authorial responsibility with the speaker" (Rajadhyaksha 2009:175).

Second, if the grievance is that the work is not being properly engaged, then what kind of engagement would be adequate? As soon as the question is put this way, a certain implicit ideal begins to emerge: a well-tuned continent spectator who sits through the film from beginning to end with rigorously focused attention, who carries out the properly patient work of aesthetic judgment, that is to say, who responsibly evaluates every element of the film vis-à-vis the formal structure of the work as a whole. In other words, pretty much the model censor according to the Khosla Report (see chapter 2). But then, is that kind of censor not supposedly necessary precisely because most people do not watch films that way?

The possibility of other kinds of less well-tuned viewing opens up here. What, for example, of distracted viewers, whether in the cinema or at home in front of the television? What of those who only see the trailer? What of those who see nothing more than a still reproduced in a newspaper? Filmic elements proliferate beyond the cinema hall into "an array of mediatized effects all around us, from low-end streaming video to high-definition screens in homes and public places . . . [conditioning our] experience of going into workplaces, . . . of waiting at a railway platform, traveling in a bus, entering a restaurant or *dhaba* [roadside food stall], or simply standing on the crowded pavement of a city" (Rajadhyaksha 2009: 103; see A. Rai 2009). As a result, the conditions of spectatorship become more dispersed: "The public congregational dimensions of the cinema have been displaced in this enactment, as have viewing circumstances that invite immersion in the screen. This circuit of film viewing takes place at home or in the slum settlement, is subject to the distractions of domestic circumstances and ambient noise and the interruptions of advertising that are more generally the condition of the domestic apparatus of television" (Vasudevan 2010:407). If such distracted spectators decide to join a protest against a certain film that they may have encountered in one of these ways, then it is perhaps fair to say that their protest is not "about the film" in a sense that would satisfy any formal hermeneutic standard. But one might also say that the protest could not have opened up the political resonances it did without the specific ways in which elements of the film potentiated its social context (see Asad 1993).

I raise these questions here because I want to resist the too-quick dismissal of these protests as "entirely dictated by politics" (K. Sharma 1999)—which is to say not "properly" political. Can we glean something other than a diagnosis of political failure from these contestations? On the one hand, there is the figure of the incontinent crowd—the Indian mob that always fails to bring about the French Revolution. This represents one side of a nonfunctional performative dispensation: effervescence unmediated by symbolic order. On the other hand, there is the figure of the cynical demagogue—the Bal Thackerays of the world—who claim, in a mode of thinly disguised and manipulative self-interest, to be standing up for the silent majority. This represents the other side of the broken dispensation: a discourse of symbolic order without a genuine grounding in popular effervescence. ("Do they genuinely feel?") Anurag Kashyap's plaintive recollection of the *Water* imbroglio perfectly expresses this disjuncture between wasted commitment and cynical discourse: "Everybody was playing it but I *believed* it."

What would it mean to reconsider these tussles and tangles—as boorish and violent as they often were—neither from the standpoint of being stuck in an in-between time of arrested development nor as more or less manipulative acts of public cultural authorship, but rather as experiments in potentiated reality during a period when the open edge of mass publicity was particularly palpable? The point is not to celebrate or romanticize violent and often ignorant forms of political action, but rather to reconsider them as part of a series of gambles on the potentials that may dwell in public cultural fields. Sometimes the "excitable speech" (Butler 1997) of an influential individual does seem, in a way that looks like (irresponsible) authorship, to enable a public ruction, as when the Shiv Sena's Pramod Navalkar incited a rampage against M. F. Husain's paintings in October 1996: "Would the paintings have caused outrage if Navalkar had not presented their 'offensiveness' to the public in the first place? In this case, publicly voicing a protest in the name of the public did not simply register as an act of desecration but actively constructed it and with it the possibility of retaliatory violence" (Jain 2007:296). But, in general, the capacity to *incite* is less based on some perfect *insight* into the ways that public affect will actualize than on experimental attempts at performative potentiation. Kajri Jain notes, mobilizing the familiar metaphors, that "to the extent that [the power of images] unfolds in a trans-subjective arena it is not fully controllable by individual subjects, whether at the point of 'production' or of 'reception': to create images is to play with magic, with fire" (2007:372).

If these protests were not really "about the films" in a limited sense, then nor were they only about their own manifest ideological claims: injured communal sentiments, the decadence of lesbianism, and so on. The analytical challenge, rather, is to think about the relationship between this manifest level of film content and ideological claims on the one hand, and the persistent, more structural question of cinematic spectator-citizenship on the other. It is certainly true that the battles of the cultural emergency were partly triggered by political shifts that had nothing to do with the cinema per se. But it is equally true that these battles were, in a deep sense, contests over the possibility of performative dispensations that would be adequate to the postliberalization moment. And nowhere was the central tension that animated that contest—the tension between crowd effervescence and public morality—more acute than in and around the movies.

Let me try to illustrate these points by means of a return to Mani Ratnam's *Bombay*.

BOMBAY REDUX: THE POLITICS OF REALISM

At one level, the struggle over *Bombay* was a fairly straightforward tug-of-war over content. Every interest group that was permitted to extract its pound of flesh—and, as we have seen, there were quite a few—wanted something taken out. The CBFC asked for any appearance of the words "Pakistan," "Islamic state," and "Afghanistan" to be removed, for a chant urging the destruction of the Babri mosque and the building of a Ram temple on the site to be erased, for documentary footage of the storming and demolition of the mosque to be replaced with still photos and news headlines, and so on. The Mumbai police apparently wanted to eliminate dialogue suggesting that they were prejudiced against Muslims, along with scenes showing policemen being murdered by rioters. Bal Thackeray insisted that Mani Ratnam delete one sequence showing a character obviously modeled on him driving around Mumbai in the wake of the riots wearing a remorseful expression and another in which he hands out bangles to his (male) activists, implying that they had allowed themselves to be emasculated by Muslim violence. Thackeray claimed that he objected to the scenes because they suggested that the Shiv Sena bore responsibility for instigating the carnage; others said he simply did not want to be seen expressing regrets that he did not feel. Muslim leaders asked for several cuts of their own, including a section of Q'uranic verse—"Allah show me the correct path . . ."—that accompanies the Muslim heroine's elopement with the Hindu hero (since it implied religious sanction for their union), a scene in which the heroine's veil catches a branch and gets torn off as she is running after the hero (implying that their interfaith romance liberates her from oppression at the hands of her own community), and a scene in which the heroine, having given birth to twins, declares that the babies have "two gods." At this level of manifest content, the arguments were all about balance and blame. One Muslim leader asked Mani Ratnam to rework the plot so as to accommodate a Muslim man marrying a Hindu woman. Ratnam had himself gone on record saying he wanted *Bombay* to be a balanced depiction of complicity and bravery on both sides. But many commentators felt that the very effort to produce a "balanced view"—whether formally successful or not—amounted, under the circumstances, to a shameful denial of the systematic victimization of a minority.

Communalized complaints about imbalance and misrepresentation at the movies were nothing new. During the 1930s, accusations and counter-accusations flew back and forth between Hindu and Muslim groups. Each side claimed that a cabal intent on defaming the other covertly dominated the Indian film industry, precisely at the time when the industry was trying to articulate a culturally neutral professional discourse of mass spectatorship (see chapter 2).[38] Each side routinely took offense at allegedly injurious representations of themes or personages important to their traditions. Many films of the period, both Indian and Western, angered Muslims by indulging in opulent Orientalist fantasies of Mughal India replete with lustily debauched emperors, dripping with decadence, adultery, and avarice.[39] Hindus, for their part, complained of films that appeared to "mock at idolatry and at the same time to glorify Muslim religion."[40]

What is of course missed as long as the debate stays on this level is that the cinema—like any other mass medium—does not simply *represent* communities; it helps to *make* them. The critical question is therefore not just the accuracy or fairness of images but, more fundamentally, the ways they make community identifications publicly imaginable and communicable in the first place. One of the reasons the debate over Mani Ratnam's *Bombay* was so interesting was because it kept moving back and forth between the question of the cinema as a medium that represents communities and the question of the cinema as a medium that helps to produce public structures of subjectivity.

Perhaps the central knot in the debate was the vexed question of realism. I would like to consider its contours from three angles: (a) *Bombay* as a fiction set amid recent historical events; (b) *Bombay* as a relatively innovative fusion of mainstream melodrama and edgy realism; and (c) *Bombay* as a film that prompted a postliberalization reworking of a discourse that stretches back at least to the 1920s and 1930s, a discourse in which "Islam" operates as the paradigmatic obstacle to achieving continent spectator-citizenship.

Fact and Fiction

Shekhar Kapur was accused of playing fast and loose with the facts of Phoolan Devi's life in *Bandit Queen*. But *Bandit Queen* is unambiguously a biopic; it purports to tell the true story of a real-life individual and was, as such, judged against an empirical yardstick of historical verisimilitude. *Bombay*'s blend of fiction and (recent, raw) fact presented more complex problems.

Despite their many disagreements, censors and liberal critics agreed that Mani Ratnam's decision to dramatize real events meant that his breezy claim that the film was only "a love story against the backdrop of the riots" was just not good enough. A. Ramakrishnan, then Mumbai regional officer of the CBFC, complained that it was unacceptable for *Bombay* to pin blame on particular identifiable individuals and communities—read Bal Thackeray and Hindus—at a time when the commission of inquiry into the post-Babri riots was still under way.[41] Bangalore-based journalist and cultural critic Ammu Joseph reached the opposite conclusion from the same starting point. In an open letter to Ratnam, Joseph argued that the director had abdicated the critical responsibility that inhered in his decision to reference specific historical events: "This is because you deliberately chose to locate your love story about a Hindu-Muslim couple in a particular place at a particular time in recent history which is still fresh in public memory, when you could just as well have opted for a more generic but equally relevant backdrop of communal tension and violence. In addition, you have given your film a documentary touch with the mention of specific events, significant dates, a collage of newspaper clippings, and at least one recognizable character" (Joseph 1995). The reference to actual events did, of course, beg the question of literal verisimilitude. Had Ratnam shown events "as they really happened?" Some believed that he had: "It is fair to say that few films in recent memory can have been as grittily uncompromising with the facts. Everything featured in the backdrop really happened: the murder of Mathadi workers; the burning of a tenement in Jogeshwari; the provocative *maha aartis* [public rituals of Hindu devotion, designed to compete with Muslims' Friday prayer]; the allegations of police indifference; and, of course, those who led the rioters" (Radhakrishna et al. 1995). Others worried that Ratnam had allowed himself too much latitude: "Nobody is quarreling with the director's right to a creative and imaginative portrayal of events, but creativity cannot be an excuse for distortion that does violence to reality" (Athreya 1995). In some cases, inaccuracy was the reason for objecting to a scene; in others, that it seemed too real for comfort. As we shall see, the sheer recency of the riots meant that the question of verisimilitude was never separable from the question of volatile public affect and its possible mediations.

Realism and Melodrama

Measured by the prevailing conventions of mainstream Hindi cinema, Shekhar Kapur's *Bandit Queen* was shot in a soberly realist style: no songs, no dances, theater actors from Delhi rather than Bollywood stars from Mumbai. Its critics as well as its supporters understood the work it was doing as a kind of unveiling. For conservatives like Bangalore BJP stalwart Pramila Nesargi, who organized an attempt to ban *Bandit Queen*, Kapur had simply gone too far in that clumsy, Westernized way: "*Bandit Queen*— symbolically it could have been shown. There was no need for the film to show the entire thing, completely naked [Phoolan Devi's public humiliation at the Behmai village well]. Even in the dramas in the olden days, symbolically it *can* be shown."[42] Vijay Anand, chair of the CBFC, had, on the other hand, argued that *Bandit Queen* should not be cut: "Isn't it true that Indians *should* see what's happening in their villages to their women? Rather than put on a veil and pretend that nothing of this kind is happening. The filmmaker has had the courage to show it, the audience should have the courage to see it. And no censor board should interfere with the creative expression." From a liberal point of view, *Bandit Queen*'s refusal of

"Hindi film formula signif[ied] progress towards frank and fearless film-making" (Mohamed 1996). As Justice Bharucha noted approvingly in the Supreme Court judgment that finally allowed it to be released, "It is not a pretty story. There are no syrupy songs or pirouetting around trees. It is the serious and sad story of a worm turning: a village-born female child becoming a dreaded dacoit [bandit]" (Bobby Art International v. Om Pal Singh Hoon [1996]).

At the time of *Bombay*, journalist, writer, and director Khalid Mohamed lambasted the censors and the Bollywood mainstream for their cowardice— essentially, for flinching away from realism: "Any effort to be offbeat or politically incisive is summarily dismissed by peers as well as half-witted commentators as 'arty' or '*Yeh to documentary hai*' [This is nothing but a documentary]" (Mohamed 1995). How was Indian commercial cinema ever to mature under such conditions? This assumed connection between civic maturity and a capacity to withstand and ultimately benefit from realistic representation was long-standing. In 1928 the report of the Indian Cinematograph Committee urged that "timely steps should be taken to create a national atmosphere" by means of the cinema (1928b: 61). Then, too, the main obstacle on the road to national cinematic maturity was audience "hypersensitivity," a constant readiness to take offense. Just as my interlocutors in the early 2000s would complain that Indians still had trouble, at moments of stress, transcending the particularity of their community attachments, so the ICC remarked, "We hardly think that the Christian community should object to a film discountenancing in a sober manner infant marriage or that Muslims should object to Nur Jehan [favorite wife of the Mughal emperor Jehangir] being pictured without a veil" (ICC 1928b:120).[43] The key claim here was that audiences' readiness to take offense made it difficult to deal frankly and directly with real historical events. According to the ICC, the symptom of this difficulty was Indian directors' tendency to fall back on mythology and "fictitious history" (although D. G. Phalke, often called the father of Indian cinema, told the committee that in India, historical themes had only provincial relevance whereas mythology enjoyed pan-Indian appeal).[44]

But *Bombay*, of course, was not *Bandit Queen*. To be sure, some of its cinematic devices invoked documentary naturalism. To give just one example, the scene in which the Muslim heroine arrives by train at Mumbai's Victoria Terminus was shot with a hidden camera amid real-life commuters. But *Bombay* also had songs, it had dances, it had spectacular ensemble numbers, it was driven by a melodramatically framed love story, and it sought conventional narrative resolution through patriotic pathos. Ravi Vasudevan observes that Ratnam "clearly works with certain realist concerns, at the level of restrained acting styles, and a classicism of formal construction and narrative dovetailing of cause-effect structures" (2010: 225). Unlike the realism of the "good" cinema of the 1960s and 1970s, however, Ratnam's realism is "privately financed and very much of the mainstream," designed "to celebrate middle-class modernity rather than develop a stance of social criticism" (2010:224–25). At the same time, "Melodramatic publicness rears its head determinedly: characters defined by their professionalized, middle-class modernity and through actorly economies of restraint and silence mutate into vehicles of patriotic fervour pitched in the escalated tones of public self-nomination and address" (2010:211). When asked why he had resorted to such mainstream devices, Ratnam himself replied that it would have been easier to make a smaller, more realist film; the real challenge, he suggested, lay in making "serious themes . . . palatable" in order "to reach the common man" rather than "to please a few intellectuals" (Rao 1995).

For some, like Chandan Mitra (1995), writing in the *Hindustan Times*, Ratnam had succeeded gloriously. As "the most aesthetic craftsman of passion on the screen," Ratnam was making "political cinema at its best" and should pay no heed to "secular fundamentalists" like "the incorrigible Shabana Azmi and her clones."[45] But Arun Sadhu's reflection on *Bombay* in *Frontline* magazine is perhaps a more telling expression of the ambivalence —not to say confusion—generated by the attempt to reconcile the populist pleasures of melodrama with some notion of critical and historical responsibility. Sadhu emphasized Ratnam's daring against those who reserved their admiration for grimly unflinching documentaries:

> *Bombay* is excellent entertainment with a powerful message, an intelligent golden middle ground between crass commercial cinema and thoughtful artistic film-making. . . . Mani Ratnam obviously wants to talk to common audiences. And he talks to them in their language effectively and honestly. Having committed himself to mainstream audiences, he cannot presumably do away with songs and dances, which, to be truthful, are extremely enjoyable. But choosing to stay in the mainstream imposes many limitations. The treatment has to be simplistic and often cliché-ridden. But in Mani Ratnam's handling, clichés

become beautiful moments and symbols take the form of powerful motifs which rarely fail to move. Mani Ratnam has not tried to delve deeper into the historical, political, and social questions of why and how. He has confined himself to showing what actually happened. (Sadhu 1995)

First, Sadhu presents Ratnam as a master of generic fusion, carving out a space between the aesthetic prostitution of the market and elite niche cinema. Then he appears, in more or less the same breath, both to regret the pragmatic need for analytically reductive cliché *and* to acknowledge the affectively emergent power of these same clichés in Ratnam's hands. There is an element of the intellectual's usual coy admission of guilty pleasure in popular devices ("songs and dances, which, to be truthful, are extremely enjoyable"). But there is also a sense that Ratnam's "clichés" contain a more open-ended affective potentiality ("beautiful moments," "symbols take the form of powerful motifs which rarely fail to move"). At least that is what Sadhu's next rhetorical move seems to imply, since it so definitively closes down the possibility that has just been suggested, the possibility that the affective potentiality of these "clichés" might in fact enable another way into the social truth of the world of *Bombay*. Instead, an intellectualist standard is once again asserted. ("Mani Ratnam has not tried to delve deeper into the historical, political and social questions of why and how.") And yet how do we make sense of Sadhu's final statement ("He has confined himself to showing what actually happened"), when everything he has just said suggests otherwise?

Drawing on Peter Brooks, Ravi Vasudevan notes that the categorical separation between realism and melodrama was, in the Euro-American world, a by-product of the emergence of nineteenth-century bourgeois canons of high art. Similarly, during the 1940s and 1950s, the generic characterization of mainstream Indian film as melodramatic tended, from a "refined" critical perspective, to mark its lack, its vulgarity, its aesthetic failure. Vasudevan makes a strong case for a reworked conception of the melodramatic that would highlight its "importance . . . as a public-fictional form deriving from a recalibration of the relationship between public and private spheres" (2010:10). The moment of recalibration to which Vasudevan most habitually returns is the period surrounding Indian Independence. But in the context of my argument in this book, his argument might perhaps fruitfully be extended to a consideration of both the consolidation of a public cultural regulatory discourse during the latter half of the Indian nineteenth century and to the cultural emergency of the 1990. (In that regard, it is no accident that Vasudevan lingers on Mani Ratnam's work.)

Certainly, in some respects the public debate over *Bombay* stayed on familiar ground. In the *Times of India*, Swaminathan Aiyar (1995) made a plea for romantic melodrama as a path to transcendent (yet reassuringly nationalist) humanism: "A love affair is not the forced acquisition of one community's property by another; it represents two human beings rising above the narrow sectarian passions that surround them. It ennobles both them and the nation, for it means that they are seeing each other as human beings and not as the property of any community." The following day in the *Economic Times*, Chitra Padmanabhan (1995) questioned the conflation of secularism and nationalism implied in such an argument and the naïve equation drawn between the hero's "pure love" for the heroine and his level-headed citizen's ability to transcend communal conflict in the midst of the most harrowing (and, from a cinematic point of view, possibly exploitive) violence. For Padmanabhan, Ratnam's realist gestures were simply cynical devices designed to give his sentimental agenda the appearance of a more concrete grounding in everyday life: "Ratnam uses the graphic and lovingly picturized riot scenes, with incidents that are familiar to the newspaper reader, to create a wailing wall. Little touches of authentic detail for the more towering agony of our almost otherworldly lovers. . . . The riots are just a context to highlight the helpless look on [heroine] Manisha Koirala's face." Through such devices, Padmanabhan argued, Ratnam had managed to fool both "politicians and scribes" into thinking "that the birth of a crucial contemporary political text is at hand."

But *Bombay* referred to events that had only just taken place, events that had polarized Indian publics and shattered Mumbai's long-nurtured claim to cosmopolitan tolerance. As such, the debate could never just be about the difference between criticism and cliché but also had to confront the film's live relation to fields of public affect that were still very much in motion. Some, like veteran film critic Iqbal Masud, felt that Ratnam's making "a song and dance" out of people's suffering was inherently offensive, particularly when wounds were so fresh (Ramanan 1995). Apart from the questionable ethics of capitalizing on pain, the problem of sentiment as an acceptable register of political engagement kept recurring. An editorial in the *Telegraph* argued that it was "indeed an irony that a maudlin film should be the test of as rich a legacy as cultural pluralism" ("Slam *Bombay*"

1995). But why, actually, was this such an irony? Why should a sentimental text not be a suitable medium through which to reconsider current concerns (Berlant 2008)?

Sadhu and Padmanabhan both referred to the prevalence of "cliché" in Mani Ratnam's film, and of course this is the standard critical objection to melodramatic affective techniques. But precisely because the real-life wounds were still raw, "cliché" could not here mean only an all-too-predictable mobilization of affect around reactionary ideology. The debate over *Bombay*, because it had to confront live, loose public affect, seemed to register a more profound and a more ambiguous provocation: what one might call *potentiated cliché*. Padmanabhan, seeing only the danger of an uncontainable *potency*, warned that "by its cinematic language, [*Bombay*] forces clichés into potent tools of aggression." But civic activist Sushobha Barve (1995), writing in the *Times of India*, asked, in effect, whether the film's undeniable potency might not also awaken more socially constructive *potentials*, whether precisely *Bombay*'s visceral liveness could power a project of public healing. Around the time of the film's fraught release in Mumbai, the papers had been full of vox populi interviews with audiences coming out of screenings, generally designed to convey the impression that the controversy was all a big tamasha put on by politicians and that ordinary people were taking the film in their stride as just another piece of entertainment. But Barve attended a special screening for social workers who had served in the thick of the riots and described an entirely different set of reactions: "Young Salim Mansuri of Bhendi Bazar rushed out of the film twice in an agitated state, crying out 'It's driving me mad!' Aklakhbhai from Kamathipura was so disturbed he could hardly speak and told us he would not be able to eat that night" (Barve 1995).

The Continent Spectator-Citizen

If [eighteenth-century Persian invader of India] Nadir Shah made golgothas of skulls, must we leave them out of the story because people must be made to view a historical theme without true history?
—K. A. Abbas v. Union of India (1970)

The potentiated cliché is ambiguous because it suggests two possibilities simultaneously. On the one hand, there is the "good" prospect of a cliché coming alive in such a way as to vitalize a transcendent ideal: romantic union, ethical citizenship, and so on. On the other hand, it also suggests the "bad" prospect of the cliché coming alive in a more unstable way, intensifying affect to the point of violence or paralysis. Judging from the debates it unleashed, *Bombay* pointed to both these possibilities. On one level, the responsibility for things going one way or another was, as we have seen, laid at the feet of the director. On another level, the key question seemed to be whether audience-crowds were capable of constituting themselves into the kinds of mature publics that were up to the provocation.

In chapter 2, I argued that the late 1920s and the 1930s saw a shift away from a colonial racially and culturally based theory of audience susceptibilities and toward an embryonic version of the general spectator-citizen. The idea that "uneducated" people were at risk at the movies remained in place across this change because, as it turned out, it was just as useful for a postcolonial polity that legitimated itself by reference to national development as it had been for a colonial one that justified itself vis-à-vis a civilizing mission. So far, then, I have argued that racially and culturally essentializing justifications for censorship gave way to censorship based on the permanently deferred arrival of a mature political culture. But this requires some qualification. Culturally essentializing justifications for censorship have remained alive and well (although not quite officially sanctioned) in regard to one group: Indian Muslims. Time and again, invocations of "the Muslim spectator" does the ideological work of giving the abstract figure of the pissing man all the affective and quasi-empirical particularity of a "known" fact. Consider the different ways that Hindu and Muslim objections to *Bombay* were treated. When the Shiv Sena or one of its affiliates rattled its sabers, liberals complained about a threat to secular law and order that happened to come from Hindus but which could, in principle, have come from chauvinists of any persuasion. When Muslim groups threatened to cause problems if *Bombay* was released, their actions were interpreted as symptoms of a distinctly *Muslim* unreason.

Some complained that Mani Ratnam was perpetuating the stereotype of inherently hotheaded Muslims: "While the [hero's] conservative Hindu father is projected as having a sharp tongue, the Muslim heroine's father is shown drawing his sword at the least provocation" (Rao 1995). This imbalance was only aggravated once Ratnam agreed to cut out scenes of menacing Hindu protestors while leaving sequences of rampaging Muslim mobs intact. The same logic governed the film's release schedule in the Mumbai area—it only opened in Muslim neighborhoods once screenings had gone smoothly in Hindu-majority areas. (Nor, perhaps, is it accidental that the desperately affected social workers depicted in Sushobha Barve's account above are Muslims.)

This kind of communally invidious distinction seems already to have guided film censorship practice at the time, in the 1920s and 1930s, when the modern mass spectator-citizen was being invented, and—not coincidentally—films were becoming hotly contested objects of communal acrimony. Films caricaturing Muslim subjects were often approved for exhibition, whereas films containing situations that were potentially offensive to Hindus were often either cut or banned altogether. When Muslim groups protested against a film, their protests could be dismissed as a symptom of Muslims' lamentable readiness to be whipped into a frenzy by their unscrupulous leaders.

The Bombay commissioner of police (and thus also the ex officio chairman of the Bombay Board of Film Censors), Mr. D. Healy, told the ICC that a community habituated to veiling "their" women would be more than likely to get overexcited at the sight of scantily clad screen heroines (ICC 1928a, 1:77). And while the ICC tried to remain noncommittal in its report, it did note that Muslim objections "to *any* representation whatsoever of persons venerated as holy by Islam" remained an "obstacle to the [film] producer" (ICC 1928b:41).

To be sure, this was not just an external characterization. For example, in January 1926, Muslims in Lahore objected to Cecil B. DeMille's *The Ten Commandments* (Paramount, 1923) on the grounds that its depiction of the "Holy Prophet Moses" inherently "constituted the denouncement and sacrilege of the above named venerable being." And a few months later, one Ahmed Said of the Arabgali Masjid in Bombay wrote to Police Commissioner Healy: "It is quite against our religious [*sic*] to bring the style of our God in Photoes [*sic*] and show them in Films."[46] Having suggested that a general hypersensitivity of Indian cinema audiences was retarding the development of Indian cinema by forcing directors to resort to mythology and "fictitious history," the ICC's report proceeded to specify that "Muslim opinion is particularly sensitive in certain direction regarding the presentation of historical characters" (ICC 1928b:41).

Now, of course, the distinction between "religious" and "historical" characters was ontologically problematic at best, not least in a South Asian context where devotional practice does not necessarily distinguish sacred from secular authority. It was also in a subtle way prejudicial to Muslims.

When Muslims protested against unflattering film portrayals of, say, Mughal emperors, their annoyance would be used as evidence of a regressive Muslim inability to accept historical fact (e.g., that Emperor Jehangir drank alcohol) in a continent manner. Hindu annoyance tended more consistently to be characterized as stemming from offenses against "religious sentiments" and, as such, to enjoy the protection of the Indian Penal Code. In this way, whereas Hindu complaints about cinematic misrepresentation, while couched in religious terms, could often be afforded the legitimacy of secular legal protection, Muslim complaints became symptoms of a regressive form of spectatorship that, in its inability to mediate public affect, threatened to retard India's progress toward secular modernity.

The alleged intemperance of Muslim spectators worked as a kind of constitutive otherness that at once helped to shore up the figure of the spectator-citizen and continued to threaten it from inside.[47] As Bombay became the dominant center of "national" film production in India, its reputation for business-based cosmopolitanism was also increasingly contrasted with the hotheaded zealotry attributed to northern India, where Muslim influence was historically deeper. Muslim protests against films could thus be excoriated not only as incontinent politics but also as obstacles to the supposedly neutral ability of the market in film to manifest a genuine general will. In the words of a *Filmindia* editorial from April 1936, published as communal conflict was reaching new heights of intensity, "Immediately a producer has produced a picture with an Islamic theme he is made a target of unholy attacks by these gutter sheets and with the aid of posters and fire-spitting writings, and backed by a crowd of paid hirelings the illiterate Muslim public is made to believe that the producer has distorted the teachings of their Prophet and blasphemed Islam in the picture."[48]

Muslim groups complained about insult, injury, and underrepresentation on the censor boards. But because their complaints were seen as expressions of inherently Muslim tendencies, their demands tended to be interpreted as particularistic. Thinly disguised Hindu nationalist groups, however, were quick to exploit the specter of Muslim intemperance in such a way as to equate Hindu interests with those of the general public. In the mid-1930s, for example, the Home Department of the Bombay government started receiving letters from a somewhat shady organization calling itself the All-India League of Films' Censorship (AILFC). The AILFC claimed to fight all injurious representations, but its missives soon revealed its orientation: "to

Muslim and Parsi directors no picture is complete and remains tasteless till it contains something dishonourable to Hindus."[49]

In the event, the Bombay Home Department eventually dismissed the AILFC's increasingly shrill claims as both "far-fetched" and "communalistic." Home Minister (and, decades later, Prime Minister) Morarji Desai scribbled on a memo: "No action need be taken. Squeamish attitudes on the part of communalists against exhibition of social & religious foibles should be discouraged."[50] After a brief investigation, the commissioner of police conclusively discredited the AILFC, assuring the Bombay Presidency government that it was neither a legitimate representative of the general public nor of Hindu sentiments. The field was thus cleared for film industry organizations like the Indian Motion Pictures Producers' Association to assert a market-based trade discourse against overtly communal claims. And yet "Muslim" remained the paradigmatic shorthand for both public cultural particularism and spectatorial incontinence.

Sixty-odd years later, developments following the release of *Bombay* followed a similar logic. Before the BJP–Shiv Sena coalition's electoral victory in Maharashtra was announced on March 13, 1995, Bal Thackeray had loudly and publicly deplored the film's alleged prejudice against Hindus. But once he had extracted a few cuts and the Shiv Sena was in power in the state government, Thackeray changed his tune. Having earlier addressed the film from a straightforwardly communal standpoint, he now slipped smoothly into an apparently secular idiom of aesthetic discernment. Of course, Thackeray was not about to drop his signature aggressive chauvinism completely just because his party was now in power. When the Mumbai commissioner of police, Satish Sawhney, yielded to Muslim demands to delay *Bombay*'s release by a week, Thackeray warned: "We will repent tomorrow if we bow down today." Claiming that he himself had "suggested" rather than "demanded" cuts from Ratnam, Thackeray waxed belligerent about similar requests from Muslim leaders: "Muslim fundamentalists should note that today Mahatma Gandhi and Pandit Nehru are not alive to support them. How strong are you, how strong are we, that we shall see" ("Ban on *Bombay*" 1995). But alongside the familiar growling, a new register now also appeared: both Thackeray and the new chief minister, Manohar Joshi, went on record calling *Bombay* "aesthetically excellent" ("*Bombay* Showing Portents . . ." 1995). Similarly, Nitin Govil, the general secretary of the Maharashtra branch of the BJP, urged *Bombay*'s opponents to appreciate the film "as a work of art" ("Ban on *Bombay*" 1995). The strategic genius of this move was that, once again, it made all Muslim objections seem incorrigibly partisan, as when A. S. Uraizee of the State Minorities Commission insisted against the Shiv Sena's newfound aestheticism that "art must be responsible to politics" (Ramanan 1995).

SOMETHING IN THE WAY

In some respects, then, little seemed to have changed between the mid-1930s and the mid-1990s. The figure of incontinent Muslims was still the constitutive other that helped to make plausible a majoritarian (Hindu) model of secular citizenship. And yet in other ways, the situation was quite different. In the 1930s, and for some time after, one could only claim to be espousing a secular and inclusive model of Indian citizenship by actively disavowing overtly communal appeals. Certainly, even in the mid-1990s, the BJP had to tone down its more aggressively Hindu nationalist tendencies in order to achieve national power. But in Mumbai, erstwhile seat of pragmatically inclusive Indian cosmopolitanism, it was now possible for a leader like Bal Thackeray to assert general political sovereignty in aggressively communal terms.

It was hardly incidental—despite all the other media on which the Hindu right seized during those years—that a group like the Shiv Sena should have found in the cinema such a productive site of mobilization. Right-leaning cultural nationalism, because of its investment in public sentiment as a political terrain, has generally been far more alive to the performative power of potentiated reality than its opponents on the liberal-secular left. And where better to look for potentiated clichés with mass resonance than the popular cinema? I am not, by the way, arguing that the performative efficacy of the Hindu right had to do with a corresponding deficit in liberal secularism. Some have claimed that the great shortcoming of Nehruvian nationalism was to underestimate the affective importance of everyday religiosity in Indian lifeworlds (Varma 1998). Be that as it may, I think we need to consider both the heyday of Nehruvian nationalism and the contested dispensations of the cultural emergency as historically situated responses to the challenge of producing sovereignty in a mass-mediated democracy—a challenge that is, of course, by no means restricted to India. In India these were profoundly different historical moments with very different political possibilities and equations. But both moments involved attempts to harness the affective potentials at the open edge of mass publicity to the symbolic order of community. Both moments were attempts to achieve the impossible: a reunification of the patron/police powers of Indra's banner staff on a mass scale.

Impossible, yes, but not at all fruitless. Far from it. Like all fantasies, this is a political ambition that thrives on its unattainability. Of course, its structural impossibility is not overtly admitted within the ideological discourse. Instead, the deferral of Indra's banner staff (the dream of a performative dispensation in which patron and police functions would be smoothly integrated) is blamed on "something in the way," an obstacle that is at once fascinating and contemptible. This obstacle is "extimate" in the Lacanian sense: at once apparently external—that is, inadmissible within the unified self-understanding of the would-be dispensation—and intimate, namely, actually and uncannily constitutive of that same self-understanding. The spectator-citizen's extimate obstacle is the pissing man. But the forms of his incontinence depend on the performative dispensation. On the conservative side, he is immoral and incorrigibly foreign; on the liberal side he lacks judgment and taste. The extimate obstacle is, one might say, the anthropomorphic and essentialized embodiment of the open edge of mass publicity. In its human obstacle form, the open edge reproduces the impossible dream of patron/police unification, even as the pursuit of that dream perpetually reproduces the extimate obstacle. And in its human obstacle form, the open edge also looks more amenable to political solutions, all the way from pedagogy to pogroms.

Eventually, I will be suggesting that the first step out of this vicious circle is to release the open edge from its humanoid guise; that is the subject of chapter 5. But in order to move in that direction, we will first have to explore another aspect of the cultural emergency years. If the present chapter has been an attempt to rethink the contests over public cultural sovereignty that erupted around films in the 1990s, then the next, chapter 4, explores the striking eroticization of Indian public culture during this same period.

CONCLUSION

Near the beginning of this chapter, I invoked a commonly heard argument: that the relation between impersonal, institutional power and personalized power was strictly zero-sum—the more you have of one, the less you have of the other. Applied to the Indian present, this assumption informs the ideological claim about being stuck in an exceptional in-between time, neither traditional nor modern. This liminal condition, the argument goes, is what produces the kind of irrational politics that characterized the cultural emergency: effervescent crowds without intelligent aims, manipulative leaders without genuine constituencies. I began with a reading of Shekhar Kapur's *Bandit Queen* in order to suggest that the film, which could certainly be read as an indictment of this kind of historical liminality, also opens up interesting general questions about the performative making of authority and, by the same token, presents a prescient allegory of the many challenges that the mid-1990s would bring to the CBFC's claim to regulatory sovereignty.

It is interesting, then, to note that both "liberal" and "illiberal" protagonists in the great struggle for the power to regulate public culture invoke both impersonal and personal idioms of authority. We have already seen the ease with which the Shiv Sena, at the height of its influence, was, during the struggle over Mani Ratnam's *Bombay*, able to slide from a decidedly illiberal rhetoric of communal hostility to a liberal-sounding invocation of aesthetic judgment. As Immanuel Kant proposed in his Third Critique, the importance of a transcendent standard of aesthetic judgment was that it promised to provide a spontaneous, sensuous grounding for the kind of impersonal reason that would be adequate to the abstraction of a modern public sphere. Many have argued that Kant's version of the aesthetic judgment, and the Habermasian discourse ethics that follow from it, amount to de facto authoritarianism in the de jure guise of liberal freedom (see Calhoun, ed., 1992; Robbins, ed., 1993; Warner 2002). And to be sure, Bal Thackeray certainly invoked such an impersonal aesthetic standard from within a highly personalized, charismatic, and authoritarian form of leadership. But the conclusion should not be that it was only a cynical and convenient rhetorical strategy, although it clearly had its political advantages. Rather, the tension between the impersonal and the personal elements of this performative politics might be read as a structural symptom of any attempt to assert sovereignty at the open edge of mass publicity.

On the other side, liberal critics of the Hindu right and of state censorship frequently took aim at the arbitrary and personalistic habits that seemed constantly to compromise the integrity of state institutions. Documentary filmmakers Anand Patwardhan and Rakesh Sharma both maintain websites and blogs detailing their struggles with the censors. So, for example, when the CBFC's Examining Committee viewed Rakesh Sharma's documentary *Final Solution*, Sharma made sure to keep a precise record of the committee members' comings and goings and concluded that they could not possibly even have watched the whole film, let alone had any serious discussion of its content.[51] The point is not only that a state body should conduct itself according to transparent and impersonal standards, but also that for Sharma the imprimatur of the CBFC provides a kind of legal insurance against the illegal attacks of self-styled street censors. Patwardhan, for his part, has preferred to take his battle to the courts. In response, the censors claim that Patwardhan *wants* the CBFC to try to ban his films so that he can get more attention out of going public.

In conversation with Vijay Anand about these matters, I was struck most forcefully by the very personalized tone in which Anand expressed his dismay with Patwardhan. Here, after all, was a man who had lost a great deal of sleep trying to move the censorship process in a more "professional," less personalistic direction. But what shone through his recollections of Patwardhan submitting his antinukes documentary *War and Peace* to the CBFC was a sense of affront that Patwardhan, in his hunger for public recognition, had arrogantly refused to engage a system that might well have worked in his favor. As chair of the Censor Board, Anand had put in a personal call to Patwardhan. "I said [adopting a reasonable man-to-man tone] 'these are very *minor* things, why do you want to fight?' I told him, 'there is a censor board, you have to use it. You have to listen to them. You convince them. Ninety percent of your cuts will be waived if you go and talk to the committee.'" Having arranged a meeting between Patwardhan and the CBFC's committee, Anand was then appalled at Patwardhan's demeanor: "It became a kind of ego trip. He went and abused them: 'who are you to be sitting here? You're a man of [BJP leader] Pramod Mahajan. I'll see to it that you're out. I'll see to it that my film gets passed.'"

Patwardhan has, over the years, fought lengthy legal battles to get his films shown on Doordarshan, the state television network, not only because he wants them to be seen by larger audiences but because he believes that as a public service, the network has an ethical mandate that is much broader than simply glorifying the reigning government. And, of course, Vijay Anand did not believe that Doordarshan should be a state propaganda medium. But he did, in effect, characterize it as a component of the government's performative dispensation and thus legitimately subject to its patron and police powers. His manner of expressing this again stressed an ethics of mutual, personal respect between filmmakers and the authorities: "Censor board is government, television is government. If [Patwardhan] gets a right to show [one of his films] on television, then he might as well show the version that the government has approved. If you're abusing the government and showing it on government television, then they don't like it."[52]

We might, of course, choose to interpret Anand's words as evidence of the true (regressive) authoritarian colors hiding behind a (progressive) liberal veneer. We would then proceed to sigh and shake our heads at yet more evidence of the Indian state's inability to live up to its democratic claims and let go of feudal habits. But if the argument that I have been developing so far bears any weight, then the ambiguity of the censor's discourse is not simply to be dismissed as a mark of hypocrisy. It is not simply an expression of the archaism of censorship in a democratic public sphere. Rather, it points to that much broader problem which censorship as an institutional practice both highlights and disavows: the restlessly extimate relation between the unruly potentials of mass publicity and any project of mass sovereignty.

CHAPTER 4

QUOTIDIAN ERUPTIONS

AESTHETIC DISTINCTION AND THE EXTIMATE SQUIRM

At the end of chapter 3, I proposed that asserting a performative dispensation under conditions of mass publicity involves a dynamic of constitutive
failure. In other words, the claim that patron and police powers can be
unified under a single moral order necessarily runs up against palpable
evidence of its impossibility. But the ideological fantasy that such a unified
patron/police formation *could* be achieved—even in a mass public sphere
—is sustained by blaming the failure on "something in the way." This
"something in the way" is often figured as a class of people who are lacking
or excessive in some fatal way. Depending on the performative dispensation that is being asserted, they may be Muslims or they may be south-
erners or they may be shameless women or, for anticolonial nationalists,
they may be the British. What they have in common is that their existence
prevents the full enjoyment of an idealized relation of effervescence to
symbolic order.

I hinted at the next step in my argument at the end of chapter 3: namely,
that this "something in the way" should not only be read as a way of

naming empirical social groups but that it is equally, if not more, a projection outward onto such social groups of a relation to something that feels intolerably intimate and internal to the speaker. Following Slavoj Žižek in adapting the psychoanalytic terminology of Jacques Lacan to a social relation, I called this double relation of the external and the intimate "extimate." To describe as extimate that "something in the way" which both blocks the full enjoyment of an integrated performative dispensation and sustains the desire to achieve that integration is to say that when the censor speaks of pissing men, he does so not only because there are unruly crowds that must be controlled. The constant invocation of the unruliness of these crowds, rather, is first of all a way of externalizing and thus disavowing an unruly affective potential that the censor feels in himself, but which his function as censor both constantly implies (since he must be able to recognize obscenity when he sees/feels it) and denies (since the censor must stand above all that). The pissing man is not so much the censor's empirical other as his phantom alter ego. Like a phantom limb, he has been amputated, but he nevertheless causes constant twinges in the central nervous system of the censor's discourse.

Since I use some psychoanalytically derived terms, I should emphasize that although I resist the reduction of the pissing man to actual sociological others that confront the censor "from outside," I am certainly not arguing that the extimate circuit is only an "internal" psychological reaction on the part of individual censors. Rather, my point is that what this chapter calls the extimate squirm is a symptom that runs down the middle of the whole project of asserting performative dispensations. It is, to be sure, subjectively registered as discomfort, irritation, or aversion by individuals who find themselves either formally or informally exercising judgment over the pleasures of others. But its source is structural: the impossibility of establishing stable closure at the open edge of mass publicity.

I have organized these last two chapters around the concept of obscenity, since obscenity seems to be the thing that most obviously irritates the extimate circuit. In this chapter, I delve into the aesthetic politics of this extimacy vis-à-vis the threat of obscenity. In chapter 5, by way of conclusion, I propose that "obscenity" might ultimately be a way of talking about the emergent potential of mass-mediated images in general, not only of those that would typically be classified as obscene.

Near the beginning of Mira Nair's hit film *Monsoon Wedding* (2001) is a short and relatively unremarked scene. The scene is an ironic homage to Nair's own struggles with the CBFC and with Indian public moralism around her 1997 feature adaptation of the *Kamasutra*. As such, it usefully encapsulates both the conventional stances of the cultural emergency and its more complex provocations.

The setting is a television studio, the occasion the filming of an episode of a current affairs debate show. With a knowing nod to the cargo cult of the day, the Internet economy, the show is called *Delhi.com* (Mazzarella 2010d). On the panel, arrayed around a slicked-back smoothie of a host, are the usual suspects: a liberal-cosmopolitan English-medium journalist pitching liberalization as, in part, sexual liberation; a Hindu-nationalist politician, speaking for the opposition, stressing the distinctive civilizational needs and susceptibilities of Indian audiences; and, finally, the executor of the law, a woman from the Censor Board.

We enter the conversation just as the politician is addressing the journalist: "Just because India has gone global, should we embrace everything? What about our ancient culture? Our tradition? Our values? You are saying censorship is unnecessary, absolutely unnecessary." The journalist counters with a standard move, contrasting Indian repression to global (paradigmatically American) freedom: "Let's take the example of America. The First Amendment is . . ." But the politician, entirely confident of the rhetorical resonance of his own objection, cuts him off: "This is *not* America. This is *India*." So far the discussion has been in English. But then the woman from the Censor Board intervenes in Hindi: "These are our laws. Change the Constitution, and censorship will follow." The liberal journalist, now exasperated, retorts, moving mid-sentence from Hindi back to English: "What do you think? Just because you wear handloom [cotton] and you speak in Hindi, that you represent the common man? You *don't!*"

Thus far, the conversation has followed the genre conventions of cultural emergency debates flawlessly: first, the juxtaposition of a universalist claim to juridico-libidinal liberation against a particularist claim to Indian cultural integrity; then, the making explicit of the question of specific publics and the political subtexts of language and class. But it is what happens next that is so telling.

At the invitation of the host, a shy-looking, middle-aged woman in a sari, distinctly unnerved by the flashy young audience and the dazzle of the studio lights, emerges and is introduced amid scattered applause as "one of our top dubbists in Delhi."[1] As the timid lady stations herself in front of a monitor and puts on a pair of headphones, it becomes clear that she is a voiceover artist who dubs Hindi dialogue onto foreign films. It also quickly becomes clear, however, that we are not dealing with the latest Hollywood blockbuster. This embodiment of the respectable citizen-housewife, eyes fixed on the monitor in front of her, suddenly starts emitting orgasmic moans and snatches of Hindi porno-flick dialogue: "Give it to me, give it to me. More, big boy, more. I like it like that," and so on.

The Hindu nationalist politician shakes his head in disgust. But the response of the studio audience is interesting: a kind of awkward amusement somewhere between a smile and a squirm, a strained snickering that is something more complex than the response to an unexpected eruption of obscenity. Had the dialogue been in English rather than Hindi, the scene seems to imply, the audience might have guffawed or chuckled in a worldly way, taken it in their cosmopolitan stride. But the juxtaposition of this carnal import with the Hindi voicing seems, in an uncanny way, to open up an uncomfortable third space. With an I-rest-my-case air, the panelist from the Censor Board proclaims: "That is what the common man hears!" as, over rather feeble protests from the liberal journalist, the show cuts to a commercial break.

"The common man" is a polite name for the pissing man, invoked as always in the third person; in other words, an imagined audience "out there" from which the hip folks in the audience—the second-person addressees of the statement "that is what the common man hears!"—imagine themselves to be separated by education, class, and in this case also language. So why are *they* squirming?

Analysts of the new Indian consumerism that unfolded during the 1980s and 1990s often use the terms *liberalization* and *globalization* interchangeably. But the squirm that ripples through the closing seconds of the Delhi .com scene in *Monsoon Wedding* suggests that the relation between the two terms could also be conflictual. The crucial thing about this squirm is that it is *not* just another example of the consuming elites' demonstrative distaste for vernacular affects. Rather, the squirm registers the more uncertain surprise of an unexpectedly extimate affect suddenly bubbling up out of an object and a viewing context that has, by this audience, strenuously been marked as a site of cosmopolitan composure and sensuous discernment: the "blue film."

One way to read the squirm would be as an index of the clash between liberalization and globalization: a moment of discomfort at the volatile point where the mass extension of eroticized consumer pleasure (liberalization) comes up against an elite need to mark a boundary between the down-market local and the aspirational global (globalization). If we follow this line of argument, the squirm would be a sign of the friction that occurs when consumerism seems to be *moving too quickly*; when elite attempts to manage the terms under which commodity desire may be translated into social prestige—through advertising, through branding, through moralizing performative dispensations—are unable to keep up with the mass extension of these pleasurable provocations.

This is certainly part of the story: social distinction struggling to keep up with rapid public cultural change, the work of keeping the pissing man out of the club even as the entrance keeps widening. But something more ambivalent is also going on. The squirm that for a moment ruffles the smooth cosmopolitan surface of the Delhi.com studio set marks the moment, passing but palpable, when the extimacy of the pissing man is felt, and felt collectively.

QUOTIDIAN ERUPTIONS

One of the most distinctive symptoms of the public cultural politics of the early to mid-1990s was a sense of spatial and symbolic disorientation in which obscenity was suddenly anywhere and everywhere. Advertising was an important site. I have written at length about the Kama Sutra condom controversy elsewhere (Mazzarella 2003), and I mention the Tuff Shoes ad in chapter 3. I will be discussing some other contested objects of this period, notably the film song "Choli ke Peeche" later in this chapter. But it is important to note that these high-profile, rather overdetermined controversies took place within a public cultural climate of generalized anxiety about the possibility of quotidian eruptions of obscenity, often in the places where it was least expected. Nothing illustrates this better than the curious and compelling story of the pornographic shirts.

In April 1995, a reporter for the venerable Calcutta daily the *Statesman* told of how a mild-mannered, aging Jain chemistry teacher in Delhi, leafing unsuspectingly through his local paper, came across an ad for fine cotton shirts from Mafatlal Mills. Seeing that the shirts were apparently on sale for only Rs 110 (about $3.40 at that time), the chemistry teacher decided, in the company of his wife, to visit the advertised retail outlet in the bustling shopping center at Karol Bagh.[2] In his subsequent interview with the *Statesman*'s scribe, the shaken old gentleman recounted: "I asked the dealer to show me the export quality cotton shirts. But I was appalled at what was shown me. These shirts had all kinds of obscene prints on them."

Despite his shock and his outraged modesty, and with the misleading advertisement defiantly in hand, the teacher stood his ground as citizen and consumer and repeated his request. This time the salesman curtly informed him that the rude shirts were all that Rs 110 would buy; the Mafatlal shirts started at Rs 600. The *Statesman*'s report continued by relating that "shocked by the 'audacity' of the dealers who were selling such 'off-colour' clothes right in front of the police station, the elderly teacher bought a shirt and walked straight into the police station." But here he was in for another surprise: "'I was shocked at the attitude of the policemen. Not only did they refuse to lodge a complaint, [but] a crowd of policemen gathered around me, each one wanting to have a closer look at the shirt'" ("Plaint Against 'Pornographic' Shirts" 1995). The reader is left with the image of a circle of leering constables, inexorably closing in on the hapless teacher who, still clutching his evidence for the decent majority, now has nowhere left to turn.

In all its tragicomic pathos, the story of the pornographic shirts compresses a series of key tropes into the most skeletal of narratives. Among these, one might isolate the anxiously ambiguous line between the licit erotics of the new advertising and its contemporaneous illicit twin, the booming pornography business (of which more in a moment). We see the confrontation between the uncouth, exploitive hucksterism of a pushy new entrepreneurialism and the threadbare moral dignity of an increasingly archaic public service class. At the denouement, we encounter a police force compromised not only by its widely reported complicity with organized crime and communal violence, but now also by its corporeal susceptibility to the new mass erotics.

But most of all, the story of the pornographic shirts is spectacularly mundane. No protesters chanting themselves hoarse and smashing display windows. No indignant celebrities insisting on the right to free speech while casting aspersions on the aesthetic discernment of their accusers.

What emerges here, rather, is a sense of a newly volatile space of everyday publicity, one in which the shock of obscenity is no longer confined to known zones but liable at any moment to pervert the most ordinary routines. A paranoid space, then, an intimation of an unknowable pornoterroristic calculus in which precisely the most unremarkable spaces are most urgently threatened by sudden surges.

It was not just the shirts. In 1989 a story made the rounds about railway passengers in Patna, the state capital of Bihar, whose commute was raucously disrupted when someone in the station house flipped the wrong switch and the platform video monitors suddenly started blasting the hardcore porn video with which the railway employees had been entertaining themselves after hours. Throughout the 1990s, newspapers carried rumors of nocturnal cowboy cable television providers bent on infiltrating even the interior spaces of middle-class homes with filth and to that end beaming pornography from mobile transmitter vans, constantly staying one street ahead of the police. The arrival of the Internet opened yet other vistas. Web surfers were hit with the insidious strategies of smut vendors who would seize on a domain name similar to that of a legitimate, preferably august commercial concern in order to snare upstanding consumer-citizens.[3]

"Interpolation" had long been a headache for the film censors, particularly at the lower end of the market. Steamy footage—sometimes shot by specialized producers of "bits," sometimes pirated from an entirely different movie—would be inserted without regard for narrative continuity into films that had already been passed by the censors (see Hoek 2008). Here again, part of the anxiety had to do with a sense that the distinction between continent and incontinent viewing practices was crumbling. It was not just a matter of the usual corruption. In Mumbai, street vendors of magazines and videos had long nurtured a *hafta* relationship with the police: a carefully calibrated relation of give-and-take, of bribes and crackdowns. It was also a worry, as conveyed by the story of the pornographic shirts, that the authorities who were supposed to be keeping public spaces decent were as susceptible to moral corruption as anyone else. The reported account of one Mumbai cop on the smut beat gives an inadvertently revealing sense of the thin line between the rhythms of policing and those of pleasure:

> As many as a dozen obscene scenes may be re-included in a movie. So we have to watch such flicks closely, note the scenes, and report back to

the Censor Board. Then we may watch the movie some more times to confirm that these scenes are in violation of the Censor Board directives. We have to make rounds of various theatres showing these blue films, and watch several movies throughout the day. Some blue films are exhibited at morning shows, so we have to begin the day by going to those theatres and watching them. (Islam 2002)

One account suggested that in Kerala, along with the usual bribes, porn video dealers kept the police supplied with their own weekend TV/VCR/ videotape packages. Nor did the complicity necessarily restrict itself to humble police officers. Starting in 1992, it became possible for Indians to make exorbitantly expensive long-distance phone calls to sex lines in Hong Kong. This innovation resulted in an unexpected windfall for the government's international telecommunications gateway, VSNL. In 1998 Sushma Swaraj, then the BJP government's information and broadcasting minister, attempted to live up to her name (*swaraj* literally means "self-rule") by making sure that Indians remained free of such global enslavement. For some months, the government paid workers to keep track of the appearance of new numbers and then swiftly to block them. But by 2000, VSNL had reopened access, citing an annual revenue loss on the order of more than $1 million. More embarrassingly, as one report noted, "When Swaraj banned the calls, it was discovered that about 65 percent of these were made from telephones installed at government offices and official residences" (Rajendran 2000). Who was the pissing man now?

PARA-GLOBALIZATION

Like many other successful industries, [pornography] is one where
import substitution has paid off.
—Chakravarti et al. 1989

By the late 1980s, relatively affordable video technology meant that a new indigenous pornographic film business was springing up in the suburbs of (what was then still) Bombay and other major cities. Celluloid blue films had an older history of production in some parts of the country, notably Kerala. And, of course, there had always been a specialized market in smuggled imports. In August 1921 (in other words, only a year after the censor boards had been established), an official at the Home Department in Delhi wrote to the regional administrations complaining about a related practice: "It is . . . suggested that often the whole of a film is not exhibited before the censors; this gives the opportunity, of which advantage is reported to be freely taken, of smuggling obscene films into the country by tacking them on as the last 400 or 500 feet of a large six-reel film."[4] The proceedings of the ICC also contain scattered references to obscene films. One member of the Bombay Censor Board, Mr. Watkins, told the committee with just a hint of wistfulness, "We have of course from time to time obtained obscene films, usually toy size, bits of films, and I can remember now a little toy cinema which worked quite well" (ICC 1928a, 1:104). Elsewhere, Chairman Rangachariar himself admitted having been shown bits of something "really excessively indecent . . . on the Bombay side" (ICC 1928a, 3:117). Evidence taken in camera suggested that some of the rulers of the princely states helped to smuggle pornographic film into India, but also that a studio in the Bombay suburb Santa Cruz had been known to produce domestic fare (ICC 1928a, 5:7).

The new video business of the 1980s was, as it were, the flip side of liberalization. According to one estimate, an enterprising director could rent a cheap hotel room, make a rough and ready blue film for around Rs 28,000 (then just over $2,000), including Rs 1,000 (about $75) for the female actor and, within the parameters of an informal market, expect to sell tapes at around Rs 300 ($23) a pop (Sayani 1988). Bemused commentators in the liberal press characterized the new *desi* (Indian) porn as a kind of shady double of the consumerist cornucopia that was beginning to emerge during those years: "You name it and you can get it. Whatever your inclination—and your budget—the booming porn market has something for you."[5]

At first the video revolution appears largely to have involved pirating and dubbing foreign films into Indian languages. But just as the "newspaper revolution" (Jeffrey 2000) of the late 1970s saw the beginning of an unexpected upsurge in Indian-language print, so the video boom of the late 1980s invoked an imagined community in vernacular porn.[6] Titles mentioned in the press around this time include both Hindi videos aimed at a more "national" market (*Sardar, Miss India, Bombay Fantasy*) and regionally specific efforts in Marathi (*Champabai, Gangubai*), Gujarati (*Prem*), and Malayalam (*Thirakal*). If the sheer variety of choice risked shaming the legitimate consumer goods market, then the mise-en-scène of these pioneering productions seemed often to have involved a kind of protoglobalized eclecticism: "a soundtrack of orgasmic noises, Dave Brubeck's jazz classic *Take Five*, and Anup Jalota *ghazals*."[7] Some films were even shot in London with subcontinental casts; others, like *Garam Mirch*, featured interracial couplings (Agarwal 1991). Just as marketing gurus would, at the height of globalization fever in the mid-1990s, celebrate Indians' newfound pride in Bollywood, so there were those who hailed the new Indian-made porn as a kind of libidinal homecoming: "'About time too,' says Sorab Dalal, a young management consultant in Bombay. 'The foreign stuff is good, but I was always curious about seeing a local porn movie.'"

Nor was homegrown flesh a domestic endeavor only at the level of content. Producers as well as exhibitors liked to argue that, as small businessmen struggling to survive outside the highly capitalized charmed circle of the legitimate cinema and publishing businesses, porn offered them the kind of margins that represented a fair opportunity to compete as well as a real shot at social mobility. Porn entrepreneurs were converting filthy lucre into cultural capital by buying flats in middle-class neighborhoods and sending their children to convent schools (Parmar 1991). And video parlor operators were keen to stress the respectability of their trade, carving out "family" and "couples" niches as well as claiming to cater to a significant number of housewives who, apparently, especially enjoyed films featuring "a brazen woman who seduces the hapless *brahmachari* [celibate] hero" (Agarwal 1991).[8]

At the same time in a different market niche, within the world of English-language magazine publishing, a whole new wave of "men's magazines" were hitting the stands (see Srivastava 2007). The legendary *Debonair* had since 1972 attempted to combine "erotica" in words and pictures with socially and culturally progressive editorial content. By the mid-1990s, titles like *Chastity, Fantasy,* and *Playway* were jostling for space on the same shelves, positioning themselves—in the words of *Chastity* editor Joseph Zuzarte—as "on-the-table fare, unlike other magazines which are under-the-bed" (Kesnur 1994) or, as in the case of *Fantasy*, as "awareness" magazines ("Scribes Flay Arrest . . ." 1994). In their claims to "beauty" and "aesthetic values," these magazines strenuously dissociated themselves from the down-market world of porn, even if commentators like Vir Sanghvi (1994) did their best to puncture their pretensions: "Obviously, the target reader is the average pervert in [provincial Madhya Pradesh city] Jabalpur." For Sanghvi, moreover, the boom in Indian-language porn signaled a provincial failure to manifest a more cosmopolitan desire: "a whole new class which now possesses video recorders but cannot identify with the blond bomb-shells of Scandinavian blue movies wants plump local girls who moan reas-suringly in Hindi or Marathi."

Several factors were coming together here. The rise of television as the most "mass" of all consumer goods advertising media during the 1980s required the invention of an equally "mass" idiom of commodity desire, one that could connect market segments that had previously been as dis-tant from each other as South Bombay was from small-town India. The coming of more affordable video technology allowed for provocative im-ages to be both produced and consumed in new, much more privatized and localized ways. After decades of frowning on consumer desire as inimi-cal to the interests of a developing economy, marketing was coming in from the cold and being hailed as a key driver of national development. By the same token, starting in the mid-1980s, consumerism started looking like an acceptable social aspiration (Mazzarella 2003).

One of the consequences of all this was that the debate over how to manage the erotics of the new consumerism took on a new urgency. This was not just because there were more of these provocative images around. Rather, the urgency was also a symptom of a public cultural field that, in an entirely new way, brought into uncomfortable proximity the consuming desires of groups that had previously been kept separate. As I have sug-gested in earlier chapters, the figure of the pissing man had long done the work of locating the performative excesses of public affect in the bodies of subaltern others. But with the broad-basing of consumerist desire, the dividing line between incontinent and continent practices of spectator-citizenship became harder and harder to draw.

One important index of this ambiguity was the explosion of debate about the Indian middle class/classes (Baviskar and Ray, eds., 2011; Fer-nandes 2006; Mazzarella 2005a). At one level, to speak of the middle classes was to invoke a generic term for those groups where the highest levels of untapped consumer energy were supposed to reside. At another level, the constant oscillation between singular and plural forms (middle class/mid-dle classes) signaled the uncertainty about whether this field of latent consumer enthusiasm could be imagined as a single, continuous field of aspiration (in which one might hope to move from "lower-middle" to "upper-middle" class consumption habits) or whether the Indian middle classes were in fact groups with wildly divergent needs and tastes (often identified as the "old" versus the "new" middle classes).

The important point is that while these debates touched on many things —political habits, public civility, consumption patterns, and so on—they were in an important sense symptoms of an underlying transformation that could not simply be explained in straightforwardly sociological terms, that is, as new configurations of class, caste, and so on. The key feature of this transformation was the emergence of a consumerist public culture that was, potentially, polymorphously perverse. In other words, the voluptuous language of consumerism—the language of the new advertising, the new television programming, the new cinema, and the new magazines— was in significant part a sensuous language of the body. As such it was, potentially, a language in which even pissing men could be recognized as fluent speakers.

The prospect of such a polymorphously perverse public culture triggered a range of regulatory responses, all of which had in common a desire to parse—and thus to manage—public provocation in new ways. Indian feminists, alarmed at the upsurge in blatantly sexualized images of women in the media, joined hands with the cultural right to produce the Indecent Representation of Women (Prevention) Act of 1986.[9] As its name suggests, the Act attempted to establish a prosecutable standard of "indecency" that would not be weighed down by the conceptual murk and heavy evidentiary burden of obscenity cases. In a critical commentary during discussions of the Bill, Indira Jaising (2006 [1986]) argued that a clearer distinction needed to be made between indecency and obscenity. Laws designed to regulate indecency were, she suggested, aimed at preventing "public nuisance and an affront to [a] civic sense of propriety," whereas obscenity law sought to control "immoral and corrupting" conduct and images. The issue was not just the gravity or degree of the provocation. Jaising's distinction also straddled the external and the intimate aspects of the pissing man qua extimate other; indecency laws, she wrote, should be aimed at protecting citizens from others; obscenity laws were about protecting people from themselves.[10]

Whereas the language of the law was rhetorically oriented toward protecting the vulnerable, the debates of the intelligentsia seemed more preoccupied with protecting a cultivated aesthetic sensibility from the indiscriminate wrath of the regulators. To that end, subaltern sensibilities had, as usual, to be demarcated and rejected. Thus, indigenous porn videos, unlike—presumably—imported erotica, were "tackily produced, leaving little to the imagination" (Sayani 1988). The ethical cost of this desperate distancing maneuver becomes troublingly clear in the following passage, where even unequivocal evidence of real suffering is subsumed into an implacable critique of *aesthetic* failure: "Film extras, local hoods and prostitutes make up the cast. The movies usually have no dialogue, bad lighting, a scratchy soundtrack culled from international disco hits and Indian film songs. The 'stars' look uncomfortable and camera shy. Often they look up—straight at the camera—for directions on what to do next. In *Hindi xxx New*, both women in the cast grimace right through the movie in obvious pain, with tears streaming down their faces" (Chakravarti et al. 1989). One might be tempted to argue here that the paternalist impulse of the law and the aesthetic scorn of the intelligentsia were in practice of a piece; that this cruel politics of distinction was the underlying truth, the actual substance of the courts' ideology of transcendent ethico-aesthetic judgment. As Pierre Bourdieu (1984 [1979]) points out, the politics of social distinction gives "discrimination" a double meaning. We discriminate aesthetically on behalf of all only insofar as we discriminate against the aesthetics of some. Taste is fundamentally predicated on distaste.

One might go further down the Bourdieuan road and point out that aesthetic discrimination naturalizes social inequality in such a way as to displace more difficult ethical questions. All this is true. But it is not enough. The point is not only that a polymorphously perverse public sphere pushes up against the barriers that have previously kept the subalterns out of the cultural capital market and thus triggers a violent ideological reaction, as in the quotation above. As extimate other, the pissing man is just as much within as without; a self-relation as much as a definition of empirical others. To put it simply, as a sociological category, the pissing man is above all a product of what the censors cannot readily acknowledge in themselves.

An intimation of this fact has been at the root of film censorship since the beginning, even though all the while the manifest discourse of the censors has stayed on the level of supposedly empirical subjects—that is, pissing men as actual sociological others—and how to manage them in their own and society's best interests. To revisit the point I made at the end of chapter 3: film censorship is such an important institutional site because it constantly both registers the structural fact of the open edge of mass publicity *and* tries to translate that structural fact into an opposition between continent and incontinent subjects that appears amenable to political solutions.

Why is it that we can be as detailed as we like when it comes to crime, violence etc, but not when it comes to sex? We may be fulsome in our descriptions of other kinds of sensuous satisfactions—aesthetic, bodily—but not of this one. In fact, *anything* other than sex—which, after all, is at the very center of human existence—is fit for civilized conversation. If a demonstration of this singular ban on the most natural, the most necessary and, physically, mentally, and spiritually, the most important activity of human beings is needed, you have only to sit among a group of friends at your favourite club, and instead of saying "I am very thirsty; I should like a long, cool drink of something really nice," say "I feel randy, I would like a really nice fuck."
—G. D. Khosla, *Pornography and Censorship in India*, 1976

A commonly heard liberal plaint: why so much fuss about some sexy images when India has given rise to such richly elaborated representations of the arts of love? When, in 2008, Supreme Court ruled on the obscenity charges against India's most famous painter, M. F. Husain, Justice S. K. Kaul said this:

> We have been called the land of the Kama Sutra. Then why is it that in the land of the Kama Sutra, we shy away from its very name? . . . Way back then, perhaps it would not be wrong to assume that the people led exotic lives dedicated to sensuality in all its forms. It was healthy and artistic. They studied sex, practiced sex, shared techniques with friends, and passed on their secrets to the next generation. All in good spirit. Sexual pleasure was not behind closed doors or a taboo; it was in the air in different forms. There was painting, sculpture, poetry, dance and more. Sex was embraced as an integral part of a full and complete life. It is most unfortunate that India's new "Puritanism" is being carried out in the name of cultural purity and a host of ignorant people are vandalizing art and pushing us towards a pre-renaissance era. (Husain v. Pandey [2008])[11]

This is the most common argument that liberals use in the face of conservative moralist attacks on provocative films and artworks. The argument has been widely reinforced outside India as well, for instance, in the work of performance theorist and Indophile Richard Schechner, who remarks that "until the Mughal conquest and then the English, there was no anti-theatrical prejudice or Puritanism in India. Far from it—the arts, infused with intense sexual pleasure, were often part of the religious experience. India today is less open to the *rasic*[12] mix of art, sensuosity, and feasting than before the advent of the Mughals and the British" (2003b [2001]:343–44).

The notion that there was no antitheatrical prejudice in pre-Islamic India will hardly withstand the available evidence.[13] Nevertheless, the idea of an original Indian sensuousness does important work in the present, both because it can be cited as precedent—for instance, when liberals defended M. F. Husain's decision to paint Saraswati "in the nude" against right-wing claims of obscenity and sacrilege—and because it opens up the possibility that this ancient sensuous Indian self may be recuperated in the future. Starting in the 1990s, this recuperation was supposed to come about through the generalized erotics of consumerist liberalization—if only the censors and the self-styled cultural police would get out of the way.

I was curious to hear a response from the other side, so in December 2003 I put the point to Pramila Nesargi, a Bangalore-based lawyer and BJP politician who made waves in the mid- to late 1990s by leading protests against the 1996 Miss World pageant and films like *Bandit Queen* and *Fire*. Nesargi's retort was blunt: "Sex and sexuality are only for procreation. Not for other things."[14] I persisted: what about the fact that Hindu philosophy describes *kama*[15] as one of the four aims of life and certainly does not restrict the pursuit of kama to reproductive sex? Nesargi was having none of it: "No. I told you, no? It is only for the one purpose. Our Hindu culture, our Indian culture, we look at sex only for that purpose and nothing else." At most, she was willing to concede that the *Kamasutra* was written at a time when people did not have access to more civilized distractions: "No doubt it is one of the recreations that are available. In the olden times, people did not have any entertainment whatsoever. This was the only hope. [Otherwise] what's the difference between humans and animals?"

Liberals, conversely, tend to argue that the ancient celebration of kama is a key component of a genuinely Indian ethos that was repressed by prudish foreign invaders. The precise historical moment at which this repression occurred is debated. Some place it as far back as the Bronze Age and the alleged invasion of Aryans bearing a masculinist cosmology whose fear of the feminine principle continues to inform the sexual objectification of women in current film and advertising. More commonly, though, the idea is that a repressive conception of inherent human sinfulness was imposed on Indians by Islamic and Christian conquerors. Justice G. D. Khosla, in his

Pornography and Censorship in India (1976), argues that the unfortunate effects of this repression were evident by the sixteenth century, when Tulsidas composed his version of the *Ramayana*, the *Ramcharitmanas*: "In retelling the story, Tulsidas omitted all references to Sita's shapely limbs, her resplendent teeth, her inviting mouth and her beautiful twin bosom. There is nothing about Ravana's lustful eyes roving over her entire body, caressing each part, while for greater enjoyment he describes in words what his eyes and his desire see" (Khosla 1976:83).[16]

As a result, Indian cultural production had become not only squeamish but, quite literally, blocked when it came to sex. B. K. Karanjia said, "When you try to drive sex underground it has a worse effect. It's like constipation, you see."[17] Another film writer characterized the perversity of what the Indian censors did to filmmaking: "what happens is that when you have such heavy shackles in place, people are going to find a way around it." Of course, this "way around it" could have been sensitively poetic allegory. But because of the Great Indian Repression "that way to get around it is always sleazier than the main thing in the first place. So [you get] all this suggestive innuendo."

The informal ban on kissing in Indian films (which lasted from the 1940s to its much-fanfared breaching in the 1990s[18]) is often invoked as evidence of how sexual repression will inevitably produce cultural and creative perversion. In the wake of his resignation from the Censor Board, Vijay Anand demanded of a journalist, "Why do you think we have so much vulgarity, songs, dances, pelvic thrusts, bathtub fantasies and dream sequences?" and proceeded to answer his own question: "Because you don't allow a simple kiss" (quoted in Unnithan 2002). Thirty-odd years earlier, the Khosla Committee's report on film censorship in India had been similarly convinced of the connection, observing that

> an embargo has been placed on kissing, but vulgar and distasteful antics of an animal and highly lascivious kind are permitted. . . . We have drawn attention to the importance of regarding the entire question of taste, vulgarity, eroticism and creative experimentation with an adult and balanced mind, free from a stultifying obsession with fake morality. Pornography, eroticism and sex are part of human life. Once this basic fact is accepted, a reasonable attitude towards the whole subject of artistic freedom and obscenity is possible. Undue suppression of sex themes by law has the same effect on the minds of the people as un-

wholesome confinement of filth and dirt in their bodies. (Khosla et al. 1969:122, 137)

Anupam Kher, for his part, reflected that censorship would perhaps no longer be necessary in India once "sex education will be there in the schools, when people will not giggle at the name of a penis or a vagina."[19] But for now, the general public remained repressed and awkward. And filmmakers seemed ill equipped to greet the censors' constraints as a creative challenge. As one account from the time of Vijay Anand's resignation lamented, "in Iran, the straitjacket of the censors has only stimulated creativity, as filmmakers make their points through elliptical metaphors. In China, they situate contemporary issues in earlier centuries. In Latin America, they employ magical realism to tackle political angst. In India, they simply shoot reams of extra footage of sex and violence, which the censors can chop, leaving the rest of the film more or less intact" (Shedde and Wallia 2002). The cure for this lamentable creative constipation—the cultural laxative, as it were—was to show and speak about sex without the perverse detours that repression imposed, what Justice Khosla called getting "decent, rational people to talk about sex in a frank and uninhibited manner" (1976:9). Making sex public in this way would demystify it. Time and time again, interlocutors of a certain age recalled visiting Western cities and going to pornographic theaters only to be astonished at finding them nearly empty.

Pramila Nesargi's claim that in India sex had always been restricted to procreation was on the face of it bewilderingly easy to refute. At the same time, I was also conscious of the limitations of the *Kamasutra* argument even as I was voicing it. Invoking the *Kamasutra*—or the explicitly sexual temple carvings at Khajuraho, Konarak, and elsewhere—as evidence of a genuine Indian worldview is, of course, just as ahistorical and essentializing as the conservative desire to absorb all the dizzying diversity of Indian practice into a Hinduized version of petty bourgeois respectability.[20] The problem for the liberal argument is not just that equally "traditional" counter-examples can easily be found, such as the *Manusmrti*'s infamously barefaced moments of patriarchal misogyny (Olivelle, trans., 2009). More important for the argument I am developing here, it is clearly problematic to assume that fourth- or fifth-century social relations of class, service, learning, and performance—in other words the whole set of circumstances that defined the privileged, leisurely, face-to-face world of the *nagaraka* (man-about-town) to whom Vatsyayana addressed the *Kama Sutra*—could in any straightforward way be applied to the citizen of a twenty-first-century mass democracy.

Two Disavowals: The Front Parlor and the Cosmopolitan Ecumene

The interesting question for my purpose here, then, is not which of these positions on sex in India is historically "true." Clearly, they are both problematic; posed as such, the question is inherently unanswerable. The interesting (and answerable) question, rather, is, what kinds of censorship ideologies do each of these positions support?

The conservative argument for solely reproductive sex tended to go hand in hand with the celebration of the kind of coy patriarchal erotics that found its paradigmatic expression in the blockbuster family melodramas of the 1990s and early 2000s. Films like *Hum Aapke Hain Kaun . . . !* (Sooraj Barjatya, 1994), *Dilwale Dulhaniya Le Jayenge* (Aditya Chopra, 1995), and others were routinely and approvingly invoked by CBFC chairs like Asha Parekh (1998–2001) and Sharmila Tagore (2004–2011), both veteran actresses from the mainstream Hindi cinema, as examples of good clean Indian entertainment. A film like *Bandit Queen* foregrounded the fragility and complexity of moral community across legal and illegal domains (see chapter 3). But these blockbuster melodramas used the extended patriarchal Hindu family as a metaphor for a smoothly functioning, all-incorporating, "Indian" performative dispensation.[21]

The liberal position was less obviously grounded in an idealized model of social relations. It came across as a recipe for liberation, for an escape from artificial and oppressive moralisms. Its lodestar was "taste," and it tended to equate the tasteful with the natural. As one journalist declared, emphatically, "What we are saying is, just do it more *naturally*! Sex is a natural thing! Don't make it look abnormal!" Such a "tasteful," "frank," and "natural" approach to sex claimed neutrally universal validity but was not innocent of a certain administrative ambition. As Sanjay Srivastava remarks, "There is a point, particularly in NGO discourse, where discussions about sexuality become a site pregnant with so many *precise* possibilities of human achievement that it becomes an adjunct of statist positions on 'good citizenship,' which is, more often than not, the flip side of the will to governmentality" (2007:345). And, of course, "doing it naturally" involved its own aesthetic prescriptions. The global reputation of Vatsyayana's *Kamasutra* as a sophisticated discourse on the erotic served as such an excellent model because it signaled the naturalized ardor of an aesthetic investment that was at the same time a claim to social distinction, to a world-class refusal of the provincial vulgarity that permeated mainstream popular culture.

On the conservative side, the metaphor of the patriarchal family helped to produce the impression that mass publicity could be managed through a performative dispensation that simply scaled up the patron/police functions of the domestic patriarch to those of the state. By the same token, conservatives tended to imagine the public sphere on the model of the bourgeois front parlor. When I asked the Shiv Sena's Pramod Navalkar why people should get so upset about, say, female same-sex eroticism in a film when the practice was in any case widespread in real life, he laughed: "It's the bedroom, no? What happens in real life is the bedroom! It cannot be taken into the drawing room."[22] In the process, the open edge of mass publicity was not exactly forgotten—since its dangers were constantly mentioned— but rather transformed from a structural feature of mass publicity to the (correctable) pathology of an insufficiently integrated moral community. On the liberal side, the Great Indian Repression was the obstacle that kept Indian public culture in a state of immaturity, holding it back from a proper reintegration with both its own deep, sensuous traditions and the sophisticated, cosmopolitan ecumene in which those deep traditions had long been prized and acknowledged.

On both sides, the structural openness of mass publicity was disavowed. Both sides advocated what amounted to closed performative dispensations, one in the name of a decent Indian moral community, the other in the name of cosmopolitan good taste. If conservatives tended to imagine the national community on the model of family and the public sphere on the model of the public portion of a domestic space, then liberals, conversely, stressed the absolute importance of separating public reason from domestic sentiment. As Justice Hidayatullah complained in the course of his 1970 Supreme Court judgment on the K. A. Abbas case, neither the legislature nor the executive had done enough to observe this difference when it came to provocative films. Instead, "they have attempted to bring down the public motion picture to the level of home movies" (K. A. Abbas v. Union of India [1970]).

On both sides, the actual impossibility of patron/police unification across the open edge of mass publicity was obscured by constantly invoking "something in the way": for the conservatives, moral decadence, for the liberals, sexual repression. In both cases, colonization could be blamed as the historical event that inaugurated the alienation of Indians from themselves. And in both cases, state censorship was ultimately acknowledged as a kind of temporary fix for a society that had both lost and not yet achieved the cultural self-confidence that would render such external intervention unnecessary. Conservatives typically imagine that inhabitants of a properly moral society will spontaneously regulate themselves. But with a shift from good morality to good aesthetics, this is also the liberal fantasy. As a contributor to an edited volume on obscenity in India declared at the time of the Khosla Committee's comprehensive review of film censorship, "Let the consciousness of the beautiful increase; obscenity will take care of itself" (Achwal 1968:40).

In a sense, the conservative line was more "transparent" than its liberal counterpart. From Bal Thackeray to the BJP, the cultural right quite openly used the key metaphor of family to push a prescriptively moral community qua unified performative dispensation. The liberal argument, conversely, rested on a would-be transcendent discourse of universal aesthetic judgment (suitably modulated, as necessary, by a residual sensitivity to Indian cultural values). The signal effect of this was to enable liberals to promote an ideological performative dispensation that, in its appeal to the autonomy of aesthetic judgment, pretended not to be one.

From the very early days of film censorship in India, the naked female body has been an anxious fulcrum for debates about aesthetics and morality. When the colonial government moved to appoint the Indian Cinematograph Committee in 1927, Home Member J. Crerar remarked of the cinema, "We have to deal with what is not only a great force but what may be a great art."[23] Then as now, variously disrobed female bodies were key exhibits in the moralizing prosecution's case against the cinema. Then as now, when translated into the high-art idiom of "the nude," they also underpinned the attempt to redeem the medium according to an established aesthetic ideal. During the ICC's inquiries across India in 1927–28, committee members often suggested to respondents that an unashamed contemplation of nudity was a historical hallmark of European aesthetic maturity. The question raised by the flow of frequently racy Western films into India, then, was whether such a standard should be considered a universally valid goal of the colonial civilizing mission or whether it should be set aside out of respect for specifically Indian standards of modesty.

One or two of the ICC's Indian respondents advocated aesthetic autonomy for Indian filmmakers, so that they could "be quite free to give the fullest latitude to their artistic sense and sense of propriety consistent with the pictures they are depicting, to include such scenes as they see fit" (ICC 1928a, 1:226). In the charged political climate of the times, such a call for aesthetic self-determination was, of course, quite readily legible as a way of talking about the kind of swaraj that implied political independence. Just as the British tended to suspect that apparently "traditional" performances contained seditious allusions (see chapter 1), so the ideal of aesthetic sublimation was always open to suspicion as regards the subversive content that might be smuggled in "under the cloak of art" (ICC 1928a, 1:238). And just as in the early days of the cinema in Europe and the United States, its mass appeal meant that the ideology of aesthetic autonomy could not long float free of more pragmatic concerns with cultural regulation and pedagogy.

The discourse of Indian nationalism, nurtured during the closing decades of colonial rule, had done its best to bridge the gap between constructs that the British had largely tried to separate: on the one hand, a universal standard of aesthetics; on the other, figures of Indian particularity. By the mid-1960s, however, Nehru was dead, the initial euphoria of Independence had waned, and the political field was crowded with the clamor of competing performative dispensations. The distinction between universal aesthetic value and Indian particularity reasserted itself, but now as a domesticated opposition *within* Indian censorship debates.[24] It was this opposition that, having smoldered for decades, flared up again in the 1990s as liberalization and globalization provoked a new round of claims to regulatory authority. In the polarized ideological climate of the cultural emergency, it was all too easy to take the struggle at face value as a contest between conservative reaction and progressive liberalism.

My point is not simply that both the conservative and the liberal arguments were "really" attempts to impose normative constraints on the movement and consumption of mass-mediated image-objects. While it is important to trace the ideological implications of these discourses, it would be a mistake to assume that all that was really at issue was a contest for hegemony. I might draw a parallel here back to my argument about the extimacy of the pissing man. On one level, it is correct to say that the figure of the pissing man enables a discourse of distinction that helps elites to police subalterns. But the pissing man is at the same time also the projection onto a sociological other of an uncanny emergent potential that is sensed as internal (and intolerable) to the continent censor-subject. Similarly, the liberal and conservative arguments about how to engage with mass-mediated sex

are not only irreconcilable ideological discourses belonging to distinct social groups. Taken together, they are also the bifurcated projection onto
plausible social groups—liberals and conservatives—of an uncanny and un-
divided potential that seems to emerge from the mass-mediated image-
object. I expand on this point in chapter 5, but the important point to keep
in mind for now is that what at one level appear as irreconcilable understandings of the power and/or danger of images are at another level attempts to "fix"—in terms of recognizably liberal and conservative social
ideologies—an emergent quality in these images that is by definition dynamic and mobile.

OBSCENITY AND ITS INSULATIONS

The conservative/liberal opposition was, then, at one level a way of index-
ing different imagined performative dispensations, one grounded in a figure of moral community modeled on the patriarchal family, the other
based on a quasi-transcendent standard of aesthetic judgment. But when it
came to judging obscenity, the conservative/liberal opposition also lined
up with two different ontologies of the provocative image-object. In chapter 2, I made a distinction between the "force" and the "meaning" of the
cinematic image-object and showed how the struggle over *Bandit Queen*
involved a constant oscillation back and forth between these categories.
This same opposition recurs in obscenity cases, where it becomes a debate
over whether image-objects may be considered inherently obscene or
whether obscenity must be understood as a function of context.

The 1932 judgment against a book called the *Ramsdar Atmakatha* is a
good example of the inherentist line. The book purported to be the life
narrative of one Ramesdada, complete with detailed descriptions of his
sexual adventures. The publisher, Kailash Chandra, was charged and con-
victed under, inter alia, Section 292 of the Indian Penal Code—the obscenity section.[25] In his judgment, Justice Jack called the book "manifestly
obscene" and Justice Mitter added that "the object which the writer has in
view is really immaterial. If the publication is an obscene publication it
would be no defense to say that the law was broken for some wholesome
and salutary purpose" (Kailash Chandra v. Emperor [1932]).[26] According
to this way of thinking, then, *Ramsdar Atmakatha* was inherently obscene,
irrespective of any redeeming circumstances or intentions.

The contextualist understanding of obscenity, by contrast, holds that a

graphic depiction of sex might be justifiable vis-à-vis some morally laud-
able social purpose. Former Supreme Court justice V. R. Krishna Iyer put
the dilemma in characteristically vivid terms: "Should the writing be viewed
as a whole so that its thrust may be better evaluated or should the court
merely pick out isolated passages where obscenity oozes?" (2006 [1988]:40).
As in so much that touches on the cinema, the screen kiss has been an
important fulcrum of this debate. Precisely the de facto rather than the de
jure status of the ban on kissing has made screen kissing the paradigm of the
manifestly obscene image-object. For this reason, the prohibition has also
been a favorite target of liberal reformers. The Khosla Report argued, for
example, that "there is no justification for banning a kiss between members
of the opposite sexes or even the nude human form, if such a scene or shot is
strictly relevant to the story and is displayed in good taste, in a sensitive
artistic manner, without unduly emphasizing the erotic aspect" (Khosla et
al. 1969:93).

Broadly speaking, in U.S. and UK jurisprudence there was a mid-
twentieth-century shift from inherentist to contextualist understandings of
obscenity. But in India, frequent liberal attempts to effect a similar transition have not quite succeeded. There has been a great deal of judicial hand-
wringing, particularly at the level of the Supreme Court, over when and how
the law might intervene in the sphere of art because, as Justice Krishna Iyer
opined, "State made strait-jacket is an inhibitive prescription for a free
country unless enlightened society actively participates in the administration of justice to aesthetics." Justice Krishna Iyer, in particular, pushed beyond the conventional liberal anxiety about "law's manacles on aesthetics"
to resist the Puritan fanaticism of "prudes and prigs and State moralists":
"Social scientists and spiritual scientists will broadly agree that man lives
not alone by mystic squints, ascetic chants and austere abnegation but by
luscious love of Beauty, sensuous joy of companionship and moderate non-
denial of normal demands of the flesh." Such a well-tempered life of the
senses was all the more appropriate in India given its "lustrous heritage,"
comprising "the world's greatest paintings, sculptures, songs and dances . . .
the Konaraks and Khajurahos, lofty epics, luscious in patches" (Raj Kapoor
v. State [1979]).[27]

And yet the apparently liminal character of Indian modernity, stuck between defunct tradition and delayed development, seemed to keep thwart-
ing the liberal imperative. Consider the differing fates of D. H. Lawrence's
novel *Lady Chatterley's Lover* (1928) in the UK and in India.[28] In what

amounted to a test case of the more contextualist standards of the new Obscene Publications Act, British courts absolved the novel of obscenity in 1960. Many Indian jurists hailed the judgment as a model to be followed on the subcontinent. Nevertheless, in 1964 Supreme Court Justice Hidayatullah, an exceptionally articulate and erudite man and by no means a cultural reactionary, ruled against *Lady Chatterley's Lover* by weighing a contextualist understanding of obscenity against the persistent latent menace of the inescapably and inherently obscene Thing. As Justice Hidayatullah put it in his judgment, "An overall view of the obscene matter in the setting of the whole work would of course be necessary but the obscene matter must be considered by itself and separately to find out whether it is so gross and its obscenity is so decided that it is likely to deprave and corrupt those whose minds are open to influences of this sort."

In the event, it was a special circumstance arising out of India's supposedly incomplete modernity that tipped the scales in this case. Justice Hidayatullah wanted to protect the emergent Indian-language literatures from the temptation of relying on cheap sensationalism rather than literary integrity to achieve visibility: "Emulation by our writers of an obscene book under the aegis of this Court's determination is likely to pervert our entire literature because obscenity pays and true art finds little popular support" (Ranjit D. Udeshi v. State of Maharashtra [1964]).[29] A version of the enunciator's exception, then; "*Lady Chatterley's Lover* might not be obscene for People Like Us, but . . ." As the Indian *Chatterley* case suggests, the adjudication of obscenity is not only a formal matter of balancing inherent risk against contextual justification. Both inherent risk and contextual justification are also imagined in relation to the in-between/not-yet status of Indian modernity.

Tellingly, Section 292 of the Indian Penal Code proposes two kinds of insulations against the threat of obscenity: modern and traditional. On the one hand, the statute offers wide-ranging liberal caveats framed in terms of the progressive interests of a modern society. Passages inserted in 1969 formally stipulate what had occasionally been admitted in practice even during the late colonial period: that an exemption from charges of obscenity may be granted to an object "(i) the publication of which is proved to be justified as being for the public good on the ground that such book, pamphlet, paper, writing, drawing, painting, representation or figure is in the interest of science, literature, art or learning or objects of general concern." So, for instance, "Intimate illustrations and photographs, though in a sense immodest," are not obscene in the context of a medical textbook, "but the same illustrations and photographs collected in a book without the medical text would certainly be considered to be obscene" (M. F. Husain v. R. K. Pandey [2008]). Potentially obscene language may be justified in a work of fiction if, in the name of realism, the sociocultural context of the characters demands that they speak that way (e.g., *Samaresh Bose v. Amal Mitra* [1985]). Or a sociological study of prostitutes might, in the interests of empirical accuracy, require that the crude language of their professional context be realistically rendered (Promilla Kapur v. Yash Pal Bhasin [1989]).

On the other hand, Section 292 also effectively preserves the old British colonial policy of noninterference in native custom (see chapter 1), which nowadays absolves any object "(ii) which is kept or used *bona fide* for religious purposes." This safeguarding of tradition takes both secular and sacred forms. The 1969 addition specifies that the charge of obscenity will not apply to "any representation sculptured, engraved, painted or otherwise represented on or in (i) any ancient monument within the meaning of the Ancient Monuments and Archaeological Sites and Remains Act, 1958 (24 of 1958), or (ii) any temple, or on any car used for the conveyance of idols, or kept or used for any religious purpose" (Law Publishers [India] 2003:143). By the terms of Section 292, then, a *shivling*, no matter how manifestly phallic, is protected from any accusation of obscenity if it is "kept or used *bona fide* for religious purposes." The erotic temple carvings of Konarak or Khajuraho, for example, are thus doubly protected as both religious and heritage objects.[30]

Things get more ambiguous when we shift our attention from objects or images to people and their movements. Insofar as they are holy men, naked *sadhus* (renouncers) may not, for instance, be prosecutable under the Penal Code's obscenity provisions. But their appearances in public spaces can still be regulated by the "secular" indecent exposure clauses of municipal police acts. Trickier still are those popular performance idioms that often contain bawdy or risqué elements but which also, whatever their adaptations to contemporary contexts, have some claim to being categorized as "traditional" vis-à-vis regional cultural practice. A passage from Hari Singh Gour's commentary on Section 294 of the Penal Code—the section that deals with "obscene acts and songs"—splendidly illustrates the confusion that tends to arise when the definitional ambition of a legalistic discourse confronts obscenity as a performatively emergent phenomenon. The passage begins by asserting obscenity as a manifest property of the thing-in-itself: "As regards obscene songs, everything depends upon the songs themselves. A love song is not necessarily obscene unless it suggests coarse and indecent associations." But the commentary then immediately slips outward, as it were, into the space of social context: "A *lavni*[31] is not necessarily an obscene song. It may be, and often is, obscene. But, on the other hand, far from being obscene, it is also considered almost sacred by the Maratha people. So a *ghazal* signifies nothing. It may be sacred or profane. If the latter, it may be a mere love song or it may savour of obscenity." The passage concludes with an attempted return to the relative safety of manifest obscenity: "The question is a question of fact and it is for the prosecution to prove what the song was and what is signified" (Singh Gour 2005:910).

In practice, the knotty part of Section 294 has not so much been the question of whether a performance or action has been inherently obscene but rather whether it can reasonably be said to have taken place in a "public place" and caused "annoyance" to others (Mazzarella 2013). But Hari Singh Gour's commentary does manifest the sense that while "tradition" is supposed to insulate a person from the corroding and corrupting force of obscenity, this insulation is very fragile and unreliable. If the very same object may, depending on context, be either a "mere love song" or "savor of obscenity," if it may from one standpoint be sacred but from another profane, then what is it that determines the difference? Why did Justice Hidayatullah, in his 1970 judgment on filmmaker and writer K. A. Abbas's constitutional challenge to film censorship, remark that "we may view a documentary on the erotic tableaux from our ancient temples with equanimity or read the *Kamasutra*, but a documentary from them as a practical sexual guide would be abhorrent" (K. A. Abbas v. Union of India [1970], para. 52)?

"CHOLI KE PEECHE": FROM INSULATION TO THREAT

A return to one of the most widely publicized early skirmishes of the cultural emergency may help to clarify these questions. I begin from the assumption that we need to move beyond explanations that rely either on a formal analysis of the properties of the object itself—for example, whether obscene elements overwhelm an otherwise reasonable purpose—or on the intentions of the author or maker of the object.

As is common Bollywood practice, the songs from Subhash Ghai's

Khalnayak were released ahead of the completion of the film itself in 1993. One of them, "Choli ke Peeche" (the main line in the chorus translates as "What's behind the blouse?"), triggered something of a public uproar after a BJP-affiliated lawyer by the name of R. P. Chugh filed an obscenity case against it in a Delhi court. The legal case itself was dismissed after Chugh failed to turn up on the appointed day. Film business insiders speculated that Chugh had in any case only been angling for the kind of settlement money that Bollywood producers often shell out to avoid the hassle and delay of going to court. But the ensuing debate remains significant for the purposes of my argument. Others (for example, Mehta 2001b) have focused on the sexual and gender politics of the controversy. I would, however, like to reexamine the "Choli ke Peeche" fracas in the light of the ambiguous/treacherous status of "tradition" as an insulation against/alibi for obscenity.

Ganga (played by Madhuri Dixit) is a policewoman who is attempting to trick the villain, Ballu (Sanjay Dutt), into letting her join his gang, the better to bring him to justice. In order to seduce him, she disguises herself as a highly sexualized village belle and treats him and his lecherous gang to a performance of "Choli ke Peeche," voiced on the soundtrack in a husky, rustic manner by Ila Arun with Alka Yagnik. As Monika Mehta points out, the way the sequence is edited achieves a typical Bollywood effect: the audience is allowed to see through the lustful eyes of the villain while at the same time being aware, as the villain is not yet, that the whole performance is a trap (see Kasbekar 2001; Mazumdar 2007). Lyrically and visually, much is made of the ambiguity of what lies behind the blouse: the sacred heart and the profane breasts. Conservatives complained that the song was obscene and derogatory to women and that young men had started "eve-teasing" women with it on street corners all over the country. Liberals rolled their eyes at the coyly repressed circumlocution that Bollywood seemed to require to refer to a pair of breasts even as the camerawork exemplified the worst kind of lecherous looking.

Some of the song's defenders argued that "Choli ke Peeche" should not be considered obscene since it was fundamentally no different from the kind of songs that would commonly be sung during festivals like Holi or as part of the flirtatious tradition of wedding *sangeet*. As a female writer and media personality put it to me: "I find 'Choli ke Peeche' raunchy and delightful. I just think it's a tease, you know? As a tradition, a lot of the time it was actually a substitute for sex education. Even some of the marriage games were a very, very vital part of initiating the young girl. The songs, the teasing, the *sangeet*. It was all about preparing her for the nuptial night. Seen in that context it's all fine. There has always been a tradition of bawdy humour. Always, always."

But of course "Choli ke Peeche" was, after all, a song performed not in the face-to-face context of a village festival or a wedding but rather on a million cassette decks and thousands of screens all over the country. The interesting problem, then, was not so much whether the *content* of "Choli ke Peeche" could reasonably be compared with "traditional" or "folk" rituals. Rather, the question was to what extent the insulating function of face-to-face performance within a "folk" context—the moral authority of a localized performative dispensation—could survive the translation into the space of mass publicity.

The same writer who called "Choli ke Peeche" "raunchy and delightful" and linked its flirtation to traditions of bawdy teasing also acknowledged that "there is an anxiety about the cinema. The same kind of song or something even more up-front, within the community, it's fine—there's a certain intimacy and therefore an insulation. But the minute you see it on the large screen it becomes . . . threatening." In other words, it was a question of medium specificity: there was something about the cinema— "the minute you see it on the large screen"—that unbalanced the "intimacy" and "insulation" that kept the performance safe "within the community." Obscenity hovered, then, at the open edge of mass publicity, at the place where a "traditional" performative dispensation was no longer able to create the ideological appearance of a stable relation between performative intensity and symbolic order.

A male Hindi film actor who had served his apprenticeship on the Delhi stage noted, "If this 'Choli ke Peeche' *gana* [song] would have been in the [urban] theater nobody would have even asked 'what is it?' and people would have clapped and said *ki*, 'wow! What a song! Very nicely said—what is behind the choli is my heart! That's amazing!'" Whereas the writer imagined a face-to-face community insulated by tradition, the actor assumed that a theater audience would come to such a play insulated by an educated, reflexive relation to "folk form": "I think when we talk about this, when I talk about it, I've been exposed to theater. So I can justify it in terms of folk form. But how many people around us know about folk forms or anything? They're not in touch with folk forms of art. Even if they see *Casanova*, for example, for a normal man it'll be a porn film. He might think that it's a porn film. It's a *boring* porn film, but it's a porn film. Because after every ten minutes there is a sexual scene."

Echoing the logic of Section 292, then, the writer and the actor articulated the two modes by which one may be protected from the threat of obscenity: by the naïve insulation of tradition or by the reflexive insulation of education. Between these lies the ignorant, volatile space of the cinema's mass public: uprooted from tradition ("they're not in touch with folk forms of art") and yet still not properly educated. ("He might think it's a porn film . . . because after every ten minutes there is a sexual scene.")

The coming of mass publicity and the corollary need for censorship is, as I suggested at the beginning of chapter 2, often imagined as a kind of historical no-man's-land, a paradoxically exceptional *and* near-universal condition of being in-between, neither here nor there; in short, the barren habitat of the pissing man. The open edge of mass publicity is shadowed by a newly rigid intolerance—a self-conscious and censorious bourgeois moralism that presents itself as a transcendent standard of decency. Many of my informants who were critical of the moralistic rigidities of the censors nevertheless also implied, in an optimistically liberal way, that with better education and more development, the majority of Indians could eventually attain that state of modern maturity that would obviate the need for this kind of censorship. For them, the decline of "traditional" idioms of performance and poetry was regrettable but inevitable. What remained of, say, the tamasha "folk" theater tradition was in any case so culturally corrupted and watered down that it might as well be put out of its misery.

But others inhabited a more complex relation to past traditions. They were not so much mourning the loss of some putative cultural purity as lamenting the intolerant violence with which bourgeois moralism had insisted on separating piety from any degree of performative irreverence. A well-known Bombay novelist told me that what angered and saddened him most was the loss of "the capacity to address God as in bhakti [devotional] poetry. You know, you tell God, 'Hey, piss off, man! Where were you all this time??' They won't say 'you were fucking around,' but they'll say 'I know what you were doing.' Now this kind of easy rapport is something that we've really lost. It's not just the robustness only in sexual matters. It's just a whole range of robustness, and there's a rigour there. We have been ashamed of it for some time."

The structure of this peculiarly modern shame contains at least two strands. The first is the familiar embarrassment of the strenuously modernizing subject confronted with the earthy indelicacies of their own rustic past. But alongside this diachronic, "developmentalist" dimension of the extimate squirm we might also recognize a synchronic effect of the open edge of mass publicity. Being addressed as a member of a mass public means being interpellated as at once "oneself" but also at the same time—this is the open edge at work—a generalizable member of what is in principle the infinite, anonymous space of the "public at large" (Warner 2002).

This shame is also the intimate counterpart of the embarrassment felt by Sunhil Sippy in chapter 2 when he saw the people who would examine *Snip!* for the first time. Sippy's heart sank as the anonymously hip cosmopolitan ecumene toward which the film was oriented suddenly revealed an uncomfortably familiar, petty bourgeois face. The shame of which the novelist was speaking arose from the same place, seen from the other side: an old, familiar idiom that has lost its context and now shrinks self-consciously from an anonymous gaze. It is not that one story is about thwarted cosmopolitanism and the other about nostalgic traditionalism. Rather, both stories tell of coming face to face with the product of a torn performative dispensation: that brittle bourgeois moralism whose rigid certainty attempts to compensate for its lack of living foundations. From the standpoint of those performative dispensations that attempt to reinstate Indra's banner staff in an age of mass publics, the constant provocation of the open edge feels like shame, like the place where obscenity lurks.

One may mourn the lost coexistence of irreverence and piety, then, and lament the prudery that has replaced it in the name of public decency. But perhaps one must also accept that if that kind of "easy rapport" once existed, then it was also predicated on moral communities that were imagined as finite and knowable, even if in practice they were not. This is, one might say, the crisis that "modernity" involves all over the world: the coming of mass publicity requires reimagining the intimacies of community on the basis of anonymity, a challenge that, as we have seen throughout this book, routinely collapses back into attempts to assert moral sovereignty either from a position of fictive kinship, such as the nation as family, the ethnos as consanguine, or on the basis of apparently impersonal transcendent principles, such as secular reason and natural aesthetics.

"Madhuri Dixit" and "Michael Jackson" in Manipur

Cultural critic and dramaturge Rustom Bharucha gives us an interesting vignette. The scene is the annual performance of the Lai Haraoba festival in Imphal, the state capital of Manipur, in the extreme northeast of India. The time, I presume, is the mid-1990s. The "religious" ritual observances of the festival temporarily make way for what Bharucha calls a "secular" entertainment segment, a kind of variety or talent show.

Bharucha describes two performers. The first is a young girl who appears not in the locally auspicious guise of the Vaishnavite saint Chaitanya Mahaprabhu but rather in the Bollywood-gypsy garb of Madhuri Dixit as Ganga in *Khalnayak*. A spirited rendition of "Choli ke Peeche" ensues. Bharucha's comment at this stage of the telling is at once laconic and judgmental: "The number goes down well, and there are no problems whatsoever with its sexist content" (2001:171).

By contrast, the next performer is a young man in jeans and T-shirt: "He bows formally, and then, to a deafening blast of Michael Jackson's 'Beat It,' he begins to dance with a vigorous, uninhibited, secular assertion of energy that is not just sexual, but driven by anger and defiance. The underlying self-affirmation of the young man's dance is perceptible, and the crowd is with him." Not only does this young "Manipuri 'Michael Jackson'" bring down the house; he also quickly brings down the wrath of the local censors—that is to say, the male elders who have organized the festival. They "interrupt the performance in a flurry of white dhotis. They are like fussy old hens, clucking with disapproval." For a moment it looks as if the crowd's enthusiasm might win, but the music is soon switched off once and for all, and the young man is sent off the stage: "And this time there can be no negotiation as the organizers stop the show with formal announcements on the microphone. The secular items are abandoned, and the spectators disperse, revealing an empty site" (Bharucha 2001:171).

Bharucha remarks: "Why the prepubescent impersonation of Dixit should escape censorship while the Manipuri 'Michael Jackson' is interrupted, could reveal deeply complicated layers of sexual hypocrisy in the transmission of Indian popular culture, where obscenity can pass as family entertainment" (2001:172). The suggestion is left hanging, since Bharucha is more interested in pursuing a polemical intervention into globalization theory than in "prob[ing] these particular layers" (2001:172). And yet Bharucha's underlying assumptions are clear. (His reference to the "sexist content" of "Choli ke Peeche" already orients us.) Rightly unwilling to romanticize the young boy's dance—for all its visceral power—as "resistance,"[32] Bharucha nevertheless uses the contrast between these two performances to make a point about "the patriarchy in traditional social structures" (2001:177), a patriarchy presumably manifested in the elders' approval of the coy, flirtatious sexuality of the local "Madhuri Dixit" versus the aggressively assertive "foreign" sexuality of "Michael Jackson."

But what should we make of the approval that greeted this Manipuri "Choli ke Peeche" when Madhuri Dixit's screen version stirred up so much trouble in a more urbane public sphere? Was it just that the idiom of the song was familiar to an audience that, because it was closer to "traditional" modes of cultural production, saw it as safe? If so, what about the fact that the spectators in Imphal were certainly enjoying the performance not only as a "first order" enactment of locally intelligible tradition but also as a quotation of a well-known Bollywood song sequence? Perhaps the festival organizers liked the precocious "Madhuri Dixit" not only because of their "patriarchy" and their "sexism," but also because of the carefully calibrated way in which her performance half-domesticated the glamorous frisson of Bombay cinema within a symbolic order that could plausibly be claimed as "traditional" in that particular social context? As such, this "Choli ke Peeche" supplied a "charge" that redounded to the greater glory of the ritual over which the elders presided and, as such, to the performative dispensation that enabled the reproduction of their authority. Through the mediation of this young woman's performance, the open edge of mass publicity could, for a moment, for some, be imagined as closed.

And what of "Michael Jackson"? Why did "Michael Jackson" transgress the boundaries of the Lai Haraoba when (the real) Michael Jackson could, in 1996, be smoothly absorbed into Bal Thackeray's (no less patriarchal, no less sexist) performative dispensation (chapter 1)? Bharucha sees the apparently smooth intersection of Thackeray and Jackson as all the more "chilling" because it is *not*—in Arjun Appadurai's terms—culturally disjunctive, but, rather, evidence of "the most uncanny flow, the 'natural' collusion . . . of the most consummate agencies of communalism and globalization" (2001:177). In other words, just as Bharucha wants to read the Manipuri elders' comfort with "Choli ke Peeche" as an expression of the underlying patriarchy and sexism of self-styled traditional authority, so he wants to use the Thackeray/Jackson clinch as evidence of an underlying complicity between hyperconservative nationalism and global capitalism.

To be sure, there are plenty of reasons to suppose that the Manipuri elders' authority rests on patriarchal and sexist assumptions. Likewise, there is plenty of evidence of the Hindu right's proximity to corporate capital. But I want to argue that what makes these events—the Lai Haraoba, Michael Jackson at Bal Thackeray's house—so interesting is their open-ended performative ambiguity. These are not just open-and-shut cases of a general pathology that we always already understand. They are also wagers on the uncertain sovereign yield that may be available at the intersection of performative provocation and symbolic order. These are the places where performative dispensations encounter the open edge. These are the places where, in order to succeed (since their success, such as it may be, depends on closing something that is by definition open), they must also fail.

CONCLUSION

The head of a creative advertising shop in Mumbai told me that "censorship is self-defeating. Because the more you hide the breast the more you increase its value, OK? And therefore you increase its attention-getting power. And therefore, the more you encourage someone to somehow or other subversively try to sneak it through. Because he knows that by virtue of censorship, by hiding it from me, you have created an unnatural value in the breast. Which is ultimately just a feeding object." A breast is just a feeding object? Says an ad man? Faced with my ill-disguised incredulity, my interlocutor backed down, saying he was only exaggerating to make a point. It was a familiar one: that censorship undermines itself by foregrounding what it wants to efface. The Big No of censorship slips over into the Big Yes of heightened publicity.

But the extreme disenchantment of his example also points to the limits of the liberal invocation of the transcendent standard of nature ("Sex is a natural thing! Don't make it look abnormal!") against its perennial enemy: the coyly lecherous detours of a repressed imagination. If the liberal aesthetic judgment is ultimately supposed to be a natural faculty, then the paradox is that the breast that it tries to rescue from the perverts turns out to have no aesthetic value left at all. At the limit, this is the price of keeping the extimate pissing man at bay, of maintaining the fiction of his otherness: a total desensualization in the name of good taste. "Choli ke peeche kya hai? Kuch nahin" (What's behind the blouse? Nothing at all).

So yes, my ad man interlocutor was giving me an extreme example. But the times were extreme. In the public culture of these years, the boundaries that used to distinguish continent from incontinent consumer-subjects was breaking down, giving rise to all the intensified assertions of aesthetic distinction and moral authority that I have discussed. The extimate squirm that runs through the studio audience at the beginning of this chapter is a corporeal index (Povinelli 2000) of this breakdown. It is the moment when the complacently authoritative distancing habit of speaking about the pissing man in the third person ("that is what the common man hears") suddenly derails and becomes a shockingly intimate first-person reflex.

In Freudian terms, this queasy slide from a third-person discourse to a first-person squirm replays the foundational trauma to which the whole censorship apparatus is a reaction formation. This is the basis of all the discourses that separate the censor-subject from the pissing man, the insulation of tradition from that of modern science. It is the starting point for everything that translates the emergent affective potential at the open edge of mass publicity into a sociological opposition between (judiciously cool) elites and (helplessly hot) subalterns.

This trauma is, of course, not foundational in a literally temporal sense; it is not as if there was once a "first encounter" between the spectator-subject of mass publicity and its open edge. Rather, it is foundational in an ongoing structural sense; it is the potential/obstacle that is constantly sensed at the edge of every performative dispensation that tries to lay sovereign claim to mass publics. It is the "something in the way" that both prevents that sovereign claim from closing its symbolic circle and keeps its fascination alive.

Just now I described censorship as a reaction formation. And indeed, so far this book has largely explored censorship as a series of defensive moves vis-à-vis the potentials that are projected onto crowds as a way of dealing with the structural challenge of the open edge of mass publicity. But it would be a mistake to think that censorship is simply a reactionary discourse. In fact, it is precisely in its most reactionary moments that it reveals a radical tendency in mass publicity. That is the subject of the next and final chapter.

CHAPTER 5

OBSCENE TENDENCIES

CENSORSHIP AND THE PUBLIC PUNCTUM

An outline of the story so far: In chapter 1, I argued that the open edge of mass publicity generates a constant anxiety about whether the emergent potential ascribed to mass-mediated image-objects may be harnessed to performative dispensations in which patron and police functions are tightly integrated. The discourse of modern censorship presupposes that there was once a time when such performative dispensations really operated, when censorship was unnecessary, when rules were unspoken, when people did not have to be told because they already knew. I began chapter 2 with the observation that censorship figures the present as an exceptional in-between time, a time of disorder between defunct tradition and deferred development. The censors' present is a time of forces threateningly unmoored from meaning. They do their best to stitch these free-floating forces back into what is sometimes called "the social fabric." The pissing man is blamed for the holes that keep appearing in this fabric. He is endlessly adaptable, offering himself as a scapegoat for modern-day Indras of all persuasions. Most important, he can be relied on to keep the ideological loop of censorship going and has served faithfully in this capacity across the colonial and post-colonial periods. In chapters 3 and 4, I showed how the figure of the pissing man qua the "something in the way" of a unified performative dispensation helps to project the uncannily extimate self-relation that we all inhabit as members of mass publics onto a more conveniently manageable quasi-sociological distinction between continent spectator-citizens and incontinent pissing men. The extimate tenderness that secretly but all too palpably links the volatile pissing man to the imperturbable censor, that links state law to the outlaw, is masked by the appearance of an unbridgeable parallax gap.

This, then, is how censorship generates a scenario that is, notably, smaller than the sum of its parts: twinned subjects, the pissing man and the censor, locked in an intimately implacable struggle over something that always seems to be escaping them. But what of the objects of censorship? In chapter 4, I suggested that "obscenity" is one of the switching points where performative dispensations sort useful from dangerous provocations through a series of insulating mediations. But my description of quotidian eruptions also intimated that while obscenity often seems self-evident, it can, during times of transition, also serve as a ready-to-hand analogy for a more comprehensive, less comprehensible sense of what happens when the meaning and purpose of the most everyday objects and situations are destabilized.

The central argument of this final chapter is that understanding obscenity as a *tendency* of image-objects opens up a useful way of thinking about mass publicity in general, far beyond what we would conventionally recognize as obscene materials. As such, obscenity appears here, like the pissing man, as "something in the way" of the fantasy of a fully functional performative dispensation, although this time on the side of the object. And yet unlike the pissing man, obscenity is not just an obstacle but also, I will suggest, a usefully provisional name for the amorally generative potential that lies at the open edge of mass publicity.

MECHANIZED MORALITY

Here is one of the censors' recurrent fantasies: a form of censorship that is so foolproof that it could function automatically, a mechanism that would never get snarled up in the thorny thickets of human judgment. The machine would always already have a set of unambiguous rules that would apply to every situation. It would, in effect, mechanize morality.

This fantasy found its perfect expression in a proposal submitted in

2001 to the CBFC by one G. D. Jasuja, the self-styled Ahmedabad-based chairperson of something called the Film Censorship Guidance Bureau. Motivated by the larger aim of "preserving the rich heritage of the fast-depleting Indian culture" and painfully aware of the regularity with which filmmakers breached both the letter and spirit of the CBFC's guidelines, Jasuja suggested that filmmakers could be directly incentivized to make wholesome films by means of a simple system of fines. For example, the CBFC might charge producers Rs 1,000/second for fight sequences (Rs 2,500 if the combatants were armed). A gunshot would cost Rs 5,000, and every appearance of hand grenades Rs 10,000. In a telling equivalence, the maximum fine—Rs 100,000 (then about $2,100)—was reserved for the depiction of murder or for any scene in which "the hero's lips touch the heroine's body or vice versa" (Mishra 2001).

Such a solution might well have found its takers at CBFC headquarters in the well-heeled neighborhood of Walkeshwar near Malabar Hill in Mumbai. And, in fact, it may be that some filmmakers would have preferred it, too. Indeed, if directors often emerge from their dealings with the censors feeling "sick," "ashamed," "dirty," "exhausted," and so on, then it is not because the Censor Board operates like an implacable agency of seamless surveillance, but rather because its workings are at once so personalized and so unpredictable. That is, however, as far as most analyses go. Censorship, filmmakers say, is arbitrary and inconsistent because the principles on which it is based are arbitrary and inconsistent. Either one imagines doing away with it altogether or remaking it in a more rational direction.

To be sure, whatever one thinks of censorship in general, the particular forms that it takes often leave a great deal to be desired. But when Justice Muhammad Hidayatullah remarked that "the task of the censor is extremely delicate and his duties cannot be the subject of an exhaustive set of commands established by prior ratiocination" (K. A. Abbas v. Union of India [1970]), perhaps his words deserve to be taken as something more than convenient obfuscation. Perhaps the difficulties of the censor's task are symptoms not only of the inherent perversity of censorship but of potentials and indeterminacies that are, as it were, chronic to mass publics. Nowhere is this more evident than in the legal category of obscenity.

The modern legal understanding of obscenity dates back to the middle of the nineteenth century. It was explicitly a response to the European industrial and democratic revolutions of the late eighteenth and early nineteenth centuries. In particular, it was a response to the emergence of the kind of intimately anonymous mass public that became possible through print capitalism.[1] In British legal history, obscenity was originally a matter for the ecclesiastical authorities. As a *public* offense, it was for a long time imagined in essentially face-to-face terms, as when in 1663 Sir Charles Sedley, politician, playwright, and all-around *bon viveur* caused a commotion by drunkenly exposing himself on the balcony of a Bow Street tavern.[2]

The British Obscene Publications Act of 1857 is often taken as the point where modern obscenity legislation began. But, in fact, the previous year an obscenity statute appeared on the books in India. It prescribed a one-hundred-rupee fine or up to three months in jail for "whoever within the territories in the possession and under the Government of the East India Company, in any shop, bazaar, street, thoroughfare, high-road, or other place of public resort, distributes, sells, or offers, or exposes for sale, or willfully exhibits to public view, any obscene book, paper, print, drawing, painting, or representation; or sings, recites, or utters any obscene song, ballad, or words to the annoyance of others."[3] In fact, as Deana Heath (2010:64) usefully reminds us, events in India directly hastened the passage of the British act the following year. The upper house of the British Parliament had seemed unlikely to pass the bill when it was originally introduced. But the Great Indian Rebellion of 1857–58 hardened the resolve of British legislators to tighten social controls across the board.

The first problem that arose after the passage of the Obscene Publications Act was finding a workable legal definition of obscenity. In the 1868 London case of *Regina v. Hicklin*, a Protestant by the name of Henry Scott was prosecuted under the Act for an anti-Catholic tract he had published titled *The Confessional Unmasked: Shewing the Depravity of the Romanish Priesthood, the Iniquity of the Confessional and the Questions Put to Females in Confession*. Having intended to expose the obscenity of priestly practice, Scott himself got hit with the charge.[4] Lord Chief Justice Cockburn, presiding, determined, "I think the test of obscenity is this: whether the tendency of the matter charged as obscenity is to deprave and corrupt those whose minds are open to such immoral influences, and into whose hands a publication of this sort may fall." Thus was born the so-called Hicklin Test, the standard that is still invoked in Indian obscenity cases today.

Scholars, jurists, and journalists routinely complain that obscenity is an exceedingly vague concept. S. C. Sarkar's exhaustive commentary on the Penal Code remarks, "No arithmetical definition of the word 'obscene' covering all possible cases can be given" (2006:893). The CFBC's certificates are, as we have seen, to some extent supposed to function as a kind of insurance against subsequent harassment of filmmakers (although there is, of course, no formal obstacle in the way of suing a filmmaker under any applicable law after a film has been released).[5] But in the field of print, entrepreneurial publicists have long been frustrated by the imprecision of obscenity as a legal category. In February 1932, for example, the Bombay publisher Manilal Keshavji Shah of Messrs. P. Manilal & Co wrote to the Home Department of the Presidency Government demanding a "true definition" of obscene literature in law. Having consulted three of the ablest lawyers in town, Shah had received three different opinions: one said there was nothing wrong with his book, a Gujarati translation of a marital guide titled *Ideal Marriage*; the second suggested that a few changes might be necessary; while the third "rejected the book as quite obscene and not worth publishing. Supposing the book is brought out in the market the opinions of all these Lawyers would amount to nothing to me." In the event, the Bombay Home Department replied to Shah that the question could only be decided in court on a case-by-case basis under the terms of Section 292 of the Indian Penal Code.[6]

Indira Jaising, additional solicitor general of India, has noted more recently that the concept of obscenity, as enshrined in the Hicklin Test, is "essentially a moral one and incapable of precise definition. . . . For no one has yet been able to define what it is that has a 'tendency to deprave and corrupt'" (2006 [1986]:116, 117). U.S. Supreme Court justice Potter Stewart's 1964 remark regarding hard-core pornography is famous, if not infamous: "I can't define it, but I know it when I see it."[7] It would appear that Indian Supreme Court justice Hidayatullah had something similar in mind when he said in that same year, "The word 'obscenity' is really not vague because it is a word which is well understood, even if persons differ in their attitude to what is obscene and what is not" (Ranjit Udeshi v. State of Maharashtra [1964]).

What kind of knowing or understanding is imagined here? While the legal understanding of obscenity certainly implies a moralizing purpose, the recognition of obscenity often appears to involve something more corporeal, more affective. As Elizabeth Povinelli has observed in a different context, "I know it when I see it" generally means "I know it when I feel it."[8]

YET THERE IT IS

> It will be noticed that the control is both thematic and episodic.
> —Justice Hidayatullah in *K. A. Abbas v. Union of India* (1970)

The problem of obscenity, understood as a structural feature of mass publicity, is the acute expression of a chronic condition. On the side of the subject, censorship discourse operates, as we have seen, with a basic split between incontinent pissing men, mimetically mastered by the commandment of the image, and continently judicious censors, equipped with the kind of imperturbable judgment that allows them to, as it were, put potentials in their proper places. On the side of the object, we have the split between the forceful and the meaningful object, between the image-object imagined as immediately toxic, and the image-object as mediately redeemable. Ostensibly, the category of obscenity conforms to this scheme. An image-object is obscene if it is all force and no meaning, if its intensity cannot be referred to the soothing, moral balm of a higher social purpose. And a viewer-subject is susceptible to obscenity, that is, "corruptible," if he or she lacks the judgment that continence implies.

Now, I am sure that few will object to the observation that there is something oddly artificial about these divisions. Categorizing image-objects as either forceful or meaningful makes little sense, given that communicative force is always relative to a meaningful context and the making of meaning is never separable from the performativity of rhetorical force. And yet perhaps we still need to look a bit harder at the censors' frequent habit of insisting that some image-objects are simply so forceful that meaningful context becomes irrelevant.

But why? Have not even the censors' guidelines been moving away from the crude old inherentist logic? In the bad old days, the censors were given lists of inherently objectionable content that combined categorical vagueness with an appearance of specificity. Search and destroy: "illicit sexual relationships," "nude figures," "offensive vulgarity and impropriety in conduct or dress," "gruesome murders and strangulation scenes," and so on, and so on.[9] Nowadays, the guidelines, as objectionable as the spirit of censorship may remain, have been given a contextualist makeover. The censors are now expected not just to find and chop but to use their judgment concerning crime scenes "likely to incite the commission of any offense," "needless" cruelty, or scenes "tending to encourage, justify, or glamorize" antisocial behavior. If there must be scenes of sexual violence, then they should not exceed the amount that "is relevant to the theme."[10] Censorship seems, in this post-Khosla climate, to have shifted from an "anatomical" to an "aesthetic" approach, to "general principles instead of specific prohibitions. How something is shown rather than what is shown should be the determining factor" (Karanjia 1999).

And yet censorship seems so often to stay stupidly literal. A prominent film producer scoffed: "[The censors] say you can't show a tit, not realizing that you can show a tit to be feeding a child in an extremely touching scene, or you can show a tit as Britney Spears would show a tit." Film scholars, too, complain of the (official and unofficial) censors' lamentable literalism. In a commentary on the debates over Mani Ratnam's *Bombay* (see chapter 4), Ravi Vasudevan writes that

> the suggestion is that the depiction of certain incendiary anti-Muslim rhetoric and actions might inflame passions, presumably of the Muslims rather than of the Hindus. This means that these events are isolated from their treatment within the narrative process. The presumption is that even if a director employs a method which alienates the spectator from such scenes of anti-Muslim aggression, this would nevertheless involve the re-experiencing of the affront with possible political repercussions. (Vasudevan 2010:242)

Is not all this all evidence, after all, that censorship, whatever its occasional interpretive pretensions, is essentially an authoritarian policing practice, committed to the maintenance of social order over all other goals? Yes and no. Yes, censorship is fundamentally a police function. But no, the persistent literalism that seems to hobble all its attempts to get smart and sensitive is not just an index of this fact.

Obviously, meaning is always a function of context, and every image-object has its social and historical contexts. And yet "contextualizing" an image-object does not tell us everything we might want to know about its potential. Establishing its meaning does not quite account for its social force. One need only consider the example of so-called four-letter words or racial slurs to be reminded that representations can pack a visceral punch that is often likened, even in courts of law, to physical violence (Butler 1997; Riley 2005). The question, then, is whether such "excitable speech" occurs only in communication that is widely understood to be extreme, for example, sexually explicit utterances or hate speech. My wager here is that it is not restricted in this way, that the potential for provocation is ever present at the open edge of mass publicity, although—for reasons that I will explore below—its force is most clearly and consciously felt in these overdetermined kinds of talking and showing.

In her excellent ethnography of traveling "special drama" troupes in Tamil Nadu, Susan Seizer describes a performance during which a comical buffoon character gets away with salacious utterances by embedding them in a moralizing context. In effect, the dramatic context both declaws the potentially offending words and gestures and draws attention to their persistent provocation: "The Buffoon has created, in fact, a very special and idiosyncratic context for the potentially vulgar phrase by mentioning it only in a disclaimed usage embedded within a story told as a cautionary tale. Yet there it is" (2005:189). Filmmakers work not with the face-to-face potentialities of the stage but with the distributed, anonymously intimate possibilities of mass publics. But they, too, are aware of this effect, this "yet there it is." Sometimes they succeed in using it against the censors. The same producer who ridiculed the censors' inability to distinguish one tit from another gave me an example of the kind of simple recontextualization that could throw the censors off the scent:

> There's a line in one of my movies which says "all politicians are corrupt." And they wanted it cut out. So we changed the dialogue to have somebody saying, "Yeah, true—but that's the reason why people like me are here. To solve problems." Which is double-edged. One way of looking at it, which is the way we're looking at it, the audience will know he's a pimp. But the Censor Board will think [adopts moronic tone] "Oh that means we are not all corrupt—there are some people who are genuine and working hard to change India!" So you can beat them by being just one step ahead of them. They're a bunch of idiots!

If only it were always so easy. For every triumphant story like this I heard ten complaining about the censors' refusal to be reassured by recontextualization. "Yet there it is" is a game whose possible positions are infinite and constantly in motion.

Let us return to the wording of the Hicklin Test. Lord Cockburn established that the test of obscenity should be "whether the tendency of the matter charged as obscenity is to deprave and corrupt those whose minds are open to such immoral influences, and into whose hands a publication of this sort may fall." What is this *tendency*—a tendency that the Hicklin Test presents as a potential property of the image-object?

Justice Khosla, for one, found this usage exasperatingly vague. He complains in his *Pornography and Censorship in India*: "Anything may have a tendency for almost anything. A lamp-post may be taken as a phallic symbol, a convenient object for canine relief, a source of light, evidence of civilization, something to lean against when waiting for a bus or something to demolish in order to demonstrate a sense of rebellion or discontent. So what is the tendency of a lamp-post?" (1976:122).

From Khosla's standpoint, that of a man attempting to install "taste" as a reliable measure of obscenity, such an open-ended and protean concept was necessarily going to be irritating. And it is precisely because it is irritating to such a project that we should look more carefully at it. I would like to suggest that this little word, *tendency*—at once apparently innocuous and infuriatingly vague—contains a crucial clue to the problem of how to think beyond the antinomies of censorship as I have laid them out in these pages.

To begin with, we need to get beyond the terms of Justice Khosla's objection. The difficulty with speaking of the "tendency of a lamp-post" is not just that a lamppost may mean different things in different contexts.[11] Rather, to speak of the tendency of an image-object means to recognize that it has a virtual dimension—that is to say, potentials that may be registered as emergent forces in a mode of becoming rather than as actualized states of being meaningful.[12] As Pierre Lévy puts it, drawing on Gilles Deleuze, "the virtual is that which has potential rather than actual existence. The virtual *tends* toward actualization, without undergoing any form of effective or formal concretization" (1998:23; see Deleuze 2001).

What does it mean, then, to say that obscenity is a tendency of an object? I have already noted that the discourse of censorship seems both to be strongly invested in making comprehensive lists of Bad Things That Must Be Banned and, at the same time, to insist that the censor's judgment cannot stop there, that it must open itself to potentials in the object under examination that cannot be itemized in advance. Perhaps it is in this curious space, this space of a "content beyond content," that we find the tendency of an object—its virtual potential rather than its given forms. Perhaps it is this tendency that we are noting when we say "I know it when I feel it."

But what about the fact that all this tendency talk is really rather outmoded in relation to the contextualist drift of obscenity law in the West? If India is hanging on to the Hicklin Test long after it was abandoned in the United States and the United Kingdom, then is that not evidence of the fact that Indian modernity is failing to move beyond its perpetual not yet-ness? Actually things were not so clear-cut even in the United States and the United Kingdom. In *Roth v. United States* (1957), U.S. Supreme Court Justice Brennan, writing for the majority, did indeed introduce the yardstick of "contemporary community standards" as a replacement for the Hicklin Test. But Justices Warren's and Harlan's dissenting opinions both held on to the language of tendency. Justice Warren wanted the definition of obscenity to be an object with a "substantial tendency to corrupt by arousing lustful desires"; Justice Harlan wrote of material that would "tend to sexually impure thoughts." In the United Kingdom, the Obscene Publications Act of 1959 did away with the Hicklin Test by introducing a new definition of obscenity that was more contextually oriented and yet still retained the language of tendency: "an article shall be deemed to be obscene if its effect or (where the article comprises two or more distinct items) the effect of any one of its items is, if taken as a whole, such as to tend to deprave and corrupt persons who are likely, having regard to all relevant circumstances, to read, see or hear the matter contained or embodied in it."[13] The sense that the cinema activates such a tendency can already be discerned in the transcripts of the interviews conducted by the Indian Cinematograph Committee.

INCONTINENT LOOKING

A General Suggestiveness
Whether the cinema was thought "good" or "bad," almost everyone agreed that it had an extraordinary ability to agitate audiences. Mr. Dwarkadas, secretary of the Bombay Vigilance Association, spoke of "scenes which violently shake and upset the emotions.... They stimulate the quickly excitable emotions of children and adolescents in a wrong way" (ICC 1928a, 1:262). Others proposed that "sensuous films" were particularly likely to produce

"high excitement" in the impressionable (ICC 1928a, 1:644), to "stimulate uncontrolled passions" (ICC 1928a, 2:1085), again, particularly among sections of the population that were thought to lack proper cognitive insulation.

Still others pursued a kind of comparative ontology of media, suggesting that the cinema image was "much more striking" than the printed word and more liable to make "a lasting impression" than either print or oral discourse (ICC 1928a, 2:556, 339). The moving picture's quality of being so incomparably "full of life" (ICC 1928a, 2:509) contained both beneficial and treacherous potentialities. As a Trivandrum chemistry professor argued, the inherent fascination of moving pictures promised to make both the producer's and the consumer's tasks easier: "The demonstrative value of pictures saves a person from a heavy strain on his imagination and his faith" (ICC 1928a, 3:461). The value of the cinema lay not just in its communicative facility but also in its immersive appeal. Bhagwat Prasad, a Lucknowi judge, enthused that "the Picture House possesses all the attractions of real life. We find ourselves in the midst of people on the screen and become interested in them. Our tears for their sorrows and our delight at their successes are immediately called forth. The effect that is produced in our minds is instantaneous, and it is not soon effaced. We hear an orator and are impressed. Modern novels move us by their reality, but the greater reality of this vivid presentation of everyday life before our eyes moves us more readily and almost more deeply" (ICC 1928a, 4:108). And yet precisely this "vivid presentation" seemed to some the mark of cinema's lack vis-à-vis, say, the novel. In its apparent bypassing of reasoned judgment, the cinema was, par excellence, the medium of the crowd, of the massified aggregate of pissing men. Some worried that its facility—often imagined as conveying a kind of unmediated verisimilitude—constituted its greatest danger. Reflected a judge of Peshawar, Mufti Abdul Latiff, "In my view there is much difference between novel reading and seeing a thing in the cinema. In the one case one's brain is reasoning things out, while in the other the actual thing is shown on the screen, which is quite different" (ICC 1928a, 2:276).

Indeed, the spatial arrangement of the audience in the cinema halls during these years was itself imagined along a scale from rabidity to reason. The cheaper seats were downstairs and in front. The people who sat there were, literally, both inferior and more immediately absorbed in the image on the screen and, as such, assumed to be incapable of critical distance. The fancier folk sat in the balconies further back, at a safer distance from the mimetic force of the image as well as physically elevated above and behind the rabble, which they could survey without being so easily examined in return.

To those who inhabited a more elevated vantage point, nothing was so indubitably indicative of the dangerously regressive fusion of screen and crowd than the raucous noises emitted by the great unwashed in the cheap seats. Then, as now, the theme was obsessive. Many elite ICC respondents, frustrated by their inability to present coherent evidence of objectionable content, would often end up pointing to the palpable excitation triggered in audiences by the films as a corporeally concrete index.

At times the effect would be described as a pregnant, barely contained agitation in the cinema hall, a kind of audible thickening of the air. Lieutenant-Colonel Gidney, an all-India representative of Anglo-Indians and "domiciled Europeans," reported that "when there is anything suggestive [on the screen] there is often a sort of hushed silence and suppressed extasy [sic] over the suggestion" (ICC 1928a, 2:1082). But containment did not appear to be the rule. Karamchand Bulchand, producer of educational and propaganda films, remarked, "You have only to visit a downtown cinema to see how the lower classes of people gloat over scenes when there is kissing or embracing. . . . I wish you could come and hear the screeches and howls of the audience when the kissing is going on" (ICC 1928a, 1:679, 684). En masse, these responses conjure all the acoustic density of a veritable bestiary in the stalls: "hissing and jeering" (ICC 1928a, 1:51), "catcalls and exclamations" (ICC 1928a, 1:248), "hooting" (ICC 1928a, 2:275), "shouting and Ah-Ahing" (ICC 1928a, 2:225).

Apparently, the atmosphere sometimes became so charged that the cinema management felt obliged to stop a film and turn on the lights until the audience could be subdued (ICC 1928a, 2:380). If the perceived threat of the cinema was moral as well as physical, then it was moral *because* it was so physical. "All you have to do" averred H. W. Hogg, secretary of the Punjab Boy Scouts Association, "is sit in the cinema and listen to the remarks made by some of these young men, just to realize how this thing is getting really under their skin" (ICC 1928a, 2:69).

To his credit, the ICC chairman, T. Rangachariar, very quickly began to chafe at the contradiction between the committee's mandate to prove or disprove the cinema's socially deleterious effects and the apparent impossibility of locating the harm in identifiable and isolable kinds of content. Frustrated, Rangachariar complained that "the difficulty is that these statements [about the cinema's dangers] have been made not once or twice but several times, but when we proceed to ask persons who make those statements to give instances either of portions of the story or of the story itself they are unable to give us any particulars, not only now but for the last 5 or 6 years" (ICC 1928a, 1:249). Indeed, whatever examples the committee was able to glean were generally so vague, so obviously prejudiced, or simply so illogical as to be worthless. Exasperated by the imprecision of much of the testimony, Rangachariar was at the same time also unwilling wholeheartedly to accept the blithe Panglossianism evinced by many film business representatives. For example, after yet another cheerful industry apologia, this time from N. R. Desai, manager of Universal Pictures in Madras, Rangachariar exploded: "I suppose your opinion is that the cinema is all right, and that those who go the cinemas are not in any way affected?" Not to be outdone, Desai went him one better: "My opinion is that people by going to the cinemas have become better" (ICC 1928a, 3:376).

The sense that there was something distinctively and perhaps ominously powerful about the cinema continued to inform the committee's work. One of the proximate triggers to the appointment of the ICC had been a report published in 1927 by a Social Hygiene Delegation that toured India under the leadership of a Mrs. Neville Rolfe. The report, like Mrs. Rolfe's own statements to the press, exuded moral panic. It claimed, for example, that rising rates of venereal disease among Indian youth were a direct result of the corrupting influence of films.

In the end, the ICC found no evidence for most of the delegation's specific claims; indeed, it found evidence to suggest that they had been gratuitously concocted. But one of the delegation's more general suggestions did continue to haunt the committee's conversations. At one stage, Rangachariar quoted to a witness a passage from the delegation's report: "We would submit that general suggestiveness of a most undesirable kind may pervade a whole film without any one scene being within the meaning of the term 'obscenity' if western standards are used for film in western settings, although in the atmosphere of the different social customs of the East the whole film appears obscene and is suggestive of gross moral laxity to an Indian audience" (ICC 1928a, 1:77). Very broadly—I discuss this question at greater length elsewhere[14]—the colonial optic presumed Indians to be peculiarly susceptible to obscenity because they were supposed, paradoxically, to be both more corporeally "gestural" than Europeans (at a racial level) *and* more sexually conservative (at a sociocultural level). But with or without the element of cultural dissonance, the committee's conversations kept returning to one or another version of this "general suggestiveness"—this emergent quality that seemed to resist being reduced to any inventory of particular contents.

When pushed by the committee to identify exactly what they found troubling in the cinema, several respondents pointed to something along the lines of unstated implication; a habitus that seemed palpably and yet somehow indefinably to potentiate the individual elements of the image. L. K. Mitter, an assistant public prosecutor in Mandalay, suggested: "[It is] not exactly the scanty clothing. It is the gestures and postures which are suggestive of something more gross to which I object" (ICC 1928a, 3:675). After yet another round of thwarted specification, Owen Roberts, a member of the Legislative Council in Punjab, resorted to the example of Katherine Mayo's then-topical book *Mother India* (1927; see M. Sinha 2006): "I have been thinking how I could put it to you. You know the publication *Mother India*. Well, the facts in it may be correct but one puts it down to the feeling that the whole thing is wrong, that the perspective of the book is wrong and that it does not do justice to the country. It is the same thing with these films" (ICC 1928a, 2:196).

Disproportion

Across the vast spread of the ICC's proceedings, perhaps the single most frequently mentioned formal cinematic device was the close-up. Now, of course a close-up involves a spatial transformation of the audience's relation to that which the image represents. In a colonial setting its intimate scopophilia had potentially subversive implications. While for some, the besetting sin of the close-up was exaggeration, others identified an effect more akin to temporal—and perhaps, for the audience, cognitive—retardation. Punjabi scoutmaster Mr. Hogg explained, "What I object to is the 'close up,' where you get a man and woman standing for a considerable time, the slow movement of either the man or the woman putting his or her hands over the shoulders of the other. I mean, the whole thing is deliberately and slowly done, and that, to my mind, is certainly undesirable" (ICC 1928a, 2:73).

Scholars have suggested that the cinema threatened colonial authority because the camera seemed to reverse the ruling gaze, granting brown subjects collective access to those private spaces of European life that had until then been kept separate from the public performance of colonial authority (Arora 1995; Larkin 2010; B. Sinha 2005).[15] In fact, Chairman Rangachariar himself picked up on this, without at that point specifying that the danger might be greater to white prestige than to brown dignity: "Is not that a difficulty about the cinema, that it really removes the wall of one's private house and exhibits your private life[?] I mean to say what happens in a room is shown on a screen" (ICC 1928a, 3:997). What, as one Indian journalist sardonically put it, were the poor natives going to make of such "sidelights on the Sahib at play?"[16]

At the same time, the close-up generated anxieties that were not only about the empire looking back. Rather than just reversing the gaze, the cinema's "general suggestiveness" seemed also to encourage incontinent looking. At the most general level, the fixation on the close-up expressed a more general worry about disproportion. For example, many argued that silent films necessarily required overacting and, more generally, the kind of corporeal exaggeration of sentiment and gesture to which uncivilized people (with their "very graphic language") were thought to be prone. As the British Board of Film Censors put it in its 1920 report, "The besetting danger of the cinema in the expression of emotion is almost inevitably over-emphasis in action."[17]

The screen kiss was an important objective fulcrum for this debate over incontinent looking—in India as it had also been in Britain around the turn of the twentieth century (French 1997). The unwritten prohibition on kissing in mainstream Indian cinema between the 1940s and the 1990s became, as we have seen, both the bête noire of the liberal critique of repressed Bollywood aesthetics and, in a more allegorical mode, a figure for the apparent impossibility of conjugal intimacy within a social order premised on the patriarchal extended family (Prasad 1998). In the 1920s, however, Hollywood kissing seemed to capture the cinema's potentiating power.

The ICC transcripts are peppered with adjectivized attempts to express the crossing of a temperate boundary in which the kiss marks the crucial spot. What is objectionable, again, is not so much the literal substance or content of the representation, but rather the mode of its dramatization: the "*pregnant* sex film"[18] (ICC 1928a, 1:6), the "*frantic*" or "*gushing* love scenes" (ICC 1928a, 1:367, 373), the "*strenuous* kissing and this *violent* hugging" (ICC 1928a, 2:993; all emphases added). Visual précis of intimacy that it was, the kiss became the fount of a startling profusion of cinematic varieties. Something of this dramatic versatility was captured by Pherozeshah Marzban, editor of the stalwart Parsi periodical *Jam-e-Jamshed*: "Kissing may be here and there, but not indiscriminate kissing. You have got the long kiss, the prolonged kiss, the hot kiss and the soft kiss, all sorts of kisses" (ICC 1928a, 1:497). Some actually went so far as to suggest quantitative limits: "You can even define that the kissing should be only for one second or some such thing. But kissing for 30 seconds or even one minute is not proper, I think. It affects every man who sees the film" (ICC 1928a, 3:981).

Of course, there was a great deal of talk about the fact that Indians, unlike Europeans, did not kiss in public and that on-screen kissing in Indian cinemas—whether by Europeans or by Indians—was for this reason problematic. From that standpoint, the issue was simply one of different cultural norms of public decency. At the same time, many of the ICC's informants kept returning to the uncomfortable way that the movie camera not only showed kissing but also, more fundamentally, transformed it. There was a sense that the close-up created discomfort by *lingering*; that is to say, by disrupting the habitual—decent—proportions and rhythms of everyday life. The screen kiss, remarked J. Henderson, principal of Lahore College and member of the Punjab Board of Film Censors, was never just a "passing kiss" (ICC 1928a, 2:5). The cinema image was perceived as too slow, too fast, too close, and too distant. While on one level, film propagandists celebrated the cinema's ability to communicate directly and sensuously, others worried about the cinema's capacity to undo ideologically naturalized proportions—to distemper the colonial performative dispensation that had been inherited from the nineteenth century. As I have argued elsewhere (Mazzarella 2010a), the imperial darbar—a colonial adaptation of Mughal courtly incorporation rituals (Cohn 1983)—was more or less moribund by the 1920s. The rise of a properly mass politics in India, not least under the stewardship of M. K. Gandhi, demanded new technologies and media of legitimation. In this regard, the cinema appeared as a *pharmakon*, a drug that, depending on the constitution of the patient as well as on its deployment, might either heal or kill (see Pinney 2008)—a drug whose visceral tendencies were always in question.

ARRESTED PERCEPTION: THE FLOWERING OF OBSCENITY

As I suggested in chapter 2, the rise of mass politics in India strained the capacity of the colonial administration to compartmentalize its Indian subjects according to the culturalist categories of the ethnographic state.

Cinema spectatorship turned out, during the 1930s, to be one of the practices through which a new, generalized relation between sensuous enjoyment and citizenship could be imagined—several years before citizenship in the independent nation-state of India actually had to be enacted.

During the initial years of Independence, through the 1950s and into the 1960s, the performative dispensation of Nehruvian nationalism was still vital. It is perhaps not accidental that the late 1960s, just like the 1920s, saw a renewed concern with disproportionate and incontinent viewing. Both were moments in which a ruling dispensation—that is to say, a certain naturalized relationship between public enthusiasm and symbolic order—had run out of fuel. The colonial debate on the cinema tried to bring together several conflicting streams: a racial theory of corporeal susceptibility, a cultural theory of Indian modesty, and the most pressing question of imperial pedagogy: could a (neo)savage medium be used for a civilizing purpose? By the time of the Khosla Committee's report in 1969, the racial discourse had fallen by the wayside and the cultural argument for Indian specificity had been muted. But the uneasiness that clung to the cinema's strange potentiating power remained largely unchanged across the decades.

The Khosla Committee's report suggests that pure entertainment in the cinema is a recipe for slack citizens "because it tends to make the mind flabby, it arrests the thinking process, it dulls the creative impulse and makes people both physically and mentally lazy" (Khosla et al. 1969:69). On one level, this "arrested" state is imagined as a purely abject condition: the state of the pissing man, cognitively stuck in an entirely mimetic relation to the image and thus wide open to its predations. Five years earlier, Justice Hidayatullah had used remarkably similar language in the *Lady Chatterley* case when reflecting on the difficulty of reliably defining obscenity as a stable property of an object: "the insensitive sees only obscenity because his attention is arrested, not by the general or artistic appeal or message which he cannot comprehend, but by what he can see, and the intellectual sees beauty and art but nothing gross" (Ranjit Udeshi v. State of Maharashtra [1964]). Ostensibly, the "arrested" viewer is inert: he perceives obscenity because his thought remains grounded at the most literal level of the image. And yet at the same time, the perception of obscenity is also imagined as a kind of *un*grounded overintensification of corporeal stimulation, loose affect without proper symbolic mediation. And this is where the tendency of the image-object emerges as a threat: at the place where regular rhythms of perception and action are interrupted.

Readers above a certain age may be familiar with the traumatic experience of 8-mm home movies getting jammed in the projector, an obscene flower of melting celluloid spreading with alarming speed across the image as the heat of the lamp burns through the arrested film. The discourse of censorship imagines the incontinent flowering of obscenity in the mind of an "arrested" viewer along these lines. A spectator equipped with a suitable "adult discount" absorbs the image at a steady and respectable speed. But the same image threatens to bubble up obscenely in the minds of those who may get stuck or unduly fixated on it. On the one hand, the obscene tendency of an image appears here as the failure of all meaning. On the other hand, it suggests an uncontrolled and frightening profusion of corporeal quickenings and affective intensities.

In relation to the symbolic order of a performative dispensation (whether conservative-moralist or liberal-aesthetic), this obscene flowering might at first sight seem like a necessarily radical disruption. Against the possibility of such a disruption, the censors look something like Jacques Rancière's "police"—the agency that keeps things bumping along at a steady clip (in this case at twenty-four frames per second), the agency that tries to keep habits of seeing continent and relations of looking proportionate. In Davide Panagia's gloss, "The main ambition of the police is to increase the flow of circulation, to move traffic along when the traffic lights don't work, if you will. Rancière's 'there is nothing to see here' of the police order . . . ensure[s] the proper circulation of things within a system so as not to leave unaccounted the supplemental elements whose value has, as of yet, been unassigned" (2009:41–42). The obscene tendency of an object might from that point of view be its capacity to disrupt this "flow of circulation" that keeps the symbolic traffic moving along by arresting its motion: keeping the "supplemental elements" of life—the emergent tendencies—"unassigned" within the structure of that symbolic order by scattering them across the road.

And yet there is something unsatisfying about this scheme: namely, its fixed opposition between authority (police), which is always associated with symbolic order, and radical disruption (dissensus), which is always associated with the supplemental, the unclaimed, that which exceeds steady symbolic inscription. But I think Panagia's discussion also contains an opening to a less inert, more dialectical proposition. Reading Immanuel Kant's aesthetic theory alongside Rancière, Panagia zooms in on a sense of temporal disruption in Kant's account—a kind of immediacy as durational intensity, an arrested perception that "ungrounds our subjectivity" (2009:28) as we dwell on the object that enlivens our senses with that curious combination of impartiality and enjoyment which characterizes aesthetic judgment for Kant. Panagia then connects this interrupted subjectivity to Rancière's category of "dissensus"—the radical aesthetic disruption of hegemonic "consensus."

While provocative, Panagia's alignment of Kant and Rancière skates over a crucial ambiguity in Kant's theory of aesthetic judgment. It is true that, for Kant, the autonomy of the aesthetic judgment ensures a dissenting "dis-sensual" relation between the properly attuned subject and any external authorities that might seek to impose ready-made ideological values and judgments. But Kant's aesthetic judgment is also universal, which means that, at another level, it connects us to each other on the nonconceptual ground of a shared con-sensus. For Kant, there is freedom in this consensus precisely because it represents the possibility of a universal human attunement that is at the same time autonomously achieved and therefore domination proof.

In our hermeneutically suspicious times, it is perhaps not so easy to subscribe to Kant's faith in our ability to distinguish between aesthetic autonomy and sensuously grounded ideology. Who is to say whether the sensible ground on which one thinks one is making an autonomous judgment is not altogether prestructured by a habituated and thoroughly ideological history of the senses? The question is in any case more interesting in the present context as a problem of political pragmatics than as one of transcendent philosophical truth. As such, we might perhaps translate Kant's concern with securing the autonomy of judgment against the heteronomy of dependence into an ongoing grappling with affectively registered intimate tendencies, tendencies that are then given the "blameable" external form of vulgar heteronomy: the pissing man. In other words, the Kantian sense that the finality of a truly autonomous judgment might be possible (even if only as a regulative ideal) is purchased at the price of setting up a restlessly extimate self-relation.

I have suggested that the censors fear the possibility of the flowering of obscenity that might emerge when the film jams in the projector, when the smooth flow of traffic is disrupted in such a way as to trigger this arrested perception that "ungrounds our subjectivity." This would be the dis-sensual tendency in the pissing man that threatens the con-sensus of a stable symbolic order. But if the pissing man is an externalization of an extimate potential *within* the censor's discourse, then we would also have to acknowledge two further points. First, that dis-sensus is internally constitutive of con-sensus. And consequently, second, that dis-sensus cannot be imagined only as a space of "resistance" to "power"—although it pleases both the censors and some critical theorists to imagine that it is. Rather, dis-sensus would have to be rethought as an extimately emergent potential at the heart of every aesthetic judgment that comprises both the possibility of things being radically otherwise and the ground on which the censors' claim to ideological authority is reproduced.

So how are we to theorize obscenity qua tendency to account for its dual role: both threat to and guarantee of the censor's discourse?

HAPTICS AND THE PUBLIC PUNCTUM

Indian feminists have long noted that calling certain kinds of images obscene or indecent effectively serves as an alibi for other images that may be just as offensive but not publicly marked as such. Flavia Agnes, for example, remarks that "the equation of indecency with nudity or sex allowed all other portrayals of women to pass off as 'decent.' When women clad in saris were depicted in servile, stereotypical roles, these images were not attacked as indecent" (B. Bose 2006:xxxiii). Experimental filmmakers point out that Bollywood directors' complaints about the CBFC's clampdowns on female nudity have the effect of deflecting the censorship debate away from other kinds of images that might not conform so snugly to mainstream heteronormative conventions.

Could one make a similar argument about not only the content of image-objects but also about their tendencies? That is to say, is there a critical way of thinking about this alibi function of obscenity that does not fall back on an already-known political critique of hegemonic norms but rather turns our attention to the as yet underacknowledged potentials at work in even the most mainstream images?

Laura Marks (2002) writes of the erotics of "haptic" images. Haptic images are images to which our relation is touchlike, images in relation to which we may lose objectifying distance and thus in some sense lose ourselves. The distinction between haptic and optical viewing seems first to have been drawn by the art historian Alois Riegl. Claude Gandelman writes:

Riegl stated that one type of artistic procedure, which corresponds to a certain way of looking, is based on the scanning of objects according to their outlines. This trajectory of the regard Riegl called the optical. The opposite type of vision, which focuses on surfaces and emphasizes the value of the superficies of objects, Riegl called the haptic (from the Greek *haptein*, "to seize, grasp," or *haptikos*, "capable of touching"). . . . The optical eye merely brushes the surface of things. The haptic, or tactile, eye penetrates in depth, finding its pleasure in texture and grain. (1991:5)

Absorbed in a less self-conscious way at the movies, the optical eye moves along at twenty-four frames per second whereas the haptic eye may get stuck. Marks makes the useful point that haptic images do not have to be sexual to be erotic. They "are erotic regardless of their content, because they construct a particular kind of intersubjective relationship between beholder and images" (2002:13). A haptic image might be sexual, but it might also be a shot of, say, a freshly cut lawn. Content is less important than the mode of apprehension.[19] Something emerges as the eye seizes/is seized by the image. In Siegfried Kracauer's words: "A face on the screen may attract us as a singular manifestation of fear or happiness regardless of the events which motivate its expression. A street serving as a background to some quarrel or love affair may rush to the fore and produce an intoxicating effect. Street and face, then, open up a dimension much wider than that of the plots which they sustain" (Kracauer 1997 [1960]:303). A haptic relation to an image requires, one might say, the "arrested thinking process" that, in the censor's discourse, provides fertile soil for an obscene flowering. At first pass, the haptic effect is experienced as a kind of interruption or crisis, a failure of anticipated meaning that is at the same time a kind of unseemly swelling.[20]

The risk here is that we always assign a liberatory potential to haptic-tactile engagements and equate optical modes of looking with domination. Miriam Hansen, reading Benjamin on film, offers a salutary corrective:

With regard to cinema, we could understand the constellation of tactile and optical in terms of the dialectical entwinement of both these registers in its aesthetic *dispositif*. For cinema has the power to increase the haptic impact of material objects and events, to bring the viewer closer to them than possible in ordinary perception, but only on the condition of technological mediation, which affords the viewer distance and protection from the actual phenomena. Key to this paradoxical experience of mediated immediacy is the kinesthetic dimension of film, that is, the threefold movement of people and objects, the camera itself, and the rhythm of editing.... The haptic sense, suppressed since the Renaissance in favour of the distance senses of vision and hearing, is restored to a new, second-order tactility. This perceptual incorporation, though, depends on a simultaneous distancing, fracturing, and rendering strange of the object through technological and aesthetic mediation. (2011: 101)

In other words, not only must we understand the apparent immediacy of haptic experience as mediated in multiple ways (by image-apparatuses, by contexts of looking, by collective histories of the senses), but both sides of the dialectic—haptics and optics—play both roles in the great game of ideological inscription, ambidextrously producing at once affirmative familiarity and critical estrangement.

Marks develops her argument in relation to the kind of image-objects that would typically be classified as artworks. Here, as in avant-garde cinema, haptic potential is often a deliberate and acknowledged goal. But what about the image-objects that circulate in the public cultural mainstream: advertisements, feature films, quotidian speech acts and gestures? Does it make sense to speak of haptics here as well? If I am correct in discerning a link between the censor's discourse on the tendency of image-objects and a haptic subject-object relation, then the answer would have to be yes. What releases haptic potential in one image but not in another? This has to be an empirical question. Roland Barthes famously wrote of a photograph's "punctum": an emergent, almost unbearably poignant experience of being "pricked" by an irreducible element in a particular image-object. The punctum was, for Barthes, the sense of an excess, a felt intensity in—one might perhaps say a tendency of—certain images that exceeded their conventional symbolic legibility, which he called their "studium." Barthes took pains to distinguish the private experience of the punctum (which suddenly pricks him at the sight of an apparently innocuous snapshot of his mother) from the banal, overdetermined studium he attributed to advertising and other kinds of mass-mediated publicity. But what if something like this "pricking" can occur at a public, collective level as well? Might it make sense to speak of the obscene tendency of mass-mediated images as a kind of public punctum?

Here, again, Hansen's reading of Benjamin and Kracauer is suggestive. Having drawn a connection between Barthes's punctum and Benjamin's conception of the "aura" of certain images, Hansen asks, "Are there ways of translating aura's defining moments of disjunctive temporality and self-dislocating reflexivity into a potential for the *collective*, as the structural subject of cinema?" (2011:113). Elements of such an argument, she suggests, hover in Kracauer's *Theory of Film* (1997 [1960]): "The private stream of associations that the spectator interweaves with the film exceeds—yet has its basis in—the more objective, intersubjective dimension of 'psychophysical correspondences' that Kracauer considers an essential part of the material world that film 'assists us in discovering.'... The gaze that material objects—furniture, clothes, architecture—are capable of returning in certain films may 'spirit' the viewer 'away into the lumber room of his private self,' but this room is a historical space and thus part of a collective memory space" (2011:269, 270). In the 1970s, Alexander Kluge and his fellow travelers offered a more systematic theorization of this potentiated relation between film and collective experience in terms of an expanded and thus, they hoped, radicalized version of the Habermasian public sphere: "In addition to language, which is public, the public sphere should grant phantasy the status of a communal medium, and this includes the stream of associations and the faculty of memory" (Kluge 1982:215; see Negt and Kluge 1993 [1972]). Kluge argues that the first, most important medium is not film, television, radio, or the press. Rather, these are institutional forms by which the medium that matters most—collective experience—might be organized in more or less progressive directions. He conceives the concrete material of this collective experience (*Erfahrung*[21]) expansively as the very texture of everyday life—and as such irreducible to a Kantian-Habermasian norm of deliberative public reason or the carefully cultivated forms of bourgeois self-making (*Bildung*):

> People work at steady jobs, they toil away, which in turn means they work on their relationships, they work overtime in order to survive in both work and private relationships. This is the labour of inner balance, the work of a lifetime. Life is made up of these three powerful elements, the stuff of centuries with all its misery and errors. It is *thus* that the horizons of perception and the medium of social experience are actually produced. The so-called media feed on the returns of this labour. They only reflect something which depends on being filled out by the spectators from their own experience. (Kluge 1982:209)

For Kluge, the work of a progressive filmmaker therefore consists in providing carefully calibrated audiovisual triggers that can actualize emergent potentials in this collective "medium of social experience" and in that way help to produce a public sphere grounded in the "*unsophisticated* imagination" of everyday life (1982:210). The filmmaker's triggering agency remains necessary because the mainstream commercial media have, according to Kluge, "buried" and thus immobilized this collective imagination "under a thick layer of cultural garbage" (1982:210).

From a censor's standpoint, the emergent potentials of this "unsophisticated imagination" may well appear as symptoms of the pissing man's obscenely "arrested thinking process." But we are left with a couple of problems. First, Kluge's model, with its normative opposition between a progressive filmmaking practice and a reactionary mainstream public culture, has the effect of binding the emergence of haptic/obscene tendencies to the consciously calculated interventions of cinematic auteurs. It secures a vanguardist conception of revolutionary agency by insisting on a public culture that, for all the populist spontaneity of its underlying potential, cannot actualize this potential without the deliberate strategies of a "director." But is not one of the distinguishing marks of the haptic effect, above and beyond such calculated cultural provocation, that it takes us by surprise? That it emerges where we least expect it?

Second, the normative opposition between progressive and regressive public spheres may seem to offer a readily intelligible political compass. But it does so at the cost of acknowledging that ideology works not by "burying" and thus immobilizing the live potentials of collective experience, but rather by actualizing them in the service of would-be hegemonic performative dispensations. That this ideological conscription of collective experience is by definition unstable should, by now, go without saying. But its instability is just as much a source of its efficacy, of its power to compel attention and desire, as it is a fatal flaw.

THE OBSCENE SUPEREGO LOOP

I am reminded of the joke where a prisoner wanted an umbrella to protect
himself from the sun while going from his cell to Tyburn to be hanged!
—Indian Cinematograph Committee respondent D. P. Mukherjea

Considering these questions points us back to a problem that runs all the way through these pages: how do would-be performative dispensations, which necessarily strive toward the appearance of symbolic closure, deal with the structural challenge of the open edge of mass publicity? On the side of the subject, the recurrent figure of the pissing man is the generic form that this anxiety about the open edge takes: an imagined viewer whose open helplessness vis-à-vis the image requires the paternal guidance and incorporation of an authoritative symbolic order. The point about the pissing man is not just that he operates as an ideologically convenient excuse for the censors' authority. Rather, the affective excess and corporeal volatility of the pissing man qua spectator is a way of recognizing the symbolic instability that necessarily occurs at the open edge of mass publicity while at the same time pathologizing it. The pissing man becomes the "something in the way," the obstacle that constantly prevents would-be performative dispensations from closing their symbolic circles. As such, the structural impossibility of closing the circle—impossible to ignore for long in a context of mass publicity—is deflected onto the figure of an obstacle that in theory will one day be overcome. Hindu nationalists demand that Muslims who will not behave like Hindus should move to Pakistan; liberals invoke a future in which everyone will be mature and "developed" enough to stop taking everything so literally. But, of course, this "something in the way"—whatever it is—is at the same time the sine qua non of the flourishing of these performative dispensations. In the absence of this humanoid scapegoat/obstacle, this extimate other whose reliable blameworthiness constantly fortifies the moral orders that his very existence seems to frustrate, the open edge of mass publicity would have to be confronted in a different way. That is to say, the open edge would appear not as a pathology of an Other but as a generative indeterminacy that lies at the very heart of all claims to sovereignty and moral closure.

Now how does this work on the side of the object? Recall the remark of the advertising consultant at the end of chapter 4: "Censorship is self-defeating. Because the more you hide the breast the more you increase its value." I would like to propose that we reverse the first part of this state-ment: "Censorship is self-perpetuating. Because the more you hide the breast the more you increase its value." The point is not only that censorship perpetuates itself by attracting transgression. Beyond that, censorship invests particular (typically pornographic) image-objects with heightened value so as to produce a routinized and moralized transgression that stays within certain familiar and predictable limits. Thus, what I would call a "restricted obscenity" (the usual sex stuff) becomes an alibi for a more ubiquitous "generalized obscenity"—that is to say, emergent haptic tendencies that saturate mainstream public culture and need have nothing to do with sexual explicitness.

My argument, by the way, is not that restricted obscenity must take the form of sex. While there are obvious reasons why sexually explicit images function as efficient relays of mass affect, it is clearly also the case that their usefulness as tokens of restricted obscenity waxes and wanes depending on a range of factors, including the ease of their accessibility and the degree of their incorporation into mainstream forms of publicity. It is, of course, conventional to argue that pornographic images serve patriarchal purposes, and no doubt at the level of symbolic content (enactments of subordination, objectification, and so on) they often do. But I would add that they also serve the purposes of restricted obscenity so well because of the way that they juxtapose a very predictable symbolic economy (few genres are more formulaic) with an intensely haptic appeal. As J. M. Coetzee notes, "Legal and critical debate about visual pornography faces a special problem: no matter how plausibly one may plead that what the viewer sees is a constellation of signifiers calling up other, intertexted constellations of signifiers whose meaning is anything but obvious, this position is always in danger of being overwhelmed by the viewer's conviction—a conviction which it is in a sense the business of the film industry, by every means at its disposal, to bolster—that what he or she sees is the thing itself" (1996:x).

Pornography stands in an ambiguous relation to the "violence" that Barthes attributed to photography in general. For Barthes, a photograph is violent "not because it shows violent things, but because on each occasion *it fills the sight by force*, and because in it nothing can be refused or transformed" (1981:91). To repeat: on Barthes's scale, the snapshot of his mother that suddenly pricks him with its punctum is at one end; advertising, utterly reducible to its repetitive ideological studium is at the other. But pornography does not fit this scheme. In it, one might say, the punctum *is* the studium; pornography presents itself to us as at once untransformable in the sense of Barthes's punctum and obsessively repetitive. No wonder that, from the censor's point of view, it serves so effectively as the site of a routinized transgression. It is as if the restricted obscenity of pornography lends corporeal density to what Klaus Theweleit has called the "over-explicitness" of authoritarian symbolic language: signification as a prophylactic against experience (1989 [1978]:6). And yet alongside it, this utterly irreducible "and yet there it is" of corporeal presence. Perhaps this is also a formula for fetishism: a routinized fascination that feels just as viscerally fresh every time.

My basic point is that the logic of censorship thrives on isolating a restricted domain of representation that can serve as a literally, conventionally, "obscene" focus of public attention and thus also as a relatively manageable space within which the fantasy-economy of transgression, desire, and punishment can be comfortably routinized. Restricted obscenity is the familiar domain in which the pissing man does his bad business; these are the image-objects that supposedly make him lose control. By the same token, the obsessive moralized focus on restricted obscenity allows the complexity of our emergent affective investments in mainstream public culture—the quotidian locus of aesthetic ideology, as it were—to appear unproblematic, practical, and rational.

Slavoj Žižek (1993) captures this dynamic effectively. He argues, following Lacan, that the symbolic order—the social order of meaning—remains haunted by a void or absence that troubles all signifying projects' striving for fullness and presence. In order to deflect attention away from this problematic indeterminacy at the heart of meaning-making, the symbolic order installs compensatory prohibitions—Bad Objects that invite a manageable transgression. With each act of transgression, there is the sense that one has not quite reached the obscene Thing that was supposed to lie beyond the prohibition. Instead, one gets folded all the more tightly back into an "obscene superego loop"—that is, into a moralized attachment to the laws of the symbolic order that is inextricable from the pleasure of transgressing them.

Translated into the terms of my own argument, the void that haunts the symbolic order becomes especially palpable in mass publics, taking the form of the tendencies that hover at the open edge of mass publicity. The obscene superego loop is the circuit of restricted obscenity, in relation to which the prospect of generalized obscenity—the potentiated reality of the ordinary image-object (whether cinematic or otherwise)—serves as a kind of uncanny (because entirely naturalized) supplement. In other words, restricted obscenity serves the interests of the censors' performative dispensation because it creates the appearance that the emergent potentials of mass-mediated image objects can in fact be effectively and centrally managed and moralized. Just as the extimacy of the pissing man occasionally sends a squirm down the spine of bourgeois moralism, so generalized obscenity is a name for the intimation that unknowable affective tendencies operate at the very heart of the most normative cultural orders. Restricted obscenity is easy to describe because we always already know what it is. Generalized obscenity can only be captured as an intimation of an emergent affective tendency, or, in the words of the ICC respondent, a "general suggestiveness" that is in itself nonsymbolizable. Eventually, if it does not simply dissipate, it will be harnessed and put to work in a symbolic economy, either as valorized aspiration (consumerist, political, religious, and so forth) or as routinely demonized restricted obscenity (recall my discussion at the beginning of chapter 4 of quotidian eruptions). But as with the extimacy of the pissing man, generalized obscenity cannot be symbolized as such.

We might, then, reevaluate Coetzee's ironic remark that whereas "inexplicable" means "unable to be explained," "undesirable" certainly doesn't mean "unable to be desired." Coetzee suggests that from the censor's point of view, "What is undesirable is the desire of the desiring subject: the desire of the subject is undesired" (1996:viii). But if we follow the logic of the obscene superego loop, then this no longer holds. In fact the opposite is true: the "undesirable" (in the sense of restricted obscenity) is precisely that which the censor *would* prefer the subject to desire. Restricted obscenity, as defined in the censor's discourse, would thus be the site of a prohibition that keeps the subject locked into a familiar moralized loop of subjection and transgression. And yet at the same time, the language of "tendency"—as well as the censors' constant acknowledgment that judgment in practice exhausts and exceeds any lists that can be made in advance—implies a recognition of the generalized obscenity that is always looming around the edges of the superego loop.

Perhaps I might hazard a simile here and recall how, in Freud's essays on sexuality (2000 [1905]), the polymorphously erogenous body of the child is normatively expected to move through sexual maturation and organize itself according to the restricted *telos* of genital sexuality. The politics of performative dispensations might be understood that way, too: the unpredictable tendencies of image-objects are organized into a tacit ideological compact between approved objects of desire and standardized sites of transgression. But those polymorphous potentials nevertheless remain, ideologically framed as the persistent obstacle to lasting satisfaction and self-integration.[22] Perhaps, also, we are now in a position to take the apparently preposterous mantra of the moral police—obscenity as a threat to the moral fabric, and so on—seriously. The moral fabric—that is, the symbolic order underwritten by restricted obscenity—*is* in fact at risk of unraveling, not because of some set of image-objects that can be quarantined by law but rather because of the generalized obscenity that exists as a virtual tendency in apparently innocent images. This, then, would be the literal meaning of that phrase most beloved of the moral crusaders of the 1910s and 1920s: "demoralizing films."

Well into the "Power" section of the extraordinary *Crowds and Power*, Elias Canetti explains, through the figure of unmasking, how the power of a sovereign is grounded in setting up a routinized, controllable transgression: "A ruler wages continuous warfare against spontaneous and uncontrolled transformation. The weapon he uses in this fight is the process of *unmasking*, the exact opposite of transformation. . . . It is part of the nature of this process of unmasking that the perpetrator always knows exactly what he will find" (1984 [1960]:378). Many years later, Michael Taussig— coming at the same problem via Bataille (but also mindful of Canetti's line on unmasking)—remarks that the sacrality of sovereign power relies on defacement. Or to put it another way, it relies on the censorship that triggers transgression, "Obscenity is built into the quasi-divine right of authority, royal or common" (1999:39). The power of restricted obscenity is that it provokes the viscerally routinized transgressions that constantly reinstall a symbolic order—a moral law and the performative dispensation that sponsors and polices it. But it remains haunted by that generalized potential encoded in the Hicklin Test as the tendency of "the matter charged."

And that is the censor's confusing gesture: pointing to an opening while herding us into an enclosure.

SLIGHT RETURN

The censor's fist came crashing down onto his desk. It was November 2003. Vijay Anand was bristling at the memory of his failed attempt to reform Indian film censorship. In 2001 he got a call from Sushma Swaraj, then the minister of information and broadcasting in the BJP-led national government. I must have raised a surprised eyebrow at the very mention of her name, because Anand was quick to explain:

> I *warned* her. I warned her. I said, "OK look, I'm a man of cinema, I love cinema. I don't like censorship. I may ultimately destroy your censorship." She said, "We *want* a man like that." I knew the whole game. I

knew how a filmmaker suffers, how the Censor Board can create *hell* for a filmmaker. So I took it very seriously. I traveled all over. I found out. We are making films in nine languages. We have nine centers where the films are being censored. So I visited all the nine centers, I interacted with the members who censor the movies. I interacted with the directors, the writers and the producers. I interacted with a lot of intellectuals. University professors. I interacted with politicians. I consulted lawyers. I consulted a lot of people who matter. [My proposals were] very drastic. I had to fight with even the members who were on the Censor Board. The structure of the Censor Board. How it functions. How it affects the industry. I made it very simple and radically different from what it was. And I went through the documents of censorship of almost every country in the world that's censoring movies. I got the whole thing translated. It took me a hell of a long time. I got it from Japan too. Italy. Austria. USA. Canada. Britain. All these I read.[23]

Vijay Anand knew that many key members of Parliament, particularly in South India, relied on the film business. He was careful to cultivate the contacts that would support his reforms once they reached the national legislature. During the time that he was traveling the country and formulating his proposals, he had also been very open with the media. Too open, some said. Before he was able properly to discuss his proposals with his own committee, a draft of the plan was leaked. All hell broke loose. Questions rained thick and fast in Parliament, and Sushma Swaraj came under pressure from women's groups who were outraged by the rumors that Anand was about to institute a system of state-sanctioned porn. She pulled the plug. Anand recalled that "after ten months' work I was about to come out with that draft. Suddenly I got a call from New Delhi: 'Please don't go so far. Our government will not be able to support you to the level that you want.'" Anand resigned in a flurry of embittered publicity. Was he a victim of prudish pressure groups? Did the government use moral crusaders as a cover for their own anxiety about relinquishing control over the CBFC?

Perhaps it does not matter. If the proposal for X-rated theaters had gone through, the government might have enjoyed a windfall in new entertainment taxes at two or three times the rate for ordinary films. The symbolic economy of restricted obscenity would have stayed intact even as its political economy expanded. If Anand had gotten his way on wresting appointments to the Censor Board and its advisory panels away from direct government control, then the practical criteria for censorship might have shifted in a more interpretive, contextualist direction. Or—depending on who ended up doing the choosing—not.

None of this would have addressed the basic issue that film censorship both highlights and disavows: what to do with the haptic tendencies that the cinema brings into such exquisitely uncanny focus. While this may at first sight have seemed an esoteric point, my aim in this book has been to show how and why it remains one of the most fundamental problems of public life. Ultimately, it is the question of how mass-mediated life together becomes possible and livable, how the emergent enthusiasms of a mass society are or are not shaped into cultural and ideological projects.

It is no accident that anxieties about pissing men and obscene tendencies focus so tightly on the cinema. Perhaps more than anywhere else, it is as cinema spectators that we experience the intimate anonymity of mass publicity most acutely. In the cinema hall we are face-to-face crowd and abstract public at once, embodied and anonymous. For this reason, if the age of the cinema looks like it has passed, if "new media" seem to have made the cinema old, then I would argue that it still contains untimely provocations for a sharper understanding of many more recent machines. In our digital time, with its ever more customized and privatized forms of media consumption, the cinema hall may seem like an archaic space. As such it risks exuding the deceptive anti-erotics that Walter Benjamin attributed to recently outmoded phenomena.[24] But it was also Benjamin (2008b [1936]) who recognized the peculiar potentialities of the cinema as a mass medium. He knew that the cinema marked the definitive end of social orders organized around singularly emplaced ritual practices. Whatever political forms the future held were going to have to find a way of channeling the affective potentials of collective effervescence through the intimately anonymous forms of mass publicity.

Today, as cinema stretches and fragments across multiple digital media, film scholars are probing emergent, more distributed forms of spectatorship. Ravi Vasudevan describes them as enabling "an imaginary . . . which refuses the limits of the cinema hall, or of a unified filmic address in defining the scope of film experience. [In] these accounts, filmic experience is now substantially hybridized as it is entangled, mixed, remodeled, by its mobilization into the highly fluid forms of contemporary media experience" (2010:357; see A. Rai 2009).

Whereas some detect liberatory potentials in the brave new digital cinemascape, others mourn the loss of a vitally critical public formation around films that depended on the forms of viewing enabled by the cinema hall. Ashish Rajadhyaksha reflects that

> the period—the years between 1895 and 1990—that we are able to so accurately identify as the "time of celluloid" can be further bracketed off as determining a public engagement with the moving image. This is a particular kind of public: one that celluloid not only exemplifies but, in hindsight, may have fabricated largely on its own, and narrativized primarily as a mix of text and social action through the twin regulatory mechanisms of *containment* and *excess*. "Containment" is a formal requirement of the film frame and a social requirement of perhaps the most crucial institution of the public domain in our time of celluloid: the movie theatre. Its inherent structural instability, notwithstanding—perhaps exacerbated by—its fantasy character, has real public consequences that it does not apparently share even with sequel technologies such as, say, video. (2009:7)

In this book, I have argued that this public cultural dialectic of containment and excess finds its sharpest articulation at the cinema but also that its roots are deeper and more general, that it is ultimately a function of the structural provocation generated by the open edge of mass publicity. It preceded the cinema historically and exceeds it now.

Still, if the cinema brought this "public engagement" into acute focus, then perhaps the passing of the movie theater as the definitive site of spectatorship may also be blurring it. The point, surely, is neither to wax nostalgic over lost opportunities nor to assume that emergent formations necessarily spell freedom. Clearly, times and technologies are changing. But an untimely investigation across time may be more fruitful than either celebratory or elegiac narratives of epochal rupture. What, for example, can a focus on emergent potentialities help us to understand about the time of celluloid? And, conversely, does the cinema hall's mobile simultaneity of crowd and public still hold lessons for our engagements with digital media?

Writing on the historical knife's edge of the mid-1930s, Walter Benjamin distinguished, famously, between two possible outcomes. The cinema could become a handmaiden to the aestheticization of politics, in which case the regressive performative dispensation of movie star celebrity would join hands with the rising cult of the Führer. Or it could nudge open the door to a new mass politicization of aesthetics, potentiating the tendencies lying dormant in our collective sensoria in hitherto unsuspected ways. Our current situation may be less starkly marked as a world historical either/or. But as it palpates the public punctum, the censor's fist still struggles to keep a double grip on the ritual banner staff of sovereign authority and the nameless force of the new.

NOTES

1. IOL, MSS EUR/F191/191.

2. Examples include Derné 2000; Dickey 1993, 1995, 2001; Nakassis and Dean 2007; L. Srinivas 2002; and S. V. Srinivas 2009.

3. Efficient narrative overviews can be found in Bhowmik 2009 and Vasudev 1978.

4. I decided to pursue an immanent critique of Indian film censorship because I sensed that its internal contradictions opened up questions that a more externalist analysis would miss. At the same time, my immanentist orientation has its costs. I am aware, for example, that there is much of direct relevance to my argument that emerges out of the nonvisual aspects of cinematic experience, not least in the dimension of sound (Altman, ed., 1992). Although several passages clearly imply a movement beyond the visual and toward a more general (perhaps synaesthesic) phenomenology of spectatorship (see, for instance, Sobchack 2004), I remain conscious that I have inherited my informants' habit of imagining the cinema primarily in terms of seeing.

5. A quick word about my use of the phrase *mass publicity*. Many would argue that the age of "masses"—of "mass democracy," "mass culture," even "mass media" —has been historically supplanted by more differentiated structures of politics, marketing, and media. I cling to the term *mass* not out of some nostalgia for a

vanished, more homogeneous era but because it preserves the sense of generality that I believe still characterizes the modern notion of publics. I toyed briefly with replacing the term *publicity* with *publicness* in acknowledgment of the distinction by Jürgen Habermas (1989) between a commercial public sphere, driven by advertising and marketing, and the kind of public sphere that is premised on deliberative reason. But aside from the inelegance of the phrase "the open edge of mass publicness" (see below), I also quickly realized that one of the aims of my argument in this book was to point to the mutual imbrication of the categories that Habermas wants to separate.

6. As it turned out, Anupam Kher's tenure as CFBC chair would be just as turbulent and short as that of Vijay Anand. Anand's chairmanship had been cut short by the controversy over his proposed overhaul of the censorship process; Kher became embroiled in a struggle over the CFBC's attempt to ban *Final Solution*, Rakesh Sharma's harrowing documentary account of the origins and aftermath of the genocidal violence that killed an estimated two thousand Muslims in Gujarat in February 2002. One of Kher's final acts as CFBC chair was to oversee the granting of a censor certificate with no cuts to *Final Solution* in October 2004, but it was too little too late. Some claimed that Kher's days as censor chief had effectively been numbered since a government led by the Congress Party took over in New Delhi in May of that year. Whatever the causes that led to his departure, Kher's position was then taken over by veteran actress Sharmila Tagore, who served until 2011.

7. My intention here is not simply to participate in the easy scoffing that so often greets outbursts like Trivedi's on the part of those people against whom his accusations are directed. Instead, I think it is important historically to situate this desire to protect the "essence of Indianness" from the more brutal winds of global modernity. One strand of such a historicization leads, as I show in chapter 1, back to the British colonial policy of noninterference in Indian "custom," whereby "traditional" Indian practices, particularly those that the British understood as authentically religious, were granted relative protection from administrative intervention. Another strand leads back to the proto-nationalist distinction so influentially described by Partha Chatterjee (1993), according to which an "inner" cultural sphere of Indianness was set apart from an "outer" sphere of realpolitik. Both strategies, of course, inadvertently helped to produce what they were in the business of protecting, namely, "authentic Indian culture."

8. An earlier version of some of the material in this section appears in Mazzarella and Kaur 2009.

9. At a government/film industry forum in 1996, Bhatt startled participants by calling for a "right to pornography" for every Indian citizen and declaring himself —perhaps not entirely helpfully for his cause—the classic "Indian male junglee" (U. Rai 1996). Journalist Derek Bose notes that Bhatt provoked protests with his statements in support of pornography at a time when he was on the governing council

of the government-run Film and Television Institute of India in Pune: "In a memorandum to the Ministry of Information and Broadcasting, prominent women's organizations in the country demanded Bhatt's removal on the grounds that no Indian citizen and particularly one holding a government office can affirm the right to watch pornography" (Bose 2005:150). Discussing the U.S. culture wars of the 1980s, Wendy Steiner notes that in response to the wave of moral policing aimed at everyone from the photographer Robert Mapplethorpe to the sit-com *Married . . . With Children*, "the nation's art associations declared August 26, 1989 Art Emergency Day" (Steiner 1995:16).

10. For an inside account of the *Water* controversy, see the memoir *Shooting Water* (2005), by Deepa Mehta's daughter, Devyani Saltzman; Ghosh 2010 is an invaluable one-stop synthetic analysis of the *Fire* controversy.

11. *Rath yatra* literally means "pilgrimage by chariot." The 1990 version was a massive publicity stunt/mobilization organized by the BJP and its affiliate organizations, under the rubric Ram Rath Yatra (a rath yatra in the name of the Hindu god-king Ram). Riding a "chariot" (actually a modified truck), Advani intended to proceed, in a winding, ten-thousand-kilometer (ca. 6,200-mile) itinerary from Somnath on India's west coast (the symbolically pregnant site of a Hindu temple destroyed by Islamic invaders in the eleventh century) to Ayodhya, the town in Uttar Pradesh where Hindu nationalists claim that the sixteenth-century Babri mosque was constructed on the site of Ram's birth. In the event, and after much violence along the way, the yatra was cut short when Advani was arrested in Dhanbad in the state of Bihar on October 23, 1990. The Babri mosque was destroyed just over two years later on December 6, 1992, when it was stormed by Hindu nationalist activists.

12. Rakesh Sharma, interview with the author, Mumbai, April 9, 2004.

13. Fashion TV was founded in France in 1997 and has become a worldwide staple of satellite/cable television. During the postliberalization period in India, its steady diet of scantily clad catwalk footage was often used as a kind of shorthand for the ambient cultural transformation and/or corruption of Indian life. See Mazzarella (2006) for an example of its implied role in facilitating political corruption. STAR TV (Satellite Television for the Asian Region) is a Rupert Murdoch–owned network that, as of the time of this writing (January 2011), claims more than 300 million viewers in over fifty countries.

14. Ram Madhvani, interview with the author, Mumbai, November 10, 2003.

15. NDTV (New Delhi Television Limited) was founded as a private television channel in 1988. Its news channel, NDTV 24x7, currently enjoys the largest market share among English-language news channels. It produces news from a score of locations in India.

16. Nupur Basu, interview with the author, Bangalore, December 11, 2003. "Orange colours" is a reference to the saffron hue that symbolizes Hinduism.

17. Similar arguments have been made about censorship regimes elsewhere. Under the presidency of Georges Pompidou (1969–74), the French censor board instituted a categorical separation between "subversive" and "pornographic" content, a separation that, Martyn Auty (1997) argues, has facilitated a politically convenient diversionary liberalization of sexual imagery.

18. A quick perusal of the summer–fall issues of the *Illustrated Weekly of India*, of which Khushwant Singh was then the editor, bears out the claim. Whereas almost every issue in the two years leading up to the declaration of the Emergency in June 1975 burst at the seams with coverage of challenges to Mrs. Gandhi's legitimacy, the issues that followed suddenly contain no political coverage at all beyond officially approved analyses of India's infrastructural challenges. The bare breasts that had become a regular feature of every issue since around 1969—either in the form of snapshots of scandalously liberated Western models or ethnographically legitimated photo features in the style of *National Geographic*—continued undisturbed.

19. Tarun Tejpal, *Tehelka* editor, inveterate investigative journalist, and veteran of many a scandal (see Mazzarella 2006), tried heroically to sustain the idea that the Indian public sphere would not succumb in this way: "The sex scandal comes way down in the hierarchy. It means nothing, concerns no one, does not exist in the public domain. It is basically a first world indulgence, a means to group voyeurism and artificial excitement" (Tejpal 2001).

20. The term *sex film* did not, of course, refer to pornographic films, but rather to dramas that dealt with intimate or romantic relations. When asked by the Indian Cinematograph Committee what the term might mean, Bombay exhibitor R. N. Bharucha responded, "I do not know whether I shall be able to evolve a definition offhand but I will put it this way—any film which has for its main theme the relations of the sexes" (ICC 1928a, 1:115). S. A. Alley, a cinema manager in Calcutta, was rather more specific, suggesting that "sex films" are films "where there are passionate love-making scenes, kissing—not the ordinary kissing, but kissing passionately, all over the body" (2:822).

21. MSA, Home/Poll/1934/271.

22. Anupama Chopra, interview with the author, Mumbai, November 27, 2003. All subsequent quotations from Chopra in this chapter, unless otherwise noted, are taken from this conversation.

23. Kalpana Sharma, interview with the author, Mumbai, November 13, 2003.

24. The fact that Western directors were also now keenly experimenting with Bollywood textures and locations was, despite occasional controversies over the politics of representation embodied by the actual films, largely taken as evidence of the capacity of Hindi film melodrama to speak to universal human emotions. The culmination of this tendency came in 2008–9, with the Oscar-dominating success of Danny Boyle's *Slumdog Millionaire*. In addition, the fact that Bollywood melo-

drama, rather than the Indian "art film" aesthetic of Satyajit Ray and his heirs, had made it big in the West was, for many in the commercial film business, understandably an enormous vindication after decades of denigration by "serious" cineastes.

25. Pritish Nandy, interview with the author, Mumbai, November 22, 2003. One might note that Nandy spoke from experience; his own accession to the Rajya Sabha was on a Shiv Sena ticket—that is, as a representative of the Mumbai-based political movement and party that had, perhaps more than any other mainstream organization, become well known not only for its chauvinist violence against variously designated outsiders (at various times South Indians, Muslims, and North Indians) but—more especially—for its experiments in militant public cultural regulation (Bedi 2007, 2009; Eckert 2003; Hansen 2001; Heuzé 1996; Lele 1996).

26. Vijay Anand, interview with the author, Mumbai, November 17, 2003. All subsequent quotations from Anand in this chapter, unless otherwise noted, are taken from this conversation.

27. Javed Akhtar, interview with the author, Mumbai, March 11, 2004.

28. Anupam Kher, interview with the author, Mumbai, November 12, 2003.

29. Drawing on Lauren Berlant (1993), Srirupa Roy writes that "Nehruvian India's most frequently invoked figure was that of the 'infantile citizen' and his need for state tutelage and protection in order to realize the potentials of citizenship, itself conceptualized as an infinitely receding horizon rather than an existing bundle of rights" (2007:20).

30. Vijay Tendulkar, interview with the author, Mumbai, March 20, 2004. Christopher Pinney elegantly captures this paradoxical potentiating effect of censorship in a discussion of the colonial regulation of printed Indian images in the early twentieth century: "Proscription thus operated within a double-bind in which every denial was simultaneously a reinscription of representational potency" (2004: 109).

31. Of course, someone like Anupam Kher, in his capacity as Censor Board chair, insisted that this is precisely what the CFBC already did. It is true that the distinction between the Indian system and the American one was perhaps not quite as clear as many of my informants believed. A common belief in India, for example, is that the American censors only recommend age-appropriate certificates rather than demand cuts. As Kirby Dick's documentary *This Film Is Not Yet Rated* (2005) shows, however, the ratings board operated by the Academy of Motion Picture Arts and Sciences remains an extremely shadowy body whose demands, particularly when the commercial pressures on film producers are taken into account, can often seem just as arbitrary and tyrannical as the treatment meted out to many of my Indian informants by the CFBC. The CFBC changed the meaning of its final initial in the 1980s from Censorship to Certification, a move that had been proposed as far back as the early 1960s (NAI, Ministry of Information and Broadcasting/Film Censors/5–2–61-FC [1961]).

The problem of enforcement adds a whole other level of logistical complexity to the question of censorship versus certification. As film journalist Anupama Chopra pointed out, "The thing is, who would enforce that in India? How would you do it? Which theatre in, like, Patiala would say 'no, I'm not going to let this kid in'—he's paying 50 bucks. Even now the way the censorship is, it doesn't really function because outside of Bombay, who knows what's going on? You don't even get box office receipts for those damn theatres, how the hell are you going to know who's *watching* the movies?" Shiv Sena culture czar Pramod Navalkar, for his part, suggested spot check inspections: "Lay down the rules, leave it to the conscience of the producers. And if they are sitting in Delhi, wasting time watching movies, let them make a flying squad of fifty or five hundred people, let them go to theatres for inspection. And if they find any rules that are let down—ban it" (Pramod Navalkar, interview with the author, Mumbai, November 23, 2003). As early as 1951, the report of the Patil Committee (properly known as the Film Enquiry Committee) recommended that state governments, not exhibitors, be required to enforce age restrictions on cinema admission.

32. MSA, Home/Poll/1932–33–34–35–36/165.

33. Rahul Bose, interview with the author, Mumbai, December 1, 2003.

34. Shyam Benegal, interview with the author, Mumbai, March 18, 2004.

35. The single exception to this exception that I have found is one of the Indian Cinematograph Committee's respondents, a Mr. B. Das, a lawyer from Calcutta, who acknowledged his own susceptibility to the cinema while at the same time describing it as distinctively Indian: "I base it on my own personal experience. Before I went to England, I never saw a cinema film; but during my stay in England I saw many of these emotional films. You know the Indian social life is quite different from the western social life. Naturally when I saw those emotional films, there was a mental and moral fall in me, even in my own estimation. I felt a bit impulsive and emotional. What is natural to the West is not natural to the East" (Indian Cinematograph Committee [ICC], 1928a 3:981).

36. B. K. Karanjia, interview with the author, Mumbai, November 17, 2003. All subsequent quotations from Karanjia in this chapter, unless otherwise noted, are taken from this conversation.

37. The expression *Lakshman rekha* comes from later versions of the *Ramayana* epic in which the hero, Ram's brother Lakshman, draws a protective line (rekha) around Ram's wife Sita's dwelling before setting off to look for Ram. In the event, Sita breaches the rekha when the demon-king Ravan shows up disguised as a mendicant begging for alms.

38. Anupam Kher told me, "You must understand that people that spend money and watch movies in theatres are not there to intellectualize cinema. They are going to get entertained. And dance-singing entertains them. Crying entertains them. Fear entertains them. It's how you get entertained. That is the nature of cinema in India."

39. The term *frontbenchers*, often used in India to describe the (subaltern) men in the cheapest section of the cinema hall, is of course deliciously ironic, as it also alludes to the leading spokespeople of a parliamentary party. As such it invokes both an ideal of deliberative democracy and its negation in the rowdy vocalizations of "the pit class."

40. Anil Dharker, interview with the author, Mumbai, April 1, 2004.

41. I am grateful to a misprint on page 3 of the 1921 Cinematograph Censorship Rules for this unintentionally apt phrase (MSA, Home Dept [Poll] 1926:172).

42. Kajri Jain observes that "for a start, we need to attend to the ways in which images themselves are bearers not just of 'interior' meanings but of a habitus: they are bodies that actualize social structures, rendering these structures concrete through their engagements with other bodies (other images as well as flesh and blood beings). . . . Further, we need to attend to the corporeal registers in which these engagements occur, not just to their psychic (understood as mental) effects, or their conservative or transformative potentials at the level of ideas" (2007:317).

43. Monstrous because ostensibly oxymoronic. Miriam Hansen's reluctance to call Kracauer a vitalist, despite acknowledging the influence of Bergson on *Theory of Film* (1997 [1960]), is in this regard telling: "Kracauer's insistence on the concreteness of camera reality versus the abstractness inflicted on our perception by modern science may echo the old vitalist complaint about the mechanist reduction of life, but his notion of the flow of life does not hinge on that opposition; besides, he links the possibility of seeing and experiencing life in its concreteness to its refraction through the cinematic apparatus" (2011:272).

44. Letter to the editor, *Bombay Chronicle*, January 31, 1925 (IOL, L/P&J/6/1747 [2601/21]).

CHAPTER 1: PERFORMATIVE DISPENSATIONS

1. My sources for this unapologetically bowdlerized version of the first section of Bharata's *Natyashastra* are Rangacharya 1996, Richmond 1993, and Unni 1998.

2. I am drawing here on the splendid work of Kathryn Hansen (1989, 2001).

3. Ravi Vasudevan remarks of the Parsi stage that "while there were intimations of the hermetic, self-referential features of modern theater, and realist dimensions deriving from the human portraiture of divine and mythical figures in realist painting and stage acting, ultimately the Parsi theater appeared to reiterate a highly iconic, frontal mode of address to its audiences that broke the onward flow of a narratively self-enclosed fictive world" (2010:37).

4. This scene is based on material contained in a file at the India Office Library: L/PS/11/272 (item P 4543/1926).

5. Elements of this montage are derived from "After the Fire" 1997, Dutt 1998, "Fire-CPM . . ." 1998, Jain and Raval 1998, Malhotra 1998, Mehra 1998, and Ravindran 1998.

6. Merriam-Webster online dictionary, at http://www.merriam-webster.com/dictionary/dispensation (accessed January 17, 2011).

7. As part of its mass mobilization toward the destruction of the Babri mosque in Ayodhya in 1992, the Hindu right organized Ram shila pujas all over India, rituals devoted to the consecration of bricks that were to be used in the construction of a Ram temple on the contested site of the mosque.

8. According to Hindu traditions, Brahma emerged from a lotus, which itself emerged from Vishnu's navel.

9. I am alluding here to the dramatist Bertolt Brecht's famous *Verfremdungs-effekt*, or estrangement-effect, according to which a play should disrupt the audience's identification with the characters at key moments so as to provoke a critical evaluation of the situation being depicted.

10. Against the fascination with large-scale *son et lumière* in Bollywood, the mainstream commercial stage, and political spectacle, experiments with various forms of Indian "peoples' theater" had, over the years, attempted to introduce modernist strategies of interruption—whether of narrative identification or of the proscenium fourth wall, whether from Brecht, Grotowsky, or Boal—into activist practice. Many fascinating exercises in progressive performance had come and gone between the heyday of the Indian People's Theater Association in the 1940s and the murder of street actor Safdar Hashmi by all-too-actual *asuras* in the midst of a performance in Delhi in 1989.

11. Bharucha (1992) says, "This 'timelessness,' of course, is a construct that has been imposed by cultural authorities in their 'invention of tradition' along with concepts of purity, authenticity and cultural preservation. The seeming transcendence of politics in these categories is political in its own right, revealing forms of censorship that have yet to be challenged by contemporary artists."

12. Ibid.

13. Ibid.

14. Bharucha's argument here is reminiscent of the line that Ashis Nandy (2002) has taken on Indian secularism and its discontents. Just as Bharucha finds in indigenous performance practices a willingness to confront, mediate, and absorb complexity and contradiction, so Nandy celebrates the adaptive creativity of ordinary religious practice as against the shared brittle rigidity of Hindu nationalism and secular modernism.

15. The bill on which it was based was completed by June 1917 and introduced into the Legislative Council that September.

16. A limelight explosion had in fact killed a projectionist and his assistant in Rangoon in 1909 (NAI, Home [Poll] February 1917:82–110 [A]). The Government of India was, during the deliberations leading to the passage of CA 1918, quite conscious of the fact that because a significant proportion of Indian cinema shows at the time took place outdoors, the justification of new legislation primarily on the

basis of fire hazards would be problematic (NAI, Home [Poll] May 1918:595–604 [A]). Conversely, since limelight was also used in other kinds of public entertainments, it was not immediately obvious that this could be made a centerpiece of legislation specifically designed to regulate the cinema.

17. Not that wartime controls were foolproof, either. In a November 1916 memo, P. H. Dumbell of the Public and Judicial Department of the India Office in London noted that "in war time more can be done in the way of censorship, given the existing organizations and the wider powers wielded by Government, than is possible in peace; but there always seems to be some loophole" (IOL, L/P&J/6/1468 [5256/16]).

18. The Government of India Act of 1919 extended the franchise and boosted the power of provincial legislative councils. Nonelected, generally British officials retained control of finance, revenue, and home affairs.

19. See Mazzarella 2010a for an analysis of the challenges of legitimating the Raj through propaganda during World War II.

20. As Rudolph and Rudolph (2002) point out, the movement toward institutionalizing English-language education in India was part of the liberal-utilitarian initiative inaugurated by the transformation of Thomas Macaulay's infamous 1835 Minute on Education into official policy. After Governor-General Bentinck's administration agreed in that same year to allocate funds to English-language schooling, the process received a further boost a couple of decades later when, in 1857, Sir Charles Wood's 1854 Education Dispatch was acted upon in order to found English-medium universities in the three presidency cities: Calcutta, Madras, and Bombay.

21. According to Chatterji (1991:29), the first Indian-owned paper in English, the *Bengal Gazette*, appeared in 1816, the first Indian-language paper, the Bengali *Samband Kaumudi*, edited by Raja Ram Mohan Roy, in about 1820. *Vidanta*, a Hindi weekly, appeared in Calcutta in 1826; the first Hindi daily was *Samachar Sudha Varshan* in 1854.

22. Chandrika Kaul quotes figures stating that the Indian circulation of vernacular papers rose from 229,000 in 1885 to 817,000 in 1905 (2003:101). Tapti Roy (1995) notes that by 1911, the Bengali print industry was second only to the jute business in regional economic importance.

23. The Adam Regulation of 1823, which required the official licensing and vetting of all books and newspapers, was enacted over the vociferous objections of prominent early social reformer and the father of the Bengal Renaissance, Rammohun Roy. Charles Metcalfe, provisionally governor-general in 1835–36, later repealed the regulation, having been advised by Thomas Macaulay that it was "wholly indefensible." The Press and Registration of Books Act was passed in 1867, and the Vernacular Press Act of 1878 was enacted during the viceroyalty of Lord Lytton, only to be withdrawn in 1881 under Lord Ripon.

24. So, for example, the Irish missionary James Long compiled the first com-

prehensive list of publications in Bengal in 1852, a resource that was quickly exploited by the government for surveillance purposes. But Long also found himself on trial in 1860 for having produced an English translation of *Nil Darpan* (*The Mirror of Indigo*), a Bengali play critical of conditions on indigo plantations. On that occasion, he defended himself by arguing that the British authorities could only establish solid legitimacy in India through an intimate knowledge of the idioms of vernacular cultural production and that it was "folly to shut our eyes to the warnings the Native Press may give" (quoted in Bhattacharyya 1989:9).

25. Lutgendorf 1989 notes that the Pax Britannica, such as it was, was in some cases a boon to cultural producers, since it helped to divert the energies of Indian rulers from warfare toward arts less martial.

26. Christopher Pinney notes the publication in 1874 of two photographic exercises in feudal nostalgia: the *Lucknow Album*, aimed at a European audience, and *The Beauties of Lucknow*, "a nostalgic eulogy for Wajid Ali Shah's court," intended for "an Indian male audience eager for the scent of a 'Lucknow immemorable for the Oriental magnificence of its entertainments'" (2008:36).

27. The post-Independence version of the Dramatic Performances Act interpolates a gesture toward a liberalized conception of dramatic criticism: "Merely because a person preaches or advocates by staging a play a political ideology different from the ideology of the party in power, a prohibitory order under Section 3 is unjustified."

28. The quotation is from Horace's letter on the Art of Poetry. It is worth reproducing the surrounding lines as well, since they pertain so directly to the question of what should and should not be allowed on the blood-stirring stage:

> The business of the drama must appear
> In action or description. What we hear,
> With weaker passion will affect the heart,
> Than when the faithful eye beholds the part.
> But yet let nothing on the stage be brought
> Which better should behind the scenes be wrought;
> Nor force th' unwilling audience to behold
> What may with grace and eloquence be told.
> Let not Medea, with unnatural rage,
> Slaughter her mangled infants on the stage;
> Nor Atreus his nefarious feast prepare,
> Nor Cadmus roll a snake, nor Progne wing the air;
> For while upon such monstrous scenes we gaze,
> They shock our faith, our indignation raise. (Chalmers 1810:744)

29. The comparative reference during these debates was always to the Lord Chamberlain's role in licensing stage performances in England.

30. Shanta Gokhale, interview with the author, Mumbai, November 2003. All quotations from Gokhale in this chapter, unless otherwise noted, are taken from this conversation.

31. MSA, Judicial Dept, File no 24, 1918.

32. MSA, Judicial Dept; 24-II, 1916.

33. NAI, Home (Poll) May 1918:595–604 (A).

34. Here, as elsewhere, we see a topical correspondence between colonial regulatory and early film theoretical concerns. Some of the early writers on film, for example, Hugo Münsterberg, were at this same time addressing the question of whether or not film was essentially a variation on theater (2002 [1916]).

35. The appearance and disappearance of the qualifier "public" in such phrases as "public performance" and "public exhibition"—as well as its subtly shifting meanings—is a topic that I explore elsewhere, in the context of an analysis of the 2003–6 Campaign Against Censorship by Indian independent and documentary filmmakers.

36. *Jatra* refers specifically to a Bengali form of itinerant folk theater, but the nineteenth-century colonial administration used the term to cover several related forms of "traditional" entertainments.

37. IOL, L/P&J/6/1468 (5256/16).

38. Rachel Moore notes that Vachel Lindsay, in one of the very earliest serious works on the cinema, *The Art of the Moving Picture* (1915), expressed precisely this apprehension: that "America, like cinema itself, was . . . both primitive and advanced" (2000:54).

39. In citations to the proceedings of the ICC throughout this book, the number before the colon denotes the volume, and the number or numbers following the colon are page number(s).

40. Anupama Chopra, interview with the author, Mumbai, November 27, 2003.

41. These dynamics were always regionally inflected. So, for instance, in the south and in Tamil Nadu in particular, bourgeois North Indian modernity still represented Aryan oppression. Against this, by the early decades of the twentieth century, Tamilian regional pride was allied with an evangelically moralizing English-language social reformism (Ramaswamy 1997; Seizer 2005).

42. NAI, Home (Poll) February 1917:82–110 (A).

43. Ratna Kapur (2002) was one of the few contemporary commentators who seemed to detect something tyrannical in Bibiji's bell ringing and thus to see her as something more complex than simply a pitiable victim.

44. Shabana Azmi, interview with the author, Mumbai, December 21, 2003. All subsequent quotations from Azmi in this chapter, unless otherwise noted, are taken from this conversation.

45. Navalkar, who passed away in 2007, was a close associate of Shiv Sena founder Bal Thackeray from the party's earliest days. In 1968 he was elected to the

Bombay Municipal Corporation, and in 1972 he was the first Shiv Sainik to be elected to the state assembly of Maharashtra.

46. Ashish Rajadhyaksha (2009) reminds us that Navalkar was himself no stranger to the titillating tale. One of his stocks-in-trade as an author was a narrative style that combined loving attention to prurient detail with bracing condemnation of vice.

47. Pramod Navalkar, interview with the author, Mumbai, November 23, 2003. All subsequent quotations from Navalkar in this chapter, unless otherwise noted, are taken from this conversation.

48. Navalkar used the phrase ABCD here to suggest completeness, in the sense of "all the way through the alphabet." Ironically, this phrase is also commonly used to describe precisely the kind of diasporic South Asians—American-Born Confused Desis—who are thought to have lost touch with their subcontinental cultural roots.

49. That is, from Maharashtra, the Indian state in which Mumbai is located.

50. The concert was organized under the aegis of the Shiv Udyog Sena (SUS), an outfit started by Bal Thackeray's nephew, Raj Thackeray, to provide employment for Maharashtrian youth. Raj Thackeray split off from the Shiv Sena in 2006 after a power struggle with Bal Thackeray's son, Uddhav, and founded his own regionalist party, the Maharashtra Navnirman Sena. Rustom Bharucha notes that "registered as a society a month after Jackson had agreed to perform in Mumbai, and recognized as a charitable organization a week before the show . . . the SUS has almost flaunted its absence of credibility" (2001:222n7).

CHAPTER 2: GROUNDS OF THE CENSOR'S JUDGMENT

1. Precisely the same argument is used to justify state-managed mass pedagogy, that is, propaganda. The 1985 Joshi Report (formally known as *An Indian Personality for Television: Report of the Working Group on Software for Doordarshan*) paints the same picture of an in-between India: "Such political and social education is of immense importance in a developing country where a moral void is generated as old institutions and values tend to lose their hold on the people but new institutions and values take time to strike deep roots. We have vast areas in the country which have been newly opened up from their isolation and brought into the mainstream of modern life. This sudden exposure implies for the people a gigantic leap from tribalism to the modern world. Such traumatic changes have vast, psychologically destabilizing consequences. In such periods of transition, mass education is required for mentally preparing the people for absorbing the shocks of change and in fact, in learning to live with change. Here is a historic opportunity for the mass media for playing an *educational role* of helping to reduce the cultural or mental lag between *modern conditions of living* and a *pre-modern social outlook*" (Government of India 1985:98–99).

2. Vijay Anand, interview with the author, Mumbai, November 17, 2003. All subsequent quotations from Anand in this chapter, unless otherwise noted, are from this conversation.

3. Anupam Kher, interview with the author, Mumbai, November 12, 2003. All subsequent quotations from Kher in this chapter, unless otherwise noted, are taken from this conversation.

4. Home Member J. Crerar noted in August 1924 that while wholly government-run censorship would obviously have been more efficient, "We are, however, and were from the first, definitely committed, out of regard to the susceptibilities of the Legislature which had to pass the Act and of the public, to a large non-official element" (NAI, Home Dept [Poll] 1925/207).

5. In the colonial administrative territory of Bombay Presidency, the 1921 Cinematograph Rules specified that in cases when the inspector expressed doubts about a film, or when there had been public complaints against a film that was already being shown, a subcommittee of two board members would be appointed to examine it and write a report. Frequently, even after a film had been passed by the board, the inspector—sometimes accompanied by the secretary—would make the rounds of city cinemas in order to verify that it was in fact being screened in accordance with the terms of its certification (i.e., with no subsequently "interpolated" scenes, etc.). For rural and provincial areas outside of the major cities, the district magistrates would forward weekly programs from their districts to the board's secretary for verification (MSA, Home Dept [Poll] 1926:95). The India Office in London worried that the inspectors were not up to the task and that the paltry wages that were offered for the job would militate against securing individuals with the kind of judgment that would be effective in, as Lord Birkenhead put it in 1925, "safeguarding public morals and taste" (MSA, Home Dept [Poll] 1925:194).

6. MSA, Home Dept (Poll) 1925:194. The phrase was Lord Birkenhead's, then the British secretary of state for India.

7. Saiyid Alay Nabi, speaking in the Council of State in March 1927 against film censorship driven by any single moral code, finally arrived at the vital organs with which the equally vital energy of the cinema might resonate: "Public morals are very indefinable. They vary with the climate of a country, they vary with the stage of development of a people. They vary with the religion of a people. Even ethical standards of individuals differ. They vary with education, upbringing and the associations and surroundings of a man. They even vary with the liver and digestive capacity of a man" (IOL, L/P&J/6/1747 [2601/21]).

8. Pinney coins the term *corpothetics* to describe a sensuous engagement with images and material culture that is popular; affective; and, above all, opposed to the Kantian prescription of disinterest: "If 'aesthetics' is about the separation between the image and the beholder, and a 'disinterested' evaluation of images, 'corpothe-

tics' entails a desire to fuse image and beholder, and the elevation of efficacy (as, for example, in *barkat*) as the central criterion of value" (2004:194).

9. The key reforms brought in by the Act were greater autonomy for the provinces of British India (ending the system of "dyarchy" introduced by its 1919 predecessor, the Montagu-Chelmsford Act); the basis for a federal structure that would include both British India and some princely states; and the introduction of direct elections on the basis of a franchise that expanded eligibility from 7 million to 35 million people.

10. MSA, Home Dept (Poll) 1932–33–34–35–36:165.

11. MSA, Home Dept (Poll) 1937:176.

12. Patel was himself very nearly censored for these remarks; the Bombay Government's Home Department wanted to, but could not, put together a defamation case against him.

13. In response to increasingly vocal pressure for representation from various interest groups, S. G. Panandikar, secretary of the Bombay Board, wrote in October 1934 that formally expanding the board's field of consultation was not a good idea: "An officially recognized Advisory Committee, it is apprehended, would seriously hamper the work of the Board, and would be likely to lead to controversies in the press and in public meetings" (MSA, Home Dept [Poll] 1934:231).

14. Aruna Vasudev (1978) notes that the first steps toward the post-Independence centralization of the CBFC in Bombay were taken in the 1935 Government of India Act, when the certification of films was moved from the "provincial" to the "concurrent" list. In other words, film censorship became one of the matters where, according to the federal structure of Indian administration, national uniformity was considered desirable but not obligatory. The Cinematograph (2nd Amendment) Act of 1949 added provisions for the appointment of a single, centralized board of film censors, and the new Constitution of 1950 added films to the list of topics over which the central government would have sole authority (the "union" list). The 1949 Amendment came into effect in 1951, and the new centralized board started work in 1952, shortly after the activation of the new Cinematograph Act.

15. These are located in Bengaluru (formerly Bangalore), Chennai (formerly Madras), Hyderabad, Kolkata (formerly Calcutta), Cuttack, Delhi, Guwahati, and Thiruvananthapuram (or Trivandrum).

16. MSA, Home Dept (Poll) 1925:194.

17. Some attention to regional linguistic representation did make its way into the post-Independence calculus, although it was never formally specified in the acts and rules pertaining to film censorship (NAI, Ministry of Information & Broadcasting/Film Censors/1952/5/1/52-FII). Since a 1959 modification, the Cinematograph Act of 1952 specifies that "the Central Government may establish at such regional centres as it sees fit advisory panels each of which shall consist of such number of persons being persons, qualified in the opinion of the Central Government to judge

the effect of films on the public, as the Central Government may think fit to appoint thereto" (Law Publishers [India] 2003:8).

18. During the first few years of Independence, the CBFC was supposed to appoint the members of the advisory panels. This power was taken over by the central government in 1954. Vijay Anand, of course, was in 2002 planning to recommend an end to—or at least a reduction in—government appointment; indeed, several commentators have suggested that this, not the X-rated theaters proposal, was the main reason that he was forced out of the CBFC chair (Bhowmik 2003). The complaint is in fact as old as the second Cinematograph Act. In June 1952, Ram Gogtay—tireless defender of cinema industry interests since the 1930s—protested in the *Times of India*: "Sir, Dr B V Keskar, the Minister for Information and Broadcasting, stated in the House of the People [i.e., the Lok Sabha] that none of the film censors belongs to any political party. This is misleading. Since January 1951 there have been no 'censors' in the sense of the inspectors who examined films prior to that date. Every film is examined by two or three members of a panel of examiners, who constitute the real censors. Among the members of the panel in Bombay, Messrs Dhurandhar, Gadgil and Salivatiswaran have always been Congressmen. Even among the members of the Central Board of Film Censors, Mrs. Lilavati Munshi, Mr. C R Srinivasan, and Mr. Tushar Kanti Ghosh are members of the Congress Party. Mr. S K Patil was a member of the Central Board until a few months ago. It is, therefore, correct to say that no member of a political party other than the Congress is a film censor today" (NAI, Ministry of Information & Broadcasting/Film Censors/1952/5/1/52-FII).

The question arose again, this time as a matter of legal principle, in 1953 as a result of the Ministry of Law's effort to ensure that members of Parliament were not also officers in "statutory corporations" such as, for example, the CBFC. The matter was initially addressed by the passage of the Prevention of Disqualification (Parliament and Part C States Legislatures) Act of 1953, which allowed a member of Parliament simultaneously to function as a member of a committee set up to advise the government "in respect of any matter of public importance of for the purpose of making an inquiry into, or collecting statistics in respect of any such matter, provided that the holder of any such office is not in receipt of, or entitled to, any fee or remuneration other than 'compensatory allowance.'"

Members of the advisory panels, insofar as they were in fact operating in an advisory capacity to the government, were thus thought to be protected. Members of the Censor Board itself were in a trickier position, since certifying films was, from a legal point of view, an *executive* function. In fact, as the Ministry of Law realized, advisory panel members might also be on thin ice, since they could be construed as holding an "office of profit under the Government of India" as contemplated in Article 102(1)(a) of the Constitution—"profit" here meaning not just monetary gain but also "patronage or honour."

The position of both advisory panel and Censor Board members who were also elected legislators was at the time addressed by the Parliament and Part C States Legislatures Prevention of Disqualifications (Miscellaneous Provisions) Act of 1954, which inserted, among modifications to other existing acts, a new subsection 2 to section 3 of the Cinematograph Act, 1952: "It is hereby declared that the office of a member of the Board or of any Committee or other body set up under any rules made under Section 8 shall not disqualify its holder from being chosen as, or from being a member of either House of Parliament" (NAI, Ministry of Information & Broadcasting/Film Censors/11–3–54-FC [1954]).

Internally, the Ministry of Information and Broadcasting complained that it was unrealistic to expect them only to find appointees who did not have some kind of political leanings or affiliations: "Human beings like all other living things are not brought up in a vacuum, i.e. extraneous influences such as politics cannot be shut out altogether." Indeed, by 1954 one civil servant at the ministry was arguing that precisely *because* the censoring authority should "represent a cross-section of enlightened public opinion," it "should be composed not only of journalists, educationists, social workers etc, but also of elected representatives of the people" (NAI, Ministry of Information & Broadcasting/Film Censors/11–3–54-FC [1954]).

19. The ICC released its report in the summer of 1928. Its major recommendations were (a) to centralize film policy and planning under a national Cinema Department under the existing Department of Commerce, which would oversee and coordinate the funding, production, and management of Indian films; (b) to abandon the so-called Empire Films Scheme, which was designed to encourage of an exchange of films between different parts of the Empire, and had met with almost universal derision; and (c) to centralize the existing censorship apparatus by bringing the provincial boards under the administrative umbrella of a national headquarters at Bombay. Little more was, in fact, heard after the ICC report about any measures to boost British films in India. Indeed, because the talkies came in 1929, the ICC's report was in some respects outdated within a year of its publication. Still, through the early 1930s, it functioned adequately enough as a first-instance rebuttal to continuing parliamentary prodding in London. Meanwhile the Government of India rather reluctantly took up the question of the report's recommendations with the provincial administrations. It was not until September 1932 that the Home Department in Delhi finally wrote to London explaining that the proposal for a central Cinema Department had met with resistance from both the Indian movie business and the provincial administrations. Further, "the Government of India are not disposed to take the view suggested by some of the replies that the existing system of censorship is not capable of improvement, they are inclined to think that any change in it cannot be regarded as sufficiently urgent to justify additional expenditure in the present state of acute financial stringency. They do not therefore propose to proceed further with the matter at present" (IOL, L/P&J/

6/1995 [372/30]). More or less the only recommendation to lead to direct action seems to have been a relatively minor suggestion to waive import duties on educational films.

20. The Motion Picture Society of India started operating in 1932, followed by a series of regional associations: the Bengal Motion Picture Association in 1936, the Indian Motion Picture Producers' Association in Bombay in 1937, and the South Indian Film Chamber of Commerce in Madras in 1938 (Vasudev 1978:61).

21. Informal advisory panels consisting of film producers were in fact attached to the censor boards in Calcutta, Bombay, and Madras in 1966.

22. MSA, Home Dept, 5th Series, 963/5.

23. Thus wrote Gandhi: "Even if I was so minded, I should be unfit to answer your questionnaire, as I have never been to a cinema. But even to an outsider, the evil that it has done and is doing is patent. The good, if it has done any at all, remains to be proved" (ICC 1928a, 4:56). While Gandhi may well never have been to a cinema when he responded to the ICC's questionnaire, both Ramachandra Guha (2007:721) and Robin Jeffrey suggest that he did manage to make it to a movie at least once in his life, to see a mythological film called *Ramrajya* in June 1944. The experience does not appear to have changed his mind about the medium. "'So far as I know,' he wrote to a cousin consoling her about the frivolous habits of a young man, 'I am the only person who has never seen a film. But no, I did go once, not knowing what the thing was about, and saw a film about the exile of Janaki and Ramachandra. It was a depressing experience and I felt like running away from the place, but could not do so. It was sheer waste of time'" (quoted in Jeffrey 2008:19).

24. The 1957 U.S. Supreme Court decision in *Roth v. United States* marked the point at which U.S. law began to require that obscenity be measured not so much as a function of individual passages or aspects of a work, but rather within the context of the work taken as a whole and in relation to contemporary community standards. Taken together with the UK Obscene Publications Act of 1959, *Roth v. United States* represents a shift toward the possibility of defending allegedly obscene materials on the basis of redeeming social value. I discuss this shift from what I call "inherentist" to "contextualist" legal understandings of obscenity in chapters 4 and 5.

25. Vijay Tendulkar, interview with the author, Mumbai, March 20, 2004. All subsequent quotations from Tendulkar in this chapter, unless otherwise noted, are taken from this conversation.

26. Although *Nishant*, like Shyam Benegal's first feature, *Ankur*, was bankrolled by Blaze Advertising and thus not by the government-appointed Film Finance Corporation, it was nevertheless tightly identified with this emergent genre that Madhava Prasad calls "statist realism."

27. In this he was actively assisted by his secretary, Anwar Jamal Kidwai, who, in the early 1980s, went on to found the AJK Mass Communications Research Centre at Jamia Millia Islamia University in New Delhi.

28. Anil Dharker, interview with the author, Mumbai, April 1, 2004. All subsequent quotations from Dharker in this chapter, unless otherwise noted, are taken from this conversation.

29. K. A. Abbas v. The Union of India & Anr on September 24, 1970, at http://indiankanoon.org/doc/1719619/ (accessed August 17, 2011). Predictably, the Emergency would take this crudely quantitative logic to an extreme. Aruna Vasudev relates that "for reasons which only the Ministry could perhaps understand, secret orders were issued to the Censor Board that no more than six minutes of violence which would include fights, were to be permitted, with no single sequence exceeding 60 seconds" (1978:185).

30. The Film Finance Corporation was founded in 1960 and tasked with supporting the production of "films of good standard" (Rajadhyaksha 2009:233). The project started making waves in 1969 with the release of Mrinal Sen's *Bhuvan Shome*, Mani Kaul's *Uski Roti*, and Basu Chatterjee's *Sara Akash*.

31. According to Vijay Anand, the going rate was five lakhs (half a million) rupees. Anand was at the forefront of organizing film world resistance to the Emergency around the opposition Janata Party. But as soon as the Janata coalition had defeated Mrs. Gandhi and formed a government in 1977, it increased the excise levy on films by 300 percent (Vasudev 1978:197).

32. B. K. Karanjia, interview with the author, Mumbai, November 17, 2003. For more on their relationship, see Karanjia's recollections in his memoir *Counting My Blessings* (2005).

33. Regarding the perks of the job, Dharker remembered that "you got a little red book, you know, like a driving license, which theoretically entitled you to walk into any cinema hall at the last minute. You just flashed it—no ticket, nothing. You were there to see that the censorship guidelines had not been violated. It was a badge of some significance, to be able to do that. Plus, don't forget that this was before the age of video, not to mention DVDs and CDs. You got to see all the bloody films! Even films for which you were not on the panel. You could request the producer of the film to have a screening for you and your friends. And they would oblige. They wanted to please you. . . . This was before [the films] were censored. Especially the foreign films. Everyone used to hanker after an invitation."

34. Shyam Benegal, interview with the author, Mumbai, March 18, 2004. All subsequent quotations from Benegal in this chapter, unless otherwise noted, are taken from this conversation.

35. Notwithstanding her routine invocation of the sinister "foreign hand," Mrs. Gandhi's populist scorn for the Indian intelligentsia during the Emergency seems to have been matched only by her desire for the approbation of their counterparts in the West (Bhat 1987; Rajagopal 2011).

36. Actually, it seems to me that the scenes that follow do provide one version of this fantastic amalgam: in a kind of Brahmin compact of sacred and secular leader-

ship, the schoolteacher convinces the priest to speak in the realist language of secular social justice, while the schoolteacher himself reaches for an allegorical-mythical vocabulary rooted in the Puranas.

37. Girish Karnad, interview with the author, Bangalore, December 14, 2003. All subsequent quotations from Karnad in this chapter, unless otherwise noted, are taken from this conversation. Karnad pointed out that the feudal protagonists speak a kind of Urdu "that's used by Muslims, by people at large in the markets and so on. But that was used as the family language." Madhava Prasad (1998:195–96) makes the point that the Benegal moment in the new Hindi cinema relied, precisely, on the deployment of regional Hindi-Urdu that, from the point of view of a speaker of standard Hindi, would signify regionality even as "in real life" most of the characters in both *Ankur* and *Nishant* would probably have spoken Telugu.

38. I asked Tendulkar whether he had been present at the shoot. He told me that although Benegal had wanted him to come along, he disliked going on location because of the boredom, the difficulty of getting work done while away from home, and—most important—the temptation that his presence would generate in the actors to suggest spontaneous changes to the script. He said, "I don't allow the director to work with me. I should be left alone. Because I come from the theatre, I come from literature. I am not a professional scriptwriter in that sense. So I have my concept and I need to be left alone. . . . Changing something on the spot [during the shoot] is not acceptable to me. If a script is well-structured, like a play, then if you want to make changes, you will have to think twice, thrice, four times, five times. You cannot babble into it the way you like. . . . But the problem with the directors is that, while shooting, they think of a number of things. Though they feel that the script is excellent. And then they keep making changes. Even if I am on set at that time, I will resist, I will oppose, I will tell them that, 'look, don't do this.'"

39. Shyam Benegal, interview with the author, Mumbai, October 11, 2010.

40. On the other hand, he may have received advance notice of what the ministry had in store; at a September 6, 1975, meeting between V. C. Shukla and film industry representatives, the minister informed them that "new and rigid censor rules would be introduced shortly." While assuring the industry of his cooperation in solving other problems that it faced, he stated in no uncertain terms that "violence, rape and degradation of womanhood will not be permitted in any movie and that in case this is found beyond reasonable proportion, the film may be totally rejected" (Vasudev 1978:156).

41. Why this should have been necessary after *Nishant* had already screened at Cannes earlier in the year—presumably with English subtitles—remains unclear.

42. The distinction between "U" (universal, i.e., films for all audiences) and "A" (films for viewers over eighteen) was introduced in 1949. A further intermediate category, U/A (signaling that some scenes may be unsuitable for viewers under twelve), was introduced in 1981. The "S" rating that is very occasionally given to

special interest/audience films appears first to have been mooted in the early 1960s. A 1961 memo from the Ministry of Information and Broadcasting proposes to establish a special scientific or educational certificate for films "on medical, anthropological and allied subjects." These would be films of "exclusive interest to special groups of audiences, for instance instructional films on menstrual and sex hygiene for adolescent girls about 12 years and above, gynecological films depicting anatomy of sex, films showing actual methods of contraception etc which may be of exclusive interest to women." In fact, the point was not so much that only women would be interested, but rather that women would be embarrassed to watch such films in the "undesirable atmosphere of salacious interest" that the presence of males would produce (NAI, Ministry of Information and Broadcasting/Film Censors/5–2–61-FC [1961]). Committed, in the 1960s way, to the pursuit of "good" cinema, the Khosla Committee also suggested a "Q" certificate for "quality" films (Bhowmik 2009).

43. Bobby Art International, Etc v. Om Pal Singh Hoon & Ors on May 1, 1996, at http://indiankanoon.org/doc/1400858/ (accessed August 17, 2011).

44. Having secured a private screening after reported earlier threats to immolate herself should the CBFC pass the film, Phoolan Devi apparently complained that the film was the "worst" she had ever seen and that it misrepresented her life (Thakur and Basu 1995). After the Delhi High Court stayed Bandit Queen's exhibition in India (which it would do again the following year after Om Pal Singh Hoon's lawsuit—see below) and ordered it withdrawn from submission to the Academy Awards, Phoolan Devi agreed, in March 1995, to a cash settlement of £40,000 sterling and a handful of cuts (Someshwar and Singh 1995). Having received satisfaction, Phoolan Devi herself proceeded to condemn the CBFC's ongoing attempts to restrict the film (Kazmi 1996).

45. Similarly, during the arguments over Deepa Mehta's Fire a couple of years later, the Supreme Court noted that it was not interested in any particular film but sought instead to establish a general principle concerning the duty of the authorities to uphold the law in the face of violent protests against films (see my discussion in chapter 3).

46. A paanwallah is a street vendor of paan, a snack ubiquitous across South Asia, consisting chiefly of betel leaf, areca nut, and lime paste, along with whatever additional elements may locally be desired.

47. For obvious reasons, detailed information about how such transactions work is hard to come by. But Lotte Hoek records an informant in the Bangladeshi film industry telling her that "these days a film would not even be given a date for censorship without the right amounts distributed. An experienced producer would know exactly how to ensure a film's smooth sailing through the board" (2008:143).

48. Sunhil Sippy, interview with the author, Mumbai, November 11, 2003. All subsequent quotations from Sippy in this chapter, unless otherwise noted, are taken from this conversation.

49. *Masala*, meaning mixed spice, is often used to describe the all-in-one trans-generic content of a mainstream Bollywood film.

50. Anurag Kashyap, interview with the author, Chicago, February 26, 2009. All subsequent quotations from Kashyap in this chapter, unless otherwise noted, are taken from this conversation.

51. The phrase comes from the Estimates Committee of 1966–67 in the lead-up to the appointment of the Khosla Committee (quoted in Bhowmik 2009:179).

52. Anurag Kashyap, conversation with the author, Mumbai, October 9, 2010. For the record, *The Girl with the Yellow Boots*, a gritty urban story that depicts, inter alia, multiple scenes of hand jobs performed by the heroine in a massage parlor, was given only a handful of word cuts. For example, in a heated telephone conversation full of "fucks," it was the word *Jesus* that had to be taken out.

53. Similarly, as Ravi Vasudevan notes, Indian state television adopted Mani Ratnam's *Roja* (1992) in the late 1990s as "a programmatic patriotic film" (2010:213), to be screened every Independence Day.

54. See K A Abbas vs. The Union of India & Anr on September 24, 1970, at http://indiankanoon.org/doc/1719619/ (accessed January 22, 2011).

CHAPTER 3: CENSORSHIP TAKES TO THE STREETS

1. Putli Bai was the first documented woman *dacoit* (bandit) in the Chambal area.

2. In fact, although the chief minister presided at the ceremony, the real-life Phoolan Devi insisted that she would only surrender her arms to two images: Mahatma Gandhi and Durga.

3. Vijay Anand, interview with the author, Mumbai, November 17, 2003. All quotations from Anand in this chapter, unless otherwise noted, are taken from this conversation. During his foreshortened tenure as CBFC chair in 2003–4, Anupam Kher tried to bring television content such as music videos under the regulatory control of the CBFC. For various reasons, including the enormous power of media moguls like STAR TV head Rupert Murdoch, this proved a hard sell. But in 2005 a Mumbai professor and activist, Pratibha Naitthani, won a case in the Mumbai High Court that effectively banned the screening of A-certified films on television. See http://indiankanoon.org/doc/1779823/ (accessed August 17, 2011).

4. Shiv Sena politician Manohar Joshi was the chief minister of Maharashtra during the Shiv Sena–BJP coalition and later the speaker of the Lok Sabha (the lower house of the Indian national parliament) in 2002–4. But Vijay Tendulkar remembered him as a ringleader of the young hotheads whose rioting led to the closure of his play *Sakharam Binder* in the early 1970s.

5. Several filmmakers, especially mainstream commercial directors, argued that it made sense to go along with the censors' demands so as to have the government

on your side in case of later trouble with goon squads. At the same time, the CFCB's certificates were clearly in themselves not enough to ensure safe screening. For example, even after Rakesh Sharma got a certificate for his Gujarat documentary *Final Solution* in 2004, actually screening it in Gujarat was an exceedingly difficult business.

6. Press release archived at http://www.mail-archive.com/gay_bombay@yahoo groups.com/msg00182.html (accessed November 15, 2010).

7. Having shelled out Rs 25 million for the distribution rights to the Hindi version of *Bombay*, ABCL (Amitabh Bachchan Corporation Limited) was, apparently, quite happy to secure Thackeray's blessing in return for a smooth run in Mumbai.

8. Meanwhile, in Muslim-majority Hyderabad-Secunderabad, where *Bombay* opened earlier than in Maharashtra, two different Muslim groups were struggling to define the contours of the public debate over the film—the Majlis Ittehal ul-Muslimeen, led by Salahuddin Owaisi, and its offshoot, the Majlis Bachao Tehrik, led by Amanullah Khan.

9. *Bombay* opened on April 7 in some suburban parts of the greater Mumbai area such as Thane, where the Shiv Sena have deep roots.

10. A Muslim delegation nevertheless traveled to Delhi in an unsuccessful last-ditch effort to extract cuts from the then information and broadcasting minister, K. P. Singh Deo.

11. An already tense atmosphere was turned up another notch when a crude bomb exploded outside the New Excelsior cinema in south Mumbai on April 5.

12. In May 1995, Ratnam told a journalist: "There were a lot of things he wanted. He had wanted an entire character removed; the character was not removed. He wanted it to be re-shot with some other person; we were able to convince him that it could not be done. He wanted the name changed to *Mumbai*, we said we couldn't. . . . He told me he didn't regret what happened [in the 1992–93 violence] because he did not cause it" (Rao 1995).

13. Clearly, Thackeray's demand that the character played by Shabana Azmi should in fact be named "Shabana" was a performative assertion of the notion that the dubious moral character of Muslim actors was inevitably going to shine through any role they played. "Saira" was a pointed reference to Saira Bano, the wife of veteran actor Dilip Kumar (born Yusuf Khan), who supported *Fire* against the Shiv Sena's attacks but did not appear in it.

14. Aruna Vasudev provides a precedent. In 1973 the Hindi film *Prabhat* was "recalled and released again only after the names of the hero and heroine were changed from Ram and Sita to Ramesh and Sarita" (1978:xiii–xiv).

15. *Fire* premiered at the Toronto Film Festival on September 6, 1996, and on October 2 at the New York Film Festival.

16. Ashish Rajadhyaksha notes that "when Shabana Azmi argued, justifiably, that the film had been 'duly passed' by the Central Board of Film Certification

(CBFC) and thereby received the right to be publicly screened, she was also pointing to the seriously compromised nature of what *should* have been, in the prevailing political arena, an ally" (2009:172).

17. Bal Thackeray spread the insinuation that Shabana Azmi's personal friendship with Sushma Swaraj had facilitated *Fire*'s smooth passage through the CBFC.

18. Mukhtar Abbas Naqvi's Muslim identity was, of course, extremely valuable for the Hindu nationalist BJP in this and other connections. Pramod Mahajan, a Maharashtrian, was instrumental in forging the alliance between the BJP and the Shiv Sena in the 1990s—against the inclination of the BJP/RSS old guard who perceived the Shiv Sena as a group of thugs. Mahajan was the childhood friend and subsequently brother-in-law of Gopinath Munde, the Shiv Sainik who served as deputy chief minister under Manohar Joshi.

19. As George Rudé reflects in his classic study of European revolutionary crowds, the crowd is typically imagined as an entity that in itself is passive but is endlessly receptive to the manipulations of leaders: "Such an attitude was shared by all in authority, whether aristocratic or middle class, conservative, liberal, or revolutionary" (1964:215).

20. Girish Karnad, interview with the author, Bangalore, December 14, 2003. All subsequent quotations from Karnad in this chapter, unless otherwise noted, are taken from this conversation.

21. P. Sebastian, interview with the author, Mumbai, November 26, 2003.

22. Vijay Tendulkar, interview with the author, Mumbai, March 20, 2004. All subsequent quotations from Tendulkar in this chapter, unless otherwise noted, are taken from this conversation.

23. Srirupa Roy makes the same point in the course of a discussion of 1964 riots in the industrial township of Rourkela, Orissa: "At one level, the spontaneity of the riot was its defining characteristic: the 'out-break' of violence that 'spread' from one locality to another without any apparent organizational structure or motivated leadership. From this perspective the riot was effectively inexplicable, located in the mysterious stirrings of crowd psychology, and unknowable and therefore unpreventable. While this was the prevailing explanation in the immediate aftermath of the riot, other sets of more specific causes emerged in later days, and the question of agency became central to the understanding of the riots. Now, the spontaneity of the crowds was seen as a symptomatic effect of other, 'real' causes, namely the instrumental manipulation of gullible populations by 'anti-social elements'" (Roy 2007:152–53).

24. Pritish Nandy, interview with the author, Mumbai, November 22, 2003.

25. Saurabh Shukla, interview with the author, Mumbai, November 14, 2003.

26. Ambiance ran the ads in a specialized handful of publications. But the scandal blew up after the tabloid *Mid-Day* featured a reproduction as a spectacular news item.

27. The suit also brought charges of, inter alia, indecent exposure of a woman and, on behalf of the python, cruelty to an animal.

28. Pramod Navalkar, interview with the author, Mumbai, November 23, 2003.

29. Ashok Kurien, interview with the author, Mumbai, February 22, 2011.

30. By the time Mehta was able to shoot *Water* several years later in Sri Lanka, Azmi and Das had been replaced.

31. Anurag Kashyap, interview with the author, Chicago, February 26, 2009. All subsequent quotations from Kashyap in this chapter, unless otherwise noted, are taken from this conversation.

32. Arundhati Roy publicly accused Shekhar Kapur of (a) pandering to an overdetermined and simplified Western moralism vis-à-vis the complexities of Indian politics and (b) failing adequately to consider the interests of the real-life Phoolan Devi (see Roy 1994).

33. The first time Mayawati of the Bahujan Samaj Party became chief minister of Uttar Pradesh in 1995, she was the first Dalit ever to head a state government in India. Phoolan Devi was released from jail in 1994 after eleven years of imprisonment. Her "legitimate" political career lasted from her first election as a Samajwadi Party MP in 1996 to her assassination in 2001.

34. The BJP's relation to the Shiv Sena had always been ambivalent, and once the BJP had formed a national government in Delhi, it was also careful to distance itself from the more "vulgar" and overtly communal tactics of the Shiv Sena, such as the underwear protest against Dilip Kumar in December 1998.

35. This is a reference to the Muslim politician, lawyer, and journalist Syed Shahabuddin, who in 1988 successfully petitioned the Rajiv Gandhi administration to have Salman Rushdie's novel *The Satanic Verses* (1988) banned in India. For liberal secularists, the episode became emblematic of the need to stand firm against religious appeals; for Hindu nationalists, it came to stand as a symptom of the Congress Party's "pseudosecularist" politics of "appeasement" vis-à-vis Muslim pressure groups.

36. Likewise, Shohini Ghosh quotes theater activist Sudhanwa Deshpande's remarks on his participation in the defense of *Fire*: "It is of course imperative for all secular people to protest such attacks. Secular and feminist organizations in the country including the Left did so unhesitatingly. And many of them did so for the principle and not necessarily because they particularly agreed with what the film was saying. As a matter of fact, some including myself and my colleagues in the Jana Natya Manch [a Delhi-based street theater group] had not even seen the film when we defended its right to be shown" (quoted in Ghosh 2010:116).

37. Kiran Nagarkar, interview with the author, Mumbai, March 16, 2004.

38. Even the ostensibly nonaligned Parsis came under suspicion from Hindu nationalists as being crypto-Islamophiles because of both their proximity to the British and their historical origins in the Middle East (never mind that they fled Persia in the eighth century to escape Muslim persecution).

39. Muslim opinion was often outraged at pictures showing "scenes of Harem life . . . especially when historic Muslim queens and princesses are shown making love" (from a question raised in the Legislative Assembly by Sheikh Sadiq Hasan in September 1933, IOL, L/P&J/6/1995/372[30]). The very next day, Jagan Nath Agarwal made the same point in the same forum on behalf of Hindus as well as Muslims.

40. From a complaint sent to the Bombay Home Department from the de facto Hindu nationalist All-India League of Films' Censorship (MSA, Home Dept [Poll] 1937–38:245).

41. A similar argument was later used to delay the release of Anurag Kashyap's *Black Friday* (2004), which explores the plot that led to the Mumbai bombings of 1993 (see chapter 2).

42. Pramila Nesargi, interview with the author, Bangalore, December 13, 2003.

43. To be sure, the cinema's relation to normative models of spectatorship did not always pass through the filter of offended communal sentiments. "Secular," scientific modes of cinematic enlightenment could also be problematic. In 1933 the League of Nations resolved to facilitate the global circulation of educational films through such measures as the waiving of customs duties. But Indian regional administrations would in practice allow films dealing with matters such as birth control or venereal diseases to be screened only to specialist audiences. In fact, something of a legal contradiction appeared here. As the remembrancer of legal affairs for the Government of Bombay pointed out in 1936, commissioners of police or district magistrates were, under rules going back to the early teens, empowered to license the screening of such films. But the Cinematograph Act of 1918, while it did not provide for restricted certification, nevertheless required that all public screenings—including, arguably, such restricted screenings—required certification of the film by a censor board. Conversely, this same notion of a specialized capacity for appreciation (or immunity to offense) was, on some occasions, extended to religious communities as well. So, for instance, despite there being no provision in the Cinematograph Act for such a practice, and in the face of the police commissioner's objections that enforcement would be impossible, the Home Department of the Government of Bombay demanded that the film *Life of Christ* (which was thought to be potentially offensive to Muslims) be shown to Christians only (MSA, Home Dept [Poll] 1937:62).

44. Phalke elaborated: "The difficulty in India is this: excepting the mythological subjects, the others such as social or historical subjects won't be appreciated by the people. For example, I am coming from the Bombay side. If I produce Shivaji's life, it will never be appreciated in Bengal or Madras; or if I produce any social film, it will not be appreciated anywhere except in Bombay. That is the chief difficulty here" (ICC 1928a, 3:881).

45. Actually, the full version of Mitra's phrase was "the incorrigible Shabana Azmi and her clones in the *Economic Times*" (ET), which I take to be a reference to

the critique by Chitra Padmanabhan (1995) of *Bombay*, published in the ET a week before Mitra's piece in the *Hindustan Times*.

46. Both references are from MSA, Home Dept (Poll) 1926:55.

47. The Hindi sound film relied from the first on Urdu poetic conventions for its dialogues and especially its song lyrics. (It also drew heavily, as I suggest in chapter 1, on the dramaturgical practices of the Parsi theater.) Hindi film dramatics were, in other words, centrally structured around a linguistic and poetic idiom historically associated with Islamicate culture. When it came to film censorship, Muslim journalists often asked how non-Muslim film inspectors, particularly in regions of India that were not primarily Hindi-Urdu speaking, could be expected adequately to evaluate the nuances of Urdu poetics. Hindu journalists, conversely, insisted that the language of Bombay films was in fact "Hindi," thus emphasizing the Sanskrit-colored, Hindu-identified elements of Hindustani. This reification of "Hindi" and "Urdu" out of the vernacular continuum of northern India was, as is well known, on one level a symptom of an increasingly communalized and nationalist public sphere (see Ahmad 2000; Orsini 2002). But in light of the tendency, gathering force in the late 1920s and 1930s, to equate Muslims with affectively chaotic modes of spectator-citizenship, it is particularly notable that the affective heart of the "Hindi" film was itself in a deep sense marked as Muslim. Ravi Vasudevan refers to Mukul Kesavan's emphasis on a Muslim "cultural influence that has determined the very nature of [Indian] cinema" (quoted in Vasudevan 2010:94). One might speculate, then, that the obsessive and rigid public identification of Indian Islam as the intractable "something in the way" of a nationally unified performative dispensation has some of its roots in the intolerably ambiguous cultural identity that lies at the affective heart of the popular cinema. And yet at the same time, as we shall see in the next chapter, this is perhaps only the most politically visible way in which this volatile emergent quality of the cinema as a mass medium has been apprehended.

48. MSA, Home Dept (Poll) 1934:271.

49. MSA, Home Dept (Poll) 1937–38:245. To safeguard moviegoers against such calumny, the AILFC demanded proportional representation for Hindus on the Bombay Censor Board, boosting their numbers from one to "at least five." By 1938 the structure of the Bombay board had in fact changed. From the original six members, split equally between official and nonofficial representatives, it now comprised eleven, out of whom a majority of seven were nonofficials. And here, with three members to two for each of the other represented communities (Muslims and Parsis), Hindus were indeed in the majority.

50. MSA Home Dept (Poll) 1937–38:245. Sensing the government's reluctance to take it seriously, the AILFC's letters had grown increasingly belligerent: "If nothing is done in the next few weeks, the Hindus might be forced to take direct action to safeguard their honour." The commissioner of police soon discovered that the AILFC had been founded around 1935 by a merchant and commission agent named

Rameswardas Agarwala and one Bhagwati Prasad Nigam (alias, apparently, "A. Lenin"). The commissioner reported to the Home Department that "neither of [these] Secretaries has any status or following. Rameshwardas Agarwala is a Marwari Sanatanist and a staunch communalist. Bhagwati Prasad Nigam . . . is a man of shady character and unsteady views." The investigation into Nigam, in particular, revealed a checkered past. Alongside his association with the AILFC, he participated in another activist organization called the Cine-Goers' Association that appears to have been responsible for a handful of agitations in Bombay. Nor were Nigam's entrepreneurial energies confined to the cinema or, even, censorship. Commented the commissioner: "He was the Secretary of the Kalishanker Bajpai Memorial which tried in vain to erect a cenotaph in Bajpai's memory at Worli in 1934. He was instrumental in founding the [A]nti-Gambling League in 1933. He is the author of (1) *Love-Making: A Perfect Guide for Lovers* and (2) *Masturbation & Its Abuse*, published in 1926" (MSA, Home Dept [Poll] 1938:181).

51. Sharma said, "The fact was that my film, when it was viewed by the Censor Board, was three and a half hours in duration. This was minuted not just by my assistants but by two independent journalists because I knew that this was going to happen. So when the [Examining] Committee met, when the panel met, all of it was logged. So if panel member number one got up, went out, made a phone call for eighteen minutes, came back—even that was logged. But the startling thing was that for a three-and-a-half-hour film, to preview it completely, then to have arguments, and then to write out a detailed explanation in terms of which sections and why the film is being denied certification, this entire process took them three hours. My contention was that they never viewed the film" (Rakesh Sharma, interview with the author, Mumbai, December 31, 2006). Lotte Hoek offers her impressions of a film censorship session in Dhaka: "While the secretary served tea and snacks intermittently, few [members] were able to sit through the whole film with concentration. There was a steady amount of movement in and out of the stuffy auditorium and mobile phones kept ringing incessantly" (2008:147; see M. Mehta 2001a).

52. Despite Vijay Anand's well-known opposition to Mrs. Gandhi during the Emergency, here he sounds rather like her. When asked, in September 1975 (i.e., a few months into the Emergency), whether tight government control of television did not undermine its credibility as a medium, she famously responded "that she did not understand what the concept of 'credibility' implied, since there was no doubt that AIR [All-India Radio] was a department of government and would remain so" (Chatterji 1991:106).

1. The reticent appearance of the dubbist is, I imagine, a sly comment on the public style of that quintessentially respectable performing woman, veteran Hindi film playback singer Lata Mangeshkar. Peter Manuel (1993) and Sanjay Srivastava note that, in concert, Mangeshkar would stand stiffly and "sing with her head buried in a notebook" (Srivastava 2007:89).

2. Rs 110 for a genuine branded shirt would have seemed a good deal, although one could quite easily have picked up a pirated version from a streetside stall for that amount or less.

3. In one case of (in)felicitous transnational lexical affinity, the venerable Indian industrial house of Tata was startled to receive complaints about a ribald cyber double at http://www.tatas.com.

4. NAI, Home Department/Jails/1922/1–11.

5. My material in this paragraph and the next is, unless otherwise noted, sourced from Chakravarti et al. (1989).

6. I am alluding here, of course, to Benedict Anderson's massively influential *Imagined Communities* (2nd ed., 1991), which argues that the rise of print capitalism enabled the cognitive and affective foundations of modern nationalist consciousness. My own argument about the palpable and perpetual crisis introduced into the consolidation of performative dispensations by the appearance of the open edge of mass publicity is, then, both an extension and a critique of Anderson's thesis.

7. Ghazals are (nowadays predominantly) Urdu poems based on rhyming couplets, often sung to a harmonium accompaniment, stressing romantic themes of separation and longing in which an intensity of spiritual or romantic devotion often appears as a more or less sublimated expression of sexual desire.

8. Mark Liechty (2001) offers a suggestive analysis of urban Nepali women negotiating their ambivalent relation to pornography as at once women and middle-class consumers.

9. Many Indian feminists, now as well as at the time, have been strongly critical of the Act (Jaising 2006 [1986]; Kishwar and Vanita 1986). Objections have ranged from the conceptual incoherence of the notion of "indecency" enshrined in it to the inability of its feminist framers to distinguish socially progressive aims from moralizing conservatism. A similar debate had taken place in the United States just a few years earlier around the efforts of Catherine MacKinnon and Andrea Dworkin to secure antiporn legislation. Those of my informants who had been part of the Indian debates of the 1980s lamented the fact that these had been conducted largely in ignorance of the U.S. controversy and thus had fallen into some of the same traps—for instance, the dangers of opportunistic alliances with elements of the cultural right and the apparently indiscriminate hostility to any form of sexually explicit representation.

10. In 1985 the Supreme Court similarly emphasized the importance of "corruption" as a sine qua non of obscenity and a more superficial sense of impropriety as a defining characteristic of vulgarity: "A vulgar writing is not necessarily obscene. Vulgarity arouses a feeling of disgust and revulsion and also boredom but does not have the effect of depraving, debasing and corrupting the morals of any reader" (Samaresh Bose v. Amal Mitra [1985]).

11. Maqbool Fida Husain v. Raj Kumar Pandey on May 8, 2008, at http://indian kanoon.org/doc/1191397/ (accessed August 17, 2011).

12. Schechner is referring here to *rasa* theory, the aesthetic philosophy of ancient India, as formalized in Bharata's *Natyashastra* (200 B.C.–A.D. 200).

13. As Farley Richmond (1993) points out, ancient sources suggest that while the performance of Sanskrit drama was understood as a sacred ritual, the social status of actors was highly ambiguous. Brahmins, for example, were not supposed to accept food from their hands.

14. Pramila Nesargi, interview with the author, Bangalore, December 13, 2003. All subsequent quotations from Nesargi in this chapter, unless otherwise specified, are from this conversation.

15. Doniger and Kakar's translation of the *Kama Sutra* defines *kama* as "desire/love/pleasure/sex" (2002:xi).

16. Khosla argues that Western civilization itself underwent a similar transition from a pagan sexual frankness to Judeo-Christian prudery: "As for familiarity with sex, outside every Athenian home stood a phallic symbol, Herm, which was a square stone pillar, crowned with a bearded head of Hermes and an erect phallus protruding in front. The Herm was a sacred object that brought luck and fertility to the inmates of the home, human as well as animal. The young girls in the family would clean and dust the Herm every morning without any sense of shame when they rubbed the duster softly over and round the phallus" (1976:92). Coming to mind is Zeenat Aman "devotionally" nuzzling up to the shivling at daybreak in Raj Kapoor's *Satyam Shivam Sundaram*.

17. B. K. Karanjia, interview with the author, Mumbai, November 17, 2003.

18. Although even then many objected that Indian actors "pecked" rather than kissed properly.

19. Anupam Kher, interview with the author, Mumbai, November 12, 2003.

20. As Shohini Ghosh mischievously remarks, "Had there been no historical evidence of homosexuality in India, I would unhesitatingly recommend its import like any other desirable commodity" (2010:121).

21. Thus, in 1994 the CBFC examined the provocative lyrics of a song from Vimal Kumar's film *Dulaara* (1994) that was an adaptation of Right Said Fred's 1991 hit "I'm Too Sexy." The Board passed the lines *Meri pant bhi sexy, meri shirt bhi sexy* (My pants are sexy, my shirt is also sexy) but drew the line at the invocation of the sacred site of the family itself: *Tharo mummy bhi sexy, tharo daddy bhi sexy, thari family bhi sexy hai* (Kazmi 1994).

22. Pramod Navalkar, interview with the author, Mumbai, November 23, 2003.

23. IOL, L/P&J/6/1747/2601/21.

24. In Freudian terms, one might propose that both the liberal and the conservative positions were compensatory attempts to install a symbolic law that would replace the "murdered father"—that is to say, the performative dispensation of energetic but paternalistic Nehruvian nationalism that in retrospect seemed both foundational and intolerable.

25. Section 292, which deals with the sale and circulation of obscene materials (as opposed to Section 294, which covers obscene public behavior; see Mazzarella 2012a), was enacted in 1925, after India had become a signatory to the 1923 Geneva Convention on traffic in obscene materials.

26. Kailash Chandra v. Emperor, AIR 1932 Cal 651 (D).

27. Raj Kapoor and others v. State and others on October 26, 1979, at http://indiankanoon.org/doc/1547506/ (accessed August 17, 2011).

28. The first book to attract legal attention on grounds of obscenity in independent India was Vladimir Nabokov's *Lolita* (1955) in 1959.

29. Ranjit D. Udeshi v. State of Maharashtra on August 19, 1964, at http://indiankanoon.org/doc/1623275/ (accessed August 17, 2011).

30. Deana Heath observes that "with the law having deemed that religious imagery and contraceptive literature were not obscene, and that most material pertaining to sexuality and the body did not merit legal intervention, the net effect of the institutionalization of the Hicklin judgment in India was to give it, by the 1890s, what was undoubtedly the most liberal obscenity law in the empire" (2010:180).

31. *Lavni* or *lavani* is a popular "folk" form of song and dance in what is now the state of Maharashtra. See Pramod Navalkar's comments near the end of chapter 1 on the Shiv Sena's attempts to sponsor a "dignified" version of the tradition.

32. "The Manipuri 'Michael Jackson' has a very truncated life, not only because he is interrupted while performing, but because he has to go home, in all probability, to a world of poverty and no future" (Bharucha 2001:176).

CHAPTER 5: OBSCENE TENDENCIES

1. In its own way, the 2008 Supreme Court judgment in M. F. Husain's obscenity trial seemed to recognize this, albeit in somewhat simplified terms. Justice S. K. Kaul noted that "art and authority have never had a difficult relationship until recently. In fact, art and artists used to be patronized by various kings and the elite class" (Maqbool Fida Husain v. Raj Jumar Pandey [2008], para 8).

2. Deana Heath quotes Colin Manchester as saying that before the mid-nineteenth century, "'the court was not concerned with penalizing obscenity in literature as *obscenity*' but with 'obscenity's relationship with two other factors, religion and breach of the peace'" (2010:51).

3. NAI, Home/Public/1856/25 Jan/No 5.

4. This kind of boomerang effect is not unusual in obscenity cases, as we shall see. Insofar as a word or an image is thought to be obscene, its justification vis-à-vis a sociologically or artistically redeeming overall purpose or context does not necessarily cancel out all of its virulent potential. As the judge in the Calcutta High Court remarked in the case of *Bose v. Mitra* (a case that dragged on from 1968 to its final resolution in the Supreme Court in 1985), "When the subject is virulent, that provides all the more reasons for subdued caution, lest in the attempt to locate the virus and disclosure of [*sic*] its causes, the treatment itself spreads the poison to contaminate many more who are yet uncontaminated" (S. C. Sarkar 2006:872).

5. In 1979, Supreme Court Justice V. R. Krishna Iyer articulated the relation between CFBC authorization and subsequent court challenges in his inimitable style. On the one hand, "Once a certificate under the Cinematograph Act is issued the Penal Code, *pro tanto*, will hang limp." On the other, "There is no difficulty in laying down that in a trial for the offenses under Sections 292 and 293 of the Indian Penal Code, a certificate granted under Section 6 of the Cinematograph Act by the Board of Censors does not provide an irrebuttable defense to accused [*sic*] who have been granted such a certificate, but it is certainly a relevant fact of some weight to be taken into consideration by the Criminal Court in deciding whether the offense charged is established" (Raj Kapoor v. State [1979]).

6. MSA/Home/Poll/1932/137. The officials at the Home Department were prepared informally to suggest that Shah's book did look like a somewhat risky venture. And that is the line that the Indian courts have generally continued to take. Supreme Court justice V. R. Krishna Iyer noted in the course of his dismissal of obscenity charges against Raj Kapoor's *Satyam Shivam Sundaram* (1978) that "a besetting sin of our legal system is the tyranny of technicality in the name of finical legality, hospitably entertained sometimes in the halls of justice. Absent orientation, justicing becomes 'computering' and ceases to be social engineering" (Raj Kapoor v. State [1979]).

7. Jacobellis v. Ohio (1964). This appeal to a situated "way of knowing" has been central to U.S. judgments on censorship and obscenity for a long time. Even as early as the 1915 *Mutual v. Ohio* case, which denied freedom speech to the cinema in the United States, "The justices felt that the law could be fairly enforced because 'its terms . . . get precision from the sense and experience of men and become certain and useful guides in reasoning and conduct'" (Jowett 1999:27).

8. "Recognition, Camouflage, Espionage: Maneuvers of Power in Late Liberalism" (talk, University of Chicago, April 24, 2008).

9. I selected these examples more or less at random from a list of forty-nine illicit types of content, as presented in the 1946 "suggestions" pamphlet of the Bombay Board of Film Censors (MSA, Home Dept, 5th Series, 496/5-I).

10. Again, I have chosen more or less at random from the list, current at the time

of this writing (September 2010), as found at http://www.indianetzone.com/8/central_board_film_certification_(cbfc).htm (accessed September 2, 2010).

11. In the context of the Hindi "social" film of the 1940s and 1950s, Ravi Vasudevan reminds us, a lamppost is actually a rather charged signifier within the mise-en-scène of the street: "Above all there is the street lamp, signifier of both street and of night and therefore of a physical, social, and sexual drive" (2010:94).

12. Without going so far as to attribute crypto-Deleuzian tendencies (pun tendentially intended) to Justice Hidayatullah, we may nevertheless note that he remarked, in his *Chatterley* judgment, that the Hicklin Test's emphasis on "tendency" "lays emphasis on the *potentiality* of the impugned object to deprave and corrupt by immoral influences" (Ranjit Udeshi v. State of Maharashtra [1964]; emphasis added).

13. Obscene Publications Act of 1959, at http://ics.leeds.ac.uk/papers/vp01.cfm?outfit=ks&folder=4&paper=55 (accessed January 8, 2011).

14. Mazzarella, "Cultural Difference and the Spectatorial *Idiot Savant*" (unpublished manuscript, n.d.).

15. The word *public* bears emphasizing here, since, of course, there were many other, more domestic contexts in which Indians encountered the "private" side of white lives—for instance, as servants to Europeans (Collingham 2001; Stoler 2002).

16. From an April 26, 1926, article in the *Times of India* (MSA/Home Dept [Poll] 1925/194).

17. British Board of Film Censors (1920) in MSA/Home Dept (Poll) 1925/194.

18. See introduction, note 20, for an explanation of this term.

19. The term *apprehension* is particularly apt in relation to censorship, combining as it does associations of experience, anxiety, understanding, and arrest.

20. My argument here is parallel in some respects to that of Bill Brown in his essay "Thing Theory," where he notes that "we begin to confront the thingness of objects when they stop working for us: when the drill breaks; when the car stalls; when the windows get filthy; when their flow within the circuits of production and distribution, consumption and exhibition, has been *arrested*, however momentarily. The story of objects asserting themselves as things, then, is the story of a changed relation to the human subject and thus the story of how the thing really names less an object than a particular subject-object relation" (2001:4; emphasis added).

21. The term *Erfahrung* (experience) has been central to Germanic philosophy in the sense formalized by Hegel: as the meaningful itinerary, over the course of a life (whether of an individual or of Spirit), of cumulative self-reflective thought. Critical theorists like Adorno and Benjamin, developing this intellectual tradition, took one of the characteristic symptoms of the crisis of capitalist modernity to be the impossibility of integrative *Erfahrung* and its replacement by *Erlebnis*—sensational, episodic, and fragmented experience (as in "Wow! What an experience!")

(see Buck-Morss 1977; Hansen 2011; Jay 1984a, 1984b). In *Minima Moralia*, Adorno characterizes *Erfahrung* as "the lag between healing oblivion and healing recollection" (2005 [1951]:54) and the condition of its withering in the twentieth century as "the vacuum between men and their fate, in which their real fate lies" (2005 [1951]:55). For Adorno, Hitler's "robot-bombs" indexed the definitive end of a Hegelian conception of meaningful history: "'I have seen the world spirit,'" he declares—ironically quoting Hegel's hailing of Napoleon—continuing, "not on horseback, but on wings without a head, and that refutes, at the same stroke, Hegel's philosophy of history" (55).

22. Freud's renegade disciple, Wilhelm Reich (1946 [1933]), extended the genital sexuality argument into an explanation of authoritarianism and, ultimately, fascism as based on the kind of routinized systems of desire and shame that inhibited an engagement with less restricted libidinal possibilities.

23. Vijay Anand, interview with the author, Mumbai, November 17, 2003. All subsequent quotations from Anand in this chapter, unless otherwise noted, are taken from this conversation.

24. "A definitive perspective on fashion follows solely from the consideration that to each generation the one immediately preceding it seems the most radical anti-aphrodisiac imaginable" (Benjamin 1999b:64).

REFERENCES

ARCHIVE ABBREVIATIONS

IOL   India Office Library, British Library, London

MSA   Maharashtra State Archive, Mumbai

NAI   National Archive of India, New Delhi

BOOKS AND ARTICLES

Achwal, Madhao. 1968. "The Literary Aspect of Obscenity." In *The Roots of Obscenity: Literature and the Law*, edited by A. B. Shah, 29–40. Bombay: Lalvani.

Adorno, Theodor. 1997. *Aesthetic Theory*. Minneapolis: University of Minnesota Press.

——. 2001. *The Culture Industry*. New York: Routledge.

——. 2005 (1951). *Minima Moralia: Reflections on a Damaged Life*. New York: Verso.

"After the Fire." 1997. *Times of India* (Mumbai), November 13.

Agarwal, Amit. 1991. "Porn Free." *Times of India* (Bombay), October 13.

Agnivesh, Swami. 2001. "The Parable of Phoolan Devi." *The Hindu* (Chennai), August 5.

Ahmad, Aijaz. 2000. "In the Mirror of Urdu: Recompositions of Nation and Community, 1947–65." In *Lineages of the Present: Ideology and Politics in Contemporary South Asia*, 103–25. New York: Verso.

Aiyar, Swaminathan. 1995. "Objecting to *Bombay*: Sexism More Than Communalism." *Times of India* (Mumbai), April 15.

Altman, Rick, ed. 1992. *Sound Theory Sound Practice*. New York: Routledge.

Appadurai, Arjun, and Carol Breckenridge. 1995. "Public Modernity in India." In *Consuming Modernity: Public Culture in a South Asian World*, edited by Carol Breckenridge, 1–20. Minneapolis: University of Minnesota Press.

Arora, Poonam. 1995. "'Imperilling the Prestige of the White Woman': Colonial Anxiety and Film Censorship in British India." *Visual Anthropology Review* 11 (2):36–50.

Asad, Talal. 1993. *Genealogies of Religion: Discipline and Reasons of Power in Christianity and Islam*. Baltimore: Johns Hopkins University Press.

Athreya, Venkatesh. 1995. "Bold but Distorted." *Frontline*, June 2.

Auty, Martyn. 1997. "Politics and Porn: How France Defends Society and Human Dignity." In *Film and Censorship: The* Index *Reader*, edited by Ruth Petrie, 53–59. London: Cassell.

Bamzai, Kaveree, and Sandeep Unnithan. 2002. "Is Sex OK?" *India Today*, August 5.

Bandyopadhyay, Sibaji. 2007. "The Pre-Text: The *Fire* Controversy." In *The Phobic and the Erotic: The Politics of Sexualities in Contemporary India*, edited by Brinda Bose and Subhabrata Bhattacharyya, 17–90. London: Seagull.

Banerji, Jaya. 1998. "Fire and Fury: A Commentary on Deepa Mehta's Film *Fire*." *Biblio* 3 (11–12):22.

"Ban on *Bandit Queen* to Continue." 1996. *Times of India* (Mumbai), March 27.

"Ban on *Bombay*: Thackeray Slams Police Chief." 1995. *Deccan Herald* (Bangalore), April 9.

Barthes, Roland. 1972. *Mythologies*. New York: Hill and Wang.

——. 1981. *Camera Lucida: Reflections on Photography*. New York: Hill and Wang.

Barve, Sushobha. 1995. "*Bombay*: Testing a Fragile Peace." *Times of India* (Mumbai), April 19.

Baviskar, Amita, and Raka Ray, eds. 2011. *Elite and Everyman: The Cultural Politics of the Indian Middle Classes*. New Delhi: Routledge.

Bayly, C. A. 1996. *Empire and Information: Intelligence Gathering and Social Communication in India, 1780–1870*. Cambridge: Cambridge University Press.

Bedi, Tarini. 2007. "The Dashing Ladies of the Shiv Sena." *Economic and Political Weekly* 42 (17):1534–41.

——. 2009. "Shiv Sena Women and the Gendered Politics of Performance in Maharashtra, India." PhD diss., University of Illinois at Chicago.

Benjamin, Walter. 1996 (1928). *One-Way Street*. In his *Selected Writings*, vol. 1, *1913–1926*, edited by Marcus Bullock and Michael Jennings. Cambridge, MA: Harvard University Press.

——. 1999a (1931). "Little History of Photography." In *Selected Writings*, vol. 2, *1927–1934*, edited by Michael Jennings, 507–30. Cambridge, MA: Harvard University Press.

——. 1999b. *The Arcades Project*. Cambridge, MA: Harvard University Press.

——. 2008a. *The Work of Art in the Age of Its Mechanical Reproducibility and Other Writings on Media*. Cambridge, MA: Harvard University Press.

——. 2008b (1936). "The Work of Art in the Age of Its Mechanical Reproducibility: Second Version." In his *The Work of Art in the Age of Its Mechanical Reproducibility and Other Writings on Media*, 19–55. Cambridge, MA: Harvard University Press.

Berlant, Lauren. 1993. "The Theory of Infantile Citizenship." *Public Culture* 5:395–410.

——. 2008. *The Female Complaint: The Unfinished Business of Sentimentality in American Culture*. Durham, NC: Duke University Press.

Bernstein, Matthew, ed. 1999. *Controlling Hollywood: Censorship and Regulation in the Studio Era*. New Brunswick, NJ: Rutgers University Press.

Bharucha, Rustom. 1992. "On Interpreting 'Interruptions.'" *Economic Times* (Mumbai), May 24.

——. 2001. *The Politics of Cultural Practice: Thinking through Theatre in an Age of Globalization*. New Delhi: Oxford University Press.

Bhat, Vignesh. 1987. *Mind Managers and Defiled Doordarshan*. Jalandhar, India: ABS.

Bhatt, Mahesh. 1998. "Is the Police Asking Me to Ignore the Heart-Breaking Fact That Many Officers Looked Away While Blood Flowed on the Streets of Bombay?" *Rediff on the Net*, December 29. http://www.rediff.com/entertai/1998/dec/29zakhm.htm (accessed January 21, 2007).

Bhattacharyya, Prabhat Kumar. 1989. *Shadow over Stage*. Calcutta: Barnali.

Bhowmik, Someswar. 2003. "From Coercion to Power Relations: Film Censorship in Post-Colonial India." *Economic and Political Weekly*, July 26, 3148–52.

——. 2009. *Cinema and Censorship: The Politics of Control in India*. New Delhi: Orient BlackSwan.

"*Bombay* Showing Portents of Becoming Serious Law, Order Issue." 1995. *Business Standard*, April 11.

Borpujari, Utpal. 2002. "'I React to the Times We Live In.'" *Deccan Herald* (Bangalore), July 7.

Bose, Brinda. 2006. "Introduction." In *Gender & Censorship*, edited by Brinda Bose, xiii–xlvi. New Delhi: Women Unlimited/Kali for Women.

——, ed. 2006. *Gender & Censorship*. New Delhi: Women Unlimited/Kali for Women.

Bose, Derek. 2005. *Bollywood Uncensored: What You Don't See on Screen and Why*. New Delhi: Rupa.

Bourdieu, Pierre. 1984 (1979). *Distinction: A Social Critique of the Judgment of Taste*. Cambridge, MA: Harvard University Press.

Brown, Bill. 2001. "Thing Theory." *Critical Inquiry* 28 (1):1–22.

Buck-Morss, Susan. 1977. *The Origin of Negative Dialectics: Theodor W. Adorno, Walter Benjamin, and the Frankfurt Institute*. Hassocks: Harvester.

——. 1989. *The Dialectics of Seeing: Walter Benjamin and the Arcades Project*. Cambridge, MA: MIT Press.

——. 2000. *Dreamworld and Catastrophe: The Passing of Mass Utopia in East and West*. Cambridge, MA: MIT Press.

Butler, Judith. 1997. *Excitable Speech: A Politics of the Performative*. New York: Routledge.

Calhoun, Craig, ed. 1992. *Habermas and the Public Sphere*. Cambridge, MA: MIT Press.

Canetti, Elias. 1984 (1960). *Crowds and Power*. New York: Farrar Straus Giroux.

Chakrabarty, Dipesh. 2000. *Provincializing Europe: Postcolonial Thought and Historical Difference*. Princeton, NJ: Princeton University Press.

Chakravarti, Sudeep, et al. 1989. "The Back-Street Boom." *Sunday*, September 9.

Chalmers, Alexander, ed. 1810. *The Works of the English Poets, from Chaucer to Cowper*. London: J. Johnson.

Chatterjee, Partha. 1993. *The Nation and Its Fragments: Colonial and Postcolonial Histories*. Princeton, NJ: Princeton University Press.

Chatterji, P. C. 1991. *Broadcasting in India*. 2nd ed. New Delhi: Sage.

Clough, Patricia, with Jean Halley, eds. 2007. *The Affective Turn: Theorizing the Social*. Durham, NC: Duke University Press.

Coetzee, J. M. 1996. *Giving Offense: Essays on Censorship*. Chicago: University of Chicago Press.

Cohn, Bernard. 1983. "Representing Authority in Victorian India." In *The Invention of Tradition*, edited by Eric Hobsbawn and Terence Ranger, 165–209. Cambridge: Cambridge University Press.

——. 1996. *Colonialism and Its Forms of Knowledge: The British in India*. Princeton, NJ: Princeton University Press.

Collingham, E. M. 2001. *Imperial Bodies: The Physical Experience of the Raj, c.1800–1947*. Cambridge: Polity.

Comaroff, Jean, and John L. Comaroff, eds. 2006. *Law and Disorder in the Postcolony*. Chicago: University of Chicago Press.

Couvares, Francis, ed. 1996. *Movie Censorship and American Culture*. Washington, DC: Smithsonian Institution Press.

Deleuze, Gilles. 1986. *Cinema 1: The Movement-Image*. Minneapolis: University of Minnesota Press.

——. 1987. *Cinema 2: The Time-Image*. Minneapolis: University of Minnesota Press.

——. 2001. *Pure Immanence: Essays on a Life*. New York: Zone Books.

Derné, Steve. 2000. *Movies, Masculinity, and Modernity: An Ethnography of Men's Filmgoing in India*. Westport, CT: Greenwood.

Dickey, Sara. 1993. *Cinema and the Urban Poor in South India*. Cambridge: Cambridge University Press.

——. 1995. "Consuming Utopia: Film Watching in Tamil Nadu." In *Consuming Modernity: Public Culture in a South Asian World*, edited by Carol Breckenridge, 131–56. Minneapolis: University of Minnesota Press.

——. 2001. "Opposing Faces: Film Star Fan Clubs and the Construction of Class Identities in South Asia." In *Pleasure and the Nation: The History, Politics and Consumption of Public Culture in India*, edited by Rachel Dwyer and Christopher Pinney, 212–46. New Delhi: Routledge.

Dirks, Nicholas. 1997. "The Policing of Tradition: Colonialism and Anthropology in Southern India." *Comparative Studies in Society and History* 39 (1):182–212.

——. 2001. *Castes of Mind: Colonialism and the Making of Modern India*. Princeton, NJ: Princeton University Press.

Doniger, Wendy, and Sudhir Kakar, trans. 2002. *Kamasutra*. Oxford: Oxford University Press.

Durkheim, Emile. 2008 (1912). *The Elementary Forms of Religious Life*. Mineola, NY: Dover.

Dutt, Nirupama. 1998. "Playing with Fire." *Indian Express* (Mumbai), December 13.

Eagleton, Terry. 1990. *The Ideology of the Aesthetic*. Oxford: Blackwell.

——. 1991. *Ideology*. New York: Verso.

Eckert, Julia. 2003. *The Charisma of Direct Action: Power, Politics, and the Shiv Sena*. New Delhi: Oxford University Press.

Eco, Umberto. 1986. *Travels in Hyperreality: Essays*. San Diego: Harcourt Brace Jovanovich.

Egginton, William. 2003. *How the World Became a Stage: Presence, Theatricality, and the Question of Modernity*. Albany: State University of New York Press.

Falk, Pasi. 1994. *The Consuming Body*. London: Sage.

Farmer, Victoria. 2003. "Television, Governance and Social Change: Media Policy through India's First Half-Century of Independence." PhD diss., University of Pennsylvania.

Fernandes, Leela. 2006. *India's New Middle Class: Democratic Politics in an Era of Economic Reform*. Minneapolis: University of Minnesota Press.

"Fire, Burn." 1998. *Telegraph* (Calcutta), December 4.

"Fire-CPM: CPI-M Condemns Centre's Decision to Refer *Fire* for Review." 1998. *Press Trust of India*, December 6.

Freedberg, David. 1989. *The Power of Images: Studies in the History and Theory of Response*. Chicago: University of Chicago Press.

Freitag, Sandria. 1989. *Collective Action and Community: Public Arenas and the Emergence of Communalism in North India*. Berkeley: University of California Press.

——. 2001. "Visions of the Nation: Theorizing the Nexus Between Creation, Consumption, and Participation in the Public Sphere." In *Pleasure and the Nation: The History, Politics and Consumption of Public Culture in India*, edited by

Rachel Dwyer and Christopher Pinney, 35–75. New Delhi: Oxford University Press.

French, Philip. 1997. "No End in Sight." In *Film and Censorship: The* Index *Reader*, edited by Ruth Petrie, 143–50. London: Cassell.

Freud, Sigmund. 2000 (1905). *Three Essays on the Theory of Sexuality*. New York: Basic Books.

Gandelman, Claude. 1991. *Reading Pictures, Viewing Texts*. Bloomington: Indiana University Press.

Ghosh, Shohini. 2010. *Fire: A Queer Film Classic*. Vancouver, BC: Arsenal Pulp Press.

Girard, René. 1977. *Violence and the Sacred*. Baltimore: Johns Hopkins University Press.

Gleig, G. R. 1830. *Life of Major General Sir Thomas Munro*. 2 vols. London: Henry Colburn and Richard Bentley.

Gopal, Sangita, and Sujata Moorti, eds. 2008. *Global Bollywood: Travels of Hindi Song and Dance*. Minneapolis: University of Minnesota Press.

Gopinath, Gayatri. 2005. "Local Sites/Global Contexts: The Transnational Trajectories of *Fire* and 'The Quilt.'" In *Impossible Desires: Queer Diasporas and South Asian Public Cultures*, 131–60. Durham, NC: Duke University Press.

Government of India. 1876. The Dramatic Performances Act (Act XIX of 1876). http://punjablaws.gov.pk/laws/6.html (accessed August 16, 2011).

———. 1918. The Cinematograph Act (Act II of 1918). http://www.indiankanoon.org/doc/1098822 (accessed July 3, 2012).

———. 1985. *An Indian Personality for Television: Report of the Working Group on Software for Doordarshan*. New Delhi: Publications Division, Ministry of Information and Broadcasting.

Gregg, Melissa, and Gregory Seigworth, eds. 2010. *The Affect Theory Reader*. Durham, NC: Duke University Press.

Guha, Ramachandra. 2007. *India after Gandhi: The History of the World's Largest Democracy*. New York: Ecco.

Guha, Ranajit. 1997. *Dominance without Hegemony: History and Power in Colonial India*. Cambridge, MA: Harvard University Press.

Guha-Thakurta, Tapati. 1992. *The Making of a New "Indian" Art: Artists, Aesthetics, and Nationalism in Bengal, ca. 1850–1920*. Cambridge: Cambridge University Press.

Gupta, Charu. 2001. *Sexuality, Obscenity, Community: Women, Muslims, and the Hindu Public in Colonial India*. New Delhi: Permanent Black.

Gupta, Dipankar. 2002. "Personalized Power." *The Hindu* (Chennai), September 14.

Gustad, Kaizad. 1999. "Of Censors, Critics, Copyright and Copycats." *The Week*, February 10.

Habermas, Jürgen. 1989 (1962). *The Structural Transformation of the Public Sphere: An Inquiry into a Category of Bourgeois Society*. Cambridge, MA: MIT Press.

Hansen, Kathryn. 1989. "The Birth of Hindi Drama in Banaras, 1868–1885." In *Culture and Power in Banaras: Community, Performance, and Environment, 1800–1980*, edited by Sandria Freitag, 62–92. Berkeley: University of California Press.

———. 2001. "The *Indar Sabha* Phenomenon: Public Theatre and Consumption in Greater India (1853–1956)." In *Pleasure and the Nation: The History, Politics and Consumption of Public Culture in India*, edited by Rachel Dwyer and Christopher Pinney, 76–114. New Delhi: Oxford University Press.

———. 2004. "Language, Community, and the Theatrical Public: Linguistic Pluralism and Change in the Nineteenth-Century Parsi Theatre." In *India's Literary History: Essays on the Nineteenth Century*, edited by Stuart Blackburn and Vasudha Dalmia, 60–86. New Delhi: Permanent Black.

Hansen, Miriam. 1987. "Benjamin, Cinema, and Experience: 'The Blue Flower in the Land of Technology.'" *New German Critique* 40 (Winter):179–224.

———. 1991. *Babel and Babylon: Spectatorship in American Silent Film*. Cambridge, MA: Harvard University Press.

———. 2011. *Cinema and Experience: Siegfried Kracauer, Walter Benjamin, and Theodor W. Adorno*. Berkeley: University of California Press.

Hansen, Thomas Blom. 1999. *The Saffron Wave: Democracy and Hindu Nationalism in Modern India*. Princeton, NJ: Princeton University Press.

———. 2001. *Wages of Violence: Naming and Identity in Postcolonial Bombay*. Princeton, NJ: Princeton University Press.

Hansen, Thomas Blom, and Finn Stepputat, eds. 2001. *States of Imagination: Ethnographic Explorations of the Postcolonial State*. Durham, NC: Duke University Press.

Hardt, Michael, and Antonio Negri. 2000. *Empire*. Cambridge, MA: Harvard University Press.

———. 2004. *Multitude: War and Democracy in the Age of Empire*. New York: Penguin.

———. 2009. *Commonwealth*. Cambridge, MA: Harvard University Press.

Hawley, John Stratton, ed. 1994. *Sati, the Blessing and the Curse: The Burning of Wives in India*. New York: Oxford University Press.

"HC Stays Screening of Bandit Queen." 1996. *Times of India* (Mumbai), March 7.

Heath, Deana. 2010. *Purifying Empire: Obscenity and the Politics of Moral Regulation in Britain, India, and Australia*. New York: Cambridge University Press.

Heuzé, Gérard. 1995. "Cultural Populism: The Appeal of the Shiv Sena." In *Bombay: Metaphor for Modern India*, edited by Sujata Patel and Alice Thorner, 213–47. New Delhi: Oxford University Press.

Hoek, Lotte. 2008. "Cut-Pieces: Obscenity and the Cinema in Bangladesh." PhD diss., University of Amsterdam.

Indian Cinematograph Committee. 1928a. *Indian Cinematograph Committee, 1927–28: Evidence*. 5 vols. Calcutta: Government of India Central Publication Branch.

——. 1928b. *Report of the Indian Cinematograph Committee*. Calcutta: Government of India Central Publication Branch.

Indian Penal Code. 2003. *The Indian Penal Code, 1860, as Amended by Information Technology Act, 2000*. Allahabad: Law Publishers (India).

Islam, Shahnawaz. 2002. "New Squad on the Trail of Blue Films." *Times of India* (Mumbai), January 10.

Jacobs, Lea. 1991. *The Wages of Sin: Censorship and the Fallen Woman Film, 1928–1942*. Madison: University of Wisconsin Press.

Jaikumar, Priya. 2006. *Cinema at the End of Empire: A Politics of Transition in Britain and India*. Durham, NC: Duke University Press.

Jain, Kajri. 2007. *Gods in the Bazaar: The Economies of Indian Calendar Art*. Durham, NC: Duke University Press.

Jain, Madhu, and Sheela Raval. 1998. "Controversy: Ire over *Fire*." *India Today*, December 21.

Jaising, Indira. 2006 (1986). "Obscenity: The Use and Abuse of the Law." In *Gender & Censorship*, edited by Brinda Bose, 116–26. New Delhi: Women Unlimited/Kali for Women.

Jay, Martin. 1984a. *Adorno*. Cambridge, MA: Harvard University Press.

——. 1984b. *Marxism and Totality: The Adventures of a Concept from Lukács to Habermas*. Berkeley: University of California Press.

Jeffrey, Robin. 2000. *India's Newspaper Revolution: Capitalism, Technology and the Indian Language Press, 1977–1999*. New York: St. Martin's Press.

——. 2008. "The Mahatma Didn't Like the Movies and Why it Matters: Indian Broadcasting Policy, 1920s–1990s." In *Television in India: Satellites, Politics and Cultural Change*, edited by Nalin Mehta, 13–31. New York: Routledge.

John, Mary, and Tejaswini Niranjana. 1999. "Mirror Politics: *Fire*, Hindutva and Indian Culture." *Economic and Political Weekly*, March 6, 581–84.

Joseph, Ammu. 1995. "An Open Letter to Mani Ratnam." *Deccan Herald* (Bangalore), May 28.

——. 2002. "Yes to Porn, No to Peace." *Indian Express* (Mumbai), July 3.

Jowett, Garth. 1999. "'A Capacity for Evil': The 1915 Supreme Court *Mutual* Decision." In *Controlling Hollywood: Censorship and Regulation in the Studio Era*, edited by Matthew Bernstein, 16–40. New Brunswick, NJ: Rutgers University Press.

Kapur, Anuradha. 2004. "Impersonation, Narration, Desire, and the Parsi Theatre." In *India's Literary History: Essays on the Nineteenth Century*, edited by Stuart Blackburn and Vasudha Dalmia, 87–118. New Delhi: Permanent Black.

Kapur, Ratna. 2002. "Too Hot to Handle: The Cultural Politics of *Fire*." In *Translating Desire: The Politics of Gender and Culture in India*, edited by Brinda Bose, 182–98. New Delhi: Katha.

Karanjia, B. K. 1999. "Sense and Censorship." *New Indian Express* (Chennai), August 27.

——. 2005. *Counting My Blessings*. New Delhi: Viking.

Kasbekar, Asha. 2001. "Hidden Pleasures: Negotiating the Myth of the Female Ideal in Popular Hindi Cinema." In *Pleasure and the Nation: The History, Politics and Consumption of Public Culture in India*, edited by Rachel Dwyer and Christopher Pinney, 286–308. New Delhi: Oxford University Press.

Kaul, Chandrika. 2003. *Reporting the Raj: The British Press and India, c 1880–1922*. Manchester, UK: Manchester University Press.

Kaur, Raminder. 2003. *Performative Politics and the Cultures of Hinduism: Public Uses of Religion in Western India*. New Delhi: Permanent Black.

Kaur, Raminder, and William Mazzarella, eds. 2009. *Censorship in South Asia: Cultural Regulation from Sedition to Seduction*. Bloomington: Indiana University Press.

Kaur, Raminder, and Ajay Sinha, eds. 2005. *Bollyworld: Popular Indian Cinema through a Transnational Lens*. New Delhi: Sage.

Kaviraj, Sudipta. 1997. "On the Construction of Colonial Power: Structure, Discourse, Hegemony." In *Politics in India*, edited by Sudipta Kaviraj, 141–58. New Delhi: Oxford University Press.

Kavoori, Anandam, and Aswin Punathambekar, eds. 2008. *Global Bollywood*. New York: New York University Press.

Kazmi, Nikhat. 1994. "Pants Can Be Sexy, Not Parents." *Times of India* (Bombay), February 17.

——. 1996. "Phoolan Joins Kapoor to Say No to Censorship." *Times of India* (Mumbai), January 19.

Kesnur, Padmaja. 1994. "It's Boomtime for 'Girlie' Magazines." *Independent*, March 3.

Khosla, G. D. 1976. *Pornography and Censorship in India*. New Delhi: Indian Book Co.

Khosla, G. D., et al. 1969. *Report of the Enquiry Committee on Film Censorship*. New Delhi: Ministry of Information and Broadcasting, Government of India.

Kishwar, Madhu. 2008 (1998). "Naïve Outpourings of a Self-Hating Indian: Deepa Mehta's *Fire*." In *Zealous Reformers, Deadly Laws: Battling Stereotypes*. Los Angeles: Sage.

Kishwar, Madhu, and Ruth Vanita. 1986. "Using Women as a Pretext for Repression." *Manushi* 37:2–8.

Kluge, Alexander. 1981–1982. "Film and the Public Sphere." *New German Critique* 24–25:206–20.

Kracauer, Siegfried. 1997 (1960). *Theory of Film: The Redemption of Physical Reality*. Princeton, NJ: Princeton University Press.

——. 2005. *The Mass Ornament: Weimar Essays*. Cambridge, MA: Harvard University Press.

Krishna Iyer, V. R. 2006 (1988). "The Jurisprudence of Obscenity." In *Gender & Censorship*, edited by Brinda Bose, 31–45. New Delhi: Women Unlimited/Kali for Women.

Kuhn, Annette. 1988. *Cinema, Censorship, and Sexuality, 1909–1925*. London: Routledge.

Kumar, Shanti. 2006. *Gandhi Meets Primetime: Globalization and Nationalism in Indian Television*. Urbana: University of Illinois Press.

Larkin, Brian. 2010. "Circulating Empires: Colonial Authority and the Immoral, Subversive Problem of American Film." In *Globalizing American Studies*, edited by Brian Edwards and Dilip Gaonkar, 155–83. Chicago: University of Chicago Press.

Law Publishers (India). 2003. *The Indian Penal Code*. Allahabad, India: Law Publishers.

Leff, Leonard, and Jerold Simmons. 2001. *The Dame in the Kimono: Hollywood, Censorship, and the Production Code*. Rev. ed. Lexington: University Press of Kentucky.

Legg, Stephen. 2007. *Spaces of Colonialism: Delhi's Urban Governmentalities*. Malden, MA: Blackwell.

Lele, Jayant. 1996. "Saffronization of the Shiv Sena: The Political Economy of City, State, and Nation." In *Bombay: Metaphor for Modern India*, edited by Sujata Patel and Alice Thorner, 185–212. New Delhi: Oxford University Press.

Lévi-Strauss, Claude. 1987. *Introduction to the Work of Marcel Mauss*. London: Routledge & Kegan Paul.

Lévy, Pierre. 1998. *Becoming Virtual: Reality in the Digital Age*. New York: Plenum.

Liang, Lawrence, Mayur Suresh, and Namita Malhotra. 2007. *The Public Is Watching: Sex, Laws and Videotapes*. New Delhi: Public Service Broadcasting Trust.

Liechty, Mark. 2001. "Women and Pornography in Kathmandu: Negotiating the 'Modern Woman' in a New Consumer Society." In *Images of the "Modern Woman" in Asia: Global Media, Local Meanings*, edited by Shoma Munshi, 34–54. Richmond: Curzon.

"Lights, Camera, Sex!" 2009. *The Telegraph* (Kolkata), June 21. http://www.telegraphindia.com/1090621/jsp/7days/story_11138851.jsp (accessed November 2, 2009).

Lutgendorf, Philip. 1989. "Ram's Story in Shiva's City: Public Arenas and Private Patronage." In *Culture and Power in Banaras: Community, Performance, and Environment, 1800–1980*, edited by Sandria Freitag, 34–61. Berkeley: University of California Press.

MacDougall, David. 2006. *The Corporeal Image: Film, Ethnography, and the Senses*. Princeton, NJ: Princeton University Press.

Malhotra, Nishi. 1998. "The Fire Woman." *Times of India* (Mumbai), December 13.

Mani, Lata. 1998. *Contentious Traditions: The Debate on Sati in Colonial India*. Berkeley: University of California Press.

Manjula, K. 1999. "An Element of Talent." *Deccan Herald* (Bangalore), September 3.

Mankekar, Purnima. 1999. *Screening Culture, Viewing Politics: An Ethnography of*

Television, Womanhood and Nation in Postcolonial India. Durham, NC: Duke University Press.

Manuel, Peter. 1993. *Cassette Culture: Popular Music and Technology in North India*. Chicago: University of Chicago Press.

Marks, Laura. 2002. *Touch: Sensuous Theory and Multisensory Media*. Minneapolis: University of Minnesota Press.

Martyris, Nina. 2002. "Films Are Our Gangotri, Don't Soil Them." *Sunday Times* (Mumbai), July 28.

Massumi, Brian. 2002. *Parables for the Virtual: Movement, Affect, Sensation*. Durham, NC: Duke University Press.

Mazumdar, Ranjani. 2007. *Bombay Cinema: An Archive of the City*. Minneapolis: University of Minnesota Press.

Mazzarella, William. 2003. *Shoveling Smoke: Advertising and Globalization in Contemporary India*. Durham, NC: Duke University Press.

——. 2005a. "Middle Class." http://www.soas.ac.uk/southasianstudies/keywords/file24808.pdf (accessed August 15, 2011).

——. 2005b. "Public Culture, Still: Tracing the Trajectory of Indian Public Culture." *Biblio: A Review of Books* 10 (9–10):13–16.

——. 2006. "Internet X-Ray: E-Governance, Transparency, and the Politics of Immediation in India." *Public Culture* 18 (3):473–505.

——. 2009. "Affect: What Is It Good For?" In *Enchantments of Modernity: Empire, Nation, Globalization*, edited by Saurabh Dube, 291–309. New Delhi: Routledge.

——. 2010a. "A Torn Performative Dispensation: The Affective Politics of British Second World War Propaganda in India and the Problem of Legitimation in an Age of Mass Publics." *South Asian History and Culture* 1 (1):1–24.

——. 2010b. "Branding the Mahatma: The Untimely Provocation of Gandhian Publicity." *Cultural Anthropology* 25 (1):1–39.

——. 2010c. "The Myth of the Multitude, or, Who's Afraid of the Crowd?" *Critical Inquiry* 36:697–727.

——. 2010d. "Beautiful Balloon: The Digital Divide and the Charisma of New Media in India." *American Ethnologist* 37 (4):783–804.

——. 2011. "The Obscenity of Censorship: Re-Thinking a Middle Class Technology." In *Elite and Everyman: The Cultural Politics of the Indian Middle Classes*, edited by Amita Baviskar and Raka Ray, 327–63. New Delhi: Routledge.

——. 2012. "Why Is Adorno So Repulsive?" In *Beyond the Anti-Aesthetic*, edited by James Elkins and Harper Montgomery. University Park: Pennsylvania State University Press.

——. 2013. "'A Different Kind of Flesh': Public Obscenity, Globalization, and the Mumbai Dance Bar Ban." In *Explode Softly: Sexualities and Contemporary Indian Visual Cultures*, edited by Brinda Bose and Shilpa Phadke. Calcutta: Seagull.

Mazzarella, William, and Raminder Kaur. 2009. "Between Sedition and Seduction: Thinking Censorship in South Asia." In *Censorship in South Asia: Cultural Regulation from Sedition to Seduction*, edited by Raminder Kaur and William Mazzarella, 1–28. Bloomington: Indiana University Press.

Mehra, Sunil. 1998. "Nuances of Loneliness." *Outlook*, November 30.

Mehta, Monika. 2001a. "Selections: Cutting, Classifying and Certifying in Bombay Cinema." PhD diss., University of Minnesota.

——. 2001b. "What Lies behind Film Censorship? The *Khalnayak* Debates." *Jouvert* 5 (3). http://english.chass.ncsu.edu/jouvert/v5i3/mehta.htm (accessed August 17, 2011).

Mehta, Nalin. 2008. *India on Television*. New York: HarperCollins.

Metcalf, Thomas. 1995. *Ideologies of the Raj*. Cambridge: Cambridge University Press.

Mishra, Vandita. 2001. "Cutting Beyond the Edge." *Indian Express* (Mumbai), November 25.

Mitra, Chandan. 1995. "A Flawed Film." *Hindustan Times* (New Delhi), April 23.

Mohamed, Khalid. 1995. "It's Outstanding!" *Times of India* (Mumbai), April 9.

——. 1996. "'Bandit Queen' Finds Itself in Hot Waters Once Again." *Times of India* (Mumbai), February 15.

Moore, Rachel. 2000. *Savage Theory: Cinema as Modern Magic*. Durham, NC: Duke University Press.

Münsterberg, Hugo. 2002 (1916). *The Photoplay: A Psychological Study and Other Writings*. New York: Routledge.

Naim, C. M. 1999. "A Dissent on 'Fire.'" *Economic and Political Weekly* 34 (16–17): 955–57.

Nakassis, Constantine, and Melanie Dean. 2007. "Desire, Youth and Realism in Tamil Cinema." *Journal of Linguistic Anthropology* 17 (1):77–104.

Nambiar, Harish. 1998. "Fire Put Out after Igniting Sena Passions." *Telegraph* (Calcutta), December 3.

Nandy, Ashis. 2002. "An Anti-Secularist Manifesto." In *The Romance of the State and the Fate of Dissent in the Tropics*, 34–60. New Delhi: Oxford University Press.

Negt, Oskar, and Alexander Kluge. 1993 (1972). *Public Sphere and Experience: Toward an Analysis of the Bourgeois and Proletarian Public Sphere*. Minneapolis: University of Minnesota Press.

Olivelle, Patrick, trans. 2009. *The Law Code of Manu*. Oxford: Oxford University Press.

Orsini, Francesca. 2002. *The Hindi Public Sphere 1920–1940: Language and Literature in the Age of Nationalism*. New Delhi: Oxford University Press.

Oshima, Nagisa. 1992. *Cinema, Censorship, and the State: The Writings of Nagisa Oshima, 1956–1978*. Cambridge, MA: MIT Press.

Padmanabhan, Chitra. 1995. "'Money' Ratnam Walks the Razor's Edge to Sell in a Communal Market." *Economic Times* (Mumbai), April 16.

Panagia, Davide. 2009. *The Political Life of Sensation*. Durham, NC: Duke University Press.

Pandian, Anand. 2011. "Reel Time: Ethnography and the Historical Ontology of the Cinematic Image." *Screen* 52 (2):193–214.

Parmar, Baljeet. 1991. "Jacks of All Sleaze." *The Daily*, September 8.

Petrie, Ruth, ed. 1997. *Film and Censorship: The* Index *Reader*. London: Cassell.

Pinney, Christopher. 1999. "Indian Magical Realism: Notes on Popular Visual Culture." In *Subaltern Studies X*, edited by Gautam Bhadra, Gyan Prakash, and Susie Tharu, 201–33. New Delhi: Oxford University Press.

——. 2001. "Introduction: Public, Popular, and Other Cultures." In *Pleasure and the Nation: The History, Politics and Consumption of Public Culture in India*, edited by Rachel Dwyer and Christopher Pinney, 1–34. New Delhi: Oxford University Press.

——. 2004. *"Photos of the Gods": The Printed Image and Political Struggle in India*. London: Reaktion.

——. 2008. *The Coming of Photography in India*. London: British Library.

——. 2009. "Iatrogenic Religion and Politics." In *Censorship in South Asia: Cultural Regulation from Sedition to Seduction*, edited by Raminder Kaur and William Mazzarella, 29–62. Bloomington: Indiana University Press.

"Plaint Against 'Pornographic' Shirts." 1995. *Statesman* (Calcutta), April 13.

Polanski, Roman. 1997. "A Matter of Perception." In *Film and Censorship: The* Index *Reader*, edited by Ruth Petrie, 169–74. London: Cassell.

Povinelli, Elizabeth. 2000. "Consuming *Geist*: Popontology and the Spirit of Capital in Indigenous Australia." In *Capitalism and the Culture of Neoliberalism*, special issue, *Public Culture* 12(2):501–28.

Prabhu, Uma. 1995. "Muslims Gear Up to Oppose *Bombay*." *Times of India* (Mumbai), March 26.

Prasad, M. Madhava. 1998. *Ideology of the Hindi Film: A Historical Construction*. New Delhi: Oxford University Press.

Procida, Mary. 2002. *Married to the Empire: Gender, Politics and Imperialism in India, 1883–1947*. Manchester, UK: Manchester University Press.

Radhakrishna, G. S., et al. 1995. *"Bombay." Sunday*, April 2–8.

Rai, Amit. 2009. *Untimely Bollywood: Globalization and India's New Media Assemblage*. Durham, NC: Duke University Press.

Rai, Usha. 1996. "Film Censorship Talks Run into Rough Weather." *Indian Express* (Mumbai), January 11.

Rajadhyaksha, Ashish. 2009. *Indian Cinema in the Time of Celluloid: From Bollywood to the Emergency*. Bloomington: Indiana University Press.

Rajadhyaksha, Radha, et al. 1995. "Kiss, Kiss, Bang, Bang." *Times of India* (Mumbai), August 6.

Rajagopal, Arvind. 2001. *Politics after Television: Hindu Nationalism and the Reshaping of the Public in India*. Cambridge: Cambridge University Press.

——. 2011. "The Emergency as Prehistory of the New Indian Middle Class." *Modern Asian Studies* 45:1003–49.

Rajendran, M. 2000. "Hot Lines Sizzle as Watchdog Winks." *Telegraph* (Calcutta), May 10.

Raman, J. Sri. 1995. "Socio-Political Censors." *Indian Express* (Mumbai), March 16.

Ramanan, Sumana. 1995. "*Bombay* Set to Roll amid Dire Threats in Scenario City." *Statesman* (Calcutta), March 30.

Ramaswamy, Sumathi. 1997. *Passions of the Tongue: Language Devotion in Tamil India, 1891–1970*. Berkeley: University of California Press.

Ramesh, Kala Krishnan, and Vijay Nambisan. 1999. "Under Fire . . . and Ice." *The Hindu* (Chennai), January 17.

Rangacharya, Adya. 1996. *The Natyasastra*. New Delhi: Munshiram Manoharlal.

Rao, Sandhya. 1995. "Censor Board Is Obsolete: Interview with Mani Ratnam." *Frontline*, June 2.

Ravindran, Visa. 1998. "Articulations of Fire and Freedom." *Deccan Herald* (Bangalore), December 7.

Reich, Wilhelm. 1946 (1933). *The Mass Psychology of Fascism*. 3rd ed. New York: Orgone Press.

Richmond, Farley. 1993. "Origins of Sanskrit Theatre." In *Indian Theatre: Traditions of Performance*, edited by Farley Richmond, Darius Swann, and Philip Zarrilli, 25–32. Delhi: Motilal Banarsidass.

Riley, Denise. 2005. *Impersonal Passion: Language as Affect*. Durham, NC: Duke University Press.

Robbins, Bruce, ed. 1993. *The Phantom Public Sphere*. Minneapolis: University of Minnesota Press.

Rodowick, David. 1997. *Gilles Deleuze's Time Machine*. Durham, NC: Duke University Press.

Roy, Arundhati. 1994. "The Truth, Nothing but the Truth." *Indian Express* (Bombay), October 16.

Roy, Srirupa. 2007. *Beyond Belief: India and the Politics of Postcolonial Nationalism*. Durham, NC: Duke University Press.

Roy, Tapti. 1995. "Disciplining the Printed Text: Colonial and Nationalist Surveillance of Bengali Literature." In *Texts of Power: Emerging Disciplines in Colonial Bengal*, edited by Partha Chatterjee, 30–62. Minneapolis: University of Minnesota Press.

Rudé, George. 1964. *The Crowd in History: A Study of Popular Disturbances in France and England, 1730–1848*. London: John Wiley.

Rudolph, Susanne, and Lloyd Rudolph. 2002. "Living with Multiculturalism: Universalism and Particularism in an Indian Historical Context." In *Engaging*

Cultural Differences: The Multicultural Challenges in Liberal Democracies, edited by Richard Shweder, 43–58. New York: Russell Sage Foundation.

Rushdie, Salman. 1980. *Midnight's Children*. New York: Knopf.

Sadhu, Arun. 1995. "Clichés, and Beyond." *Frontline*, June 2.

Saltzman, Devyani. 2005. *Shooting Water: A Mother-Daughter Journey and the Making of a Film*. Toronto: Key Porter.

Sanghvi, Vir. 1994. "The Porn Boom." *Sunday*, December 4–10.

———. 1995. "The *Bombay* Bashers." *Sunday*, April 16.

———. 1999. "Hear Us, Madame Censor." *Telegraph* (Calcutta), August 15.

———. 2003. "Fighting the Censors." *Hindustan Times* (New Delhi), November 30.

Santner, Eric. 2011. *The Royal Remains: The People's Two Bodies and the Endgames of Sovereignty*. Chicago: University of Chicago Press.

Sarkar, Kobita. 1982. *You Can't Please Everyone! Film Censorship: The Inside Story*. Bombay: IBH.

Sarkar, S. C. 2006. *Commentary on the Indian Penal Code, 1860 (Act No 45 of 1860)*. Allahabad, India: Dwivedi Law Agency.

Sayani, Sanjay. 1988. "Bombay Is New Capital of *Desi* Porn Videos." *Indian Post*, December 19.

Schechner, Richard. 2003a (1974). "From Ritual to Theater and Back: The Efficacy-Entertainment Braid." In *Performance Theory*, 112–69. New York: Routledge.

———. 2003b (2001). "Rasaesthetics." In *Performance Theory*, 333–67. New York: Routledge.

Schmitt, Carl. 2005 (1922). *Political Theology: Four Chapters on the Concept of Sovereignty*. Chicago: University of Chicago Press.

Schnapp, Jeffrey, and Matthew Tiews, eds. 2006. *Crowds*. Stanford, CA: Stanford University Press.

"Scribes Flay Arrest of *Fantasy* Editor." 1994. *Pioneer* (New Delhi), June 21.

Seizer, Susan. 2005. *Stigmas of the Tamil Stage: An Ethnography of Special Drama Artists in South India*. Durham, NC: Duke University Press.

"Shabana Surprised over Sena Objection to *Fire*." 1998. *Deccan Herald* (Bangalore), December 30.

Shah, Amrita. 1997. *Hype, Hypocrisy and Television in Urban India*. New Delhi: Vikas.

Sharma, Kalpana. 1999. "All Sound and No Substance." *The Hindu* (Chennai), November 15.

Sharma, Rakesh. 2005. "Take the Scissors Away from the Censor Board." http://rakeshindia.blogspot.com/2005/11/take-scissors-away-from-censor-board.html (accessed August 16, 2011).

Shaviro, Steven. 1993. *The Cinematic Body*. Minneapolis: University of Minnesota Press.

Shedde, Meenakshi, and Kaajal Wallia. 2002. "Censor Board Misses the Wood for the Trees." *Times of India* (Mumbai), August 2.

Singh, Khushwant. 2002. *Truth, Love & A Little Malice: An Autobiography*. New Delhi: Viking.

Singh, Tavleen. 1995. "Pampering the Minority Ego." *Indian Express* (Mumbai), April 16.

Singh Gour, Hari. 2005. *Dr. Sir Hari Singh Gour's Commentaries on the Indian Penal Code as Amended by Code of Criminal Procedure (Amendment) Act, 2005 (Act No 25 of 2005)*. Allahabad, India: Law Publishers.

Sinha, Babli. 2005. "Fearing the Close-Up: The Threat of Spatial Intimacy in Indian Cinema of the 1920s." *Biblio: A Review of Books* 10 (9–10):20–21.

Sinha, Mrinalini. 2006. *Specters of Mother India: The Global Restructuring of Empire*. Durham, NC: Duke University Press.

Sinha, Seema. 1995. "Censor Board Asks Pawar to Decide Fate of *Bombay*." *Indian Express* (Mumbai), January 11.

"Slam *Bombay*." 1995. *Telegraph* (Calcutta), April 15.

Sobchack, Vivian. 2004. *Carnal Thoughts: Embodiment and Moving Image Culture*. Berkeley: University of California Press.

Someshwar, Savera, and Onkar Singh. 1995. "Shekhar Kapur Cut Up over Deal with Phoolan." *Sunday Observer* (Mumbai), March 12.

Srinivas, Lakshmi. 2002. "The Active Audience: Spectatorship, Social Relations and the Experience of Cinema in India." *Media, Culture and Society* 24 (2):155–73.

Srinivas, S. V. 2000. "Is There a Public in the Cinema Hall?" http://www.sarai.net/research/media-city/resouces/film-city-essays/sv_srinivas.pdf (accessed August 15, 2011).

———. 2009. *Megastar: Chiranjeevi and Telugu Cinema after N T Rama Rao*. New Delhi: Oxford University Press.

Srivastava, Sanjay. 2007. *Passionate Modernity: Sexuality, Class and Consumption in India*. New Delhi: Routledge.

Steiner, Wendy. 1997. *The Scandal of Pleasure: Art in an Age of Fundamentalism*. Chicago: University of Chicago Press.

Stoler, Ann. 2002. *Carnal Knowledge and Imperial Power: Race and the Intimate in Colonial Rule*. Berkeley: University of California Press.

Ståhlberg, Per. 2002. *Lucknow Daily: How a Hindi Newspaper Constructs Society*. Stockholm: Stockholm Studies in Social Anthropology.

Swami, Praveen. 1998. "Furore over a Film." *Frontline*, December 19.

Taussig, Michael. 1999. *Defacement: Public Secrecy and the Labor of the Negative*. Stanford, CA: Stanford University Press.

Tejpal, Tarun. 2001. "The *Tehelka* Exposé: Reclaiming Investigative Journalism in India." http://www.taruntejpal.com/TheTehelkaExpose.HTM (accessed August 16, 2011).

Thakur, Punam, and Shrabani Basu. 1995. "Phoolan Surrenders." *Sunday*, March 19–25.

Theweleit, Klaus. 1989 (1978). *Male Fantasies*, vol. 2, *Male Bodies: Psychoanalyzing the White Terror*. Minneapolis: University of Minnesota Press.

Thrift, Nigel. 2008. *Non-Representational Theory: Space, Politics, Affect*. London: Routledge.

Trevelyan, John. 1973. *What the Censor Saw*. London: Michael Joseph.

"Truth or Dare." 1995. *Times of India* (Mumbai), April 2.

Unni, N. P. 1998. *Natyasastra*. Delhi: NAG.

Unnithan, Sandeep. 2002. "Interview with Vijay Anand." *India Today*, August 5.

Upadhya, Carol. 1998. "Set This House on Fire." *Economic and Political Weekly*, December 12, 3176–77.

Varma, Pavan. 1998. *The Great Indian Middle Class*. New Delhi: Viking.

Vasey, Ruth. 1997. *The World According to Hollywood, 1918–1939*. Madison: University of Wisconsin Press.

Vasudev, Aruna. 1978. *Liberty and License in the Indian Cinema*. New Delhi: Vikas.

Vasudevan, Ravi. 2010. *The Melodramatic Public: Film Form and Spectatorship in Indian Cinema*. New Delhi: Permanent Black.

Vijapurkar, Mahesh. 1995. "State Govt. Wants *Bombay* Toned Down." *The Hindu* (Madras), February 24.

Visvanathan, Shiv. 1998. "Revisiting the Shah Commission." In *Foul Play: Chronicles of Corruption*, edited by Shiv Visvanathan and Harsh Sethi, 45–87. New Delhi: Banyan.

Wajda, Andrzej. 1997. "Two Types of Censorship." In *Film and Censorship: The Index Reader*, edited by Ruth Petrie, 107–10. London: Cassell.

Warner, Michael. 2002. *Publics and Counterpublics*. New York: Zone.

Whitaker, Sheila. 1997. "Introduction." In *Film and Censorship: The Index Reader*, edited by Ruth Petrie, 1–3. London: Cassell.

Williams, Linda. 1989. *Hard Core: Power, Pleasure, and the "Frenzy of the Visible."* Berkeley: University of California Press.

———. 1995. "Introduction." In *Viewing Positions: Ways of Seeing Film*, edited by Linda Williams, 1–20. New Brunswick, NJ: Rutgers University Press.

Wittern-Keller, Laura. 2008. *Freedom of the Screen: Legal Challenges to State Film Censorship, 1915–1981*. Lexington: University Press of Kentucky.

Žižek, Slavoj. 1993. *Tarrying with the Negative: Kant, Hegel, and the Critique of Ideology*. Durham: Duke University Press.

———. 2006. *The Parallax View*. Cambridge, MA: MIT Press.

INDEX

WILLIAM MAZZARELLA is Professor of Anthropology
at the University of Chicago. He is the author of *Shoveling
Smoke: Advertising and Globalization in Contemporary India*,
and the coeditor, with Raminder Kaur, of *Censorship in South
Asia: Cultural Regulation from Sedition to Seduction*.

Library of Congress Cataloging-in-Publication Data
Mazzarella, William, 1969–
Censorium : cinema and the open edge of mass publicity /
William Mazzarella.
p. cm.
Includes bibliographical references and index.
ISBN 978-0-8223-5374-4 (cloth : alk. paper)
ISBN 978-0-8223-5388-1 (pbk. : alk. paper)
1. Motion pictures—Censorship—India—History. 2. Motion
pictures—India—History—20th century. 3. Motion pictures—
Social aspects—India. 4. Motion pictures—Political aspects—
India. I. Title.
PN1995.65.I4M39 2013
363.31—dc23   2012033714